HUNTED HERETIC

The Life and Death of Michael Servetus, 1511-1553

MICHAEL SERVETVS HISPANVS DE ARAGONIA.

ROLAND H. BAINTON

HUNTED HERETIC

The Life and Death of Michael Servetus, 1511-1553

Revised edition

edited by
Peter Hughes

with an introduction by
Ángel Alcalá

Blackstone Editions, Providence, Rhode Island 02906
© 1953 by The Beacon Press
Revised edition © 2005 by Blackstone Editions
All rights reserved. Published 2005
Printed in the United States of America

ISBN: 0-9725017-3-8

*This study of a sixteenth-century physician is dedicated
to the doctors in the family*

To the memory of ROLLIN WOODRUFF, M.D.
To his son, BRADLEY WOODRUFF, M.D.
To CHARLES EUGENE WOODRUFF, M.D.
To ROBERT BAINTON KING, M.D.
To CEDRIC ROLAND BAINTON, M.D.
and
To DOROTHY DEE FORD BAINTON, M.D.

Contents

Illustrations

Foreword

I first discovered the case of Michael Servetus shortly after joining the Unitarian Universalist church in Stamford, Connecticut in 1980. His story encapsulated for me my ambivalent feelings towards religion in general and Christianity in particular.

I had been disappointed by most instances of organized religion that I had encountered. There was no church, in my early experience, that would tolerate the views I held. In my extended family and among my acquaintance were people whose lives seemed hedged about with religious restrictions; people who believed that only the few members of their own particular congregation would be saved; people whose religious upbringing left them with persistent feelings of guilt and unworthiness; people who broke with old friends after a religious conversion; and people with whom one could not speak freely, for fear of provoking a holy war.

Yet I was drawn to the possibilities of organized religion. I had never ceased to believe in private spirituality, but this had come to seem inadequate. To my embarrassment I found that I wanted to become a preacher, although I had no church. I dreamed of a church in which people could explore the possibilities, search for truth, and learn from all others, without fear of trespassing into forbidden territories. I wanted not to dodge the issues raised in Christianity, but candidly to engage them. I wanted to be a church reformer. Even when I discovered and joined the Unitarian Universalist church, I felt that it had not gone far enough in coming to grips with the spiritual, as opposed to the intellectual, dimension of religion, and I wished at once to reform it as well.

Accordingly, Servetus's story held me appalled – and entranced. Here was a man who had been brought up in the Roman Catholic Church; had been educated during the brief period of Erasmian liberalism in Spain; who knew of the Spanish persecution of Jews and Muslims and wondered why these divisions between people had to exist; and had been revolted by the secular power and worldliness of the Church. As a young adult he discovered in books a whole new world of ideas and of the spirit. He wished to reform the church beyond the changes of the Reformation, to make a church that every thinking adult could gladly accept. For this he experienced incomprehension and deadly persecution at the hands of both Catholics and Protestants.

I asked my minister how I could learn more about Servetus. He lent me a hardcover edition of Roland Bainton's *Hunted Heretic*. I read it with growing excitement, feeling that it had some particular personal significance for me. Although I had long before made a sacred vow never to become one of those for whom borrowing a book meant permanent acquisition, I retained *Hunted Heretic*, not returning it to the church for over a year. When I finally returned the book, I hoped that the minister, having taken note of my manifest interest, would decline to take it back. To my disappointment, he walked off into another room to shelve the book. But when he returned, it was with a gift: a paperback edition of the same book. I still have it, battered and worn. It has been much consulted through the years.

As a student at Meadville/Lombard Theological School, the Unitarian Universalist seminary in Chicago, I was able to take advantage of the resources of the University of Chicago and a consortium of theological schools to pursue my interest in Servetus. At the Presbyterian school, McCormick Theological Seminary, I found the complete works of Calvin, including the Servetus trial records. Meadville/Lombard had many of the older English works on Servetus and had recently acquired the new Spanish translation of *Christianismi Restitutio* by Ángel Alcalá and Luis Betés. The University of Chicago had the 1790 reprint edition of the *Restitutio* and offered the courses in Latin I needed to help me read it. The greatest asset for the study of Servetus in Chicago was John Godbey, professor of history at Meadville/Lombard and teacher of the Radical Reformation course at the University of Chicago. For his class I wrote a paper on the early interaction of Servetus and Calvin in Paris, upon which Godbey wrote extensive and helpful comments. I wrote my Doctor of Ministry thesis on the appropriation of the story of the life and death of Servetus by modern Unitarian Universalists. The thesis was a theological interpretation, important in my preparation for ministry. I told myself that I would have time to make a more historical contribution later.

As it turned out I was called to a New England Universalist church and became interested in the history of the early American Universalists. Situated as I was, I was ideally placed to investigate the primary sources in this field. What time I had for historical research was fully occupied by this study.

After I retired on disability in 1999, I took on the task of editing the online *Dictionary of Unitarian and Universalist Biography*. Using the books, notes, and photocopies accumulated during my Chicago days, I composed the entry on Servetus myself. As a result I was invited to speak at the 450th Anniversary Conference on Servetus held by the International Council of Unitarians and Universalists at Geneva in October, 2003. While there, through the kindness and strength of several European Unitarians, I was taken in my wheelchair up and down the cobblestoned hills of old Geneva to see the places where Servetus was arrested, imprisoned, condemned, and burned at the stake.

In addition to my work on the *Dictionary*, I have worked since my retirement on the Unitarian Universalist Historical Society's project to reprint classic works of Unitarian and Universalist history. As the 2003 Servetus anniversary approached, I proposed that we reissue Roland Bainton's *Hunted Heretic*. Having been invited by Ángel Alcalá to take advantage of the enhancements offered by his 1973 Spanish translation, I decided to go beyond a simple reprint and to do the research required for a more up-to-date edition.

I am indebted to Roland Bainton for introducing me to this fascinating and absorbing topic. After nearly a quarter of a century, editing this book has brought me back to a study of Servetus, this time following in Bainton's footsteps – using internet-era resources to help me sift and organize nearly five hundred years of Servetus literature.

Anyone who tries to study Servetus in any depth, myself included, becomes caught up in theological and scholarly battles. Servetus studied or worked in so many different fields – theology, philosophy, classics, patristics, Bible commentary, comparative religion, medicine, anatomy, astrology, mathematics, geography – that nearly every scholar is out of his or her depth in one or more of these areas. Most scholars have comprehended Servetus only partially, finding him brilliant in one area and misguided in pursuing another. Others, seeing him as a dilettante in every department, have failed to understand him at all. The miracle of Roland Bainton is not so much that he was untouched by these controversies, but that he kept his balance, his sense of humor, and his all-embracing human sympathy.

Was Servetus a physician who dabbled in theology, or was he a religious reformer who, to protect himself from persecution, assumed the guise of a medical practitioner? In the late nineteenth century, Robert Willis, a retired Scottish doctor, wrote a study of Servetus, presenting him primarily as a pioneer in understanding the circulation of the blood. Willis's work was attacked by two clerical historians, Charles Dardier, a French Protestant, and Alexander Gordon, a British Unitarian. They took Willis to task for having studied a figure whose principal pre-occupation, theology, lay entirely outside his area of expertise. Traces of this particular conflict can even be observed in the pacific Bainton, who knew and admired Gordon.[1] Bainton, however, among religious scholars, was uniquely interested in the medical aspects of Servetus's career, and was a friend and collaborator of the celebrated Yale Medical School researcher and medical historian, John F. Fulton.

Servetus understood all disciplines as interrelated; that is why his insight into the circulation of the blood through the lungs appeared in the context of a theological argument in *Christianismi Restitutio*. His study of medicine was not a diversion from his work of reforming Christianity, but was an essential part of it. So it was with all the other disciplines in which he was engaged. Bainton's work reflects his understanding of this important point. He considered not only the core literature, but brought in historical witnesses from other fields to illuminate the teeming backgrounds to each of the phases of Servetus's life. He looked everywhere he could, and did not rush to judgment, but took his time. It took him over fifteen years to complete what he thought a publishable biography.[2]

Hunted Heretic was one of four studies that Bainton intended as his initial efforts in a scholarly career to be dedicated to "the reconciliation of peoples."[3] In order to understand the phenomenon of religious persecution, he knew that he would have to understand both the heretic and the heresy-hunter. He determined to treat Calvin with the same human sympathy he accorded to any of his four persecuted heroes.

This was no mean feat, for Bainton did not like Calvin at all. Writing to Fulton, he confessed his "horror for Calvin."[4] In his book on Castellion he wrote, "If Calvin ever wrote anything in favor of religious liberty it was a typographical error."[5] He had, at first, little sympathy for the views of Calvin apologists he met in Europe: "I could not see how any regime which had to liquidate its opponents could be considered Christian."[6] He was made aware of the compassionate side of Calvin by Rudolf Schwarz, the translator of Calvin's correspondence into German, whom he met in Basel after the First World War.[7] The result of Bainton's excercise in sympathy, and his sheer restraint, may be seen in *Hunted Heretic*.

In writing a biography of Servetus, Bainton had to convey an impression of his character and personality – something about which previous writers have disagreed wildly. Some assert that Servetus was executed largely because he was over-strident, incautious, unwilling to back down, intemperate, and abusive – in short, because he was obnoxious. Charles Donald O'Malley said, "All too frequently Michael Servetus appears to us as a child of calamity, but as we examine his career it must be confessed that much of the calamity was of his own making." Uncompromising and unrealistic, Servetus had, in O'Malley's estimation, a "genius for indiscretion."[8]

Others find that, on the contrary, he was cautious, restrained, and amiable. Henri Tollin described him as:

> scrupulous to a nicety; self-forgetful almost without limit; peace-loving; learned, and still learning; with an out-and-out preference for the quiet student's closet, as against the brawling forum; disliking extremes; alien from the strife of tongues; ever flexible in the expression, ever steadfast in the fact; in prosperity, unbending, in adverse fortunes, resigned to God; steadfast and child-like in his piety.[9]

And Servetus's alleged abusiveness must be measured against the polemical style of the time. Calvin, for example, could have been convicted countless times if printed vilification were a crime.

Bainton succeeded where others failed by refraining from making an explicit "character-portrait." He told the story plainly without pausing to laud or censure Servetus as a person. He assumed that Servetus had reasons for doing the things he did; that he was in his decision-making a fairly rational man. Servetus, as Bainton saw him, had a compulsion to bear witness to the truth. Yet, like most people, he had a healthy instinct for self-preservation. His story played out as a tragedy, the natural result of a unique witness being given in a time of religious fear and intolerance. Bainton did not need to analyze or to rate Servetus's character in order to study the mechanism of religious persecution.

The assessment of the value and importance of Servetus's works draws passionate responses from theologians and scholars alike. Some have asserted that Servetus was out of his depth in writing about theology and that his works are of little value. Harvard scholar Ephraim Emerton found Servetus's theology obscure, confusing, and inconsistent.[10] Émile Saisset accused Servetus of being a bad writer, of having an "incorrect and nearly barbarous" Latin style.[11] Others drew a contrasting picture of a learned and pious man, a brilliant, original, and creative theologian, perhaps even a major reformer manqué. Tollin found Servetus's theology brilliant, and centuries ahead of its time.[12] Gordon praised his Latin style, preferring it to that of the more classically learned Calvin and comparing it favorably to Emerson.[13] Much depends, it seems, upon the background, education, religion, capacities, and prejudices of the reader and interpreter of Servetus's theological writings.

In these disputes Bainton was an heir of the Servetus enthusiasts Tollin and Gordon. Yet he also respected the more critical Antonius van der Linde, and thought the Calvin advocate Émile Doumergue a worthy historian and opponent. Surveying the entire literature in his 1932 article "The Present State of Servetus Studies," Bainton judged, amongst others, Tollin and van der Linde, and extracted from each what he thought most valuable. Equally he warned against their mistakes and excesses. For example, he cautioned against the use of the information supplied by Tollin without checking it elsewhere.[14] While Tollin is much referenced in "Present State" as a guide to research, there are few citations to Tollin in the footnotes of *Hunted Heretic*. Instead, primary sources – the required corroboration – have replaced a set of studies filled with unreliable nineteenth-century speculation and interpretation.

If Bainton had any "axes to grind," they were religious liberty and peace. Religious liberty was the motivation underlying his study of the Reformation. "In this our day, religious liberty is at peril," he wrote at the beginning of *Hunted Heretic*. He addressed the issue of peace explicitly on the last page of the book, advising his readers to contemplate the ruined cities of the recently ended war – Berlin, Dresden, Hiroshima – and to consider how many we are willing to kill for our ideals, before condemning Calvin for his part in the execution of Servetus. Even here, he did not deflect the story of Servetus to dwell upon his pacifism, but made his case briefly, memorably, and to the point. He did not distort the story of Servetus to give it an anachronistic message, but reflected on the story as a preacher might (and Bainton was a preacher) in order to fashion a cautionary message for the present day. He saw the two issues as linked:

> We may inquire whether we are so tolerant and so kindly if we believe our material or national security is imperiled. Were the judge who condemned and the public which condoned the death of the Rosenbergs any less cruel than John Calvin? He believed that man's eternal salvation was at stake. We assume that the safety of our cities may be jeopardized . . . If we conceive ourselves to be imperiled, we are no more disposed to mercy than was he.[15]

Bainton's irenic evenhandedness, his ability to transcend scholarly and theological divisions, makes him a moral exemplar in academic life. Moreover, because of these virtues, his work is good scholarship. Although he took decided points of view in certain scholarly debates – as for instance when he refuted the political connection between Servetus and the Genevan Libertines – in general he arranged his material as though for a conference of peace rather than a campaign of war. This is the reason this book remains valuable after fifty years, when other, more tendentious works seem dated.

Peter Hughes

Notes

[1] See chapter 5, note 21.

[2] In the event it was thirty years before *Hunted Heretic* came out.

[3] Roland H. Bainton, *Roly: Chronicle of a Stubborn Non-Conformist* (New Haven: Yale Divinity School, 1988), 45.

[4] John F. Fulton, *Michael Servetus, Humanist and Martyr* (New York: Herbert Reichner, 1953), 7.

[5] Roland H. Bainton, introduction to Sébastien Castellion, *Concerning Heretics: Whether They Are to Be Persecuted and How They Are to Be Treated* (New York: Octagon Books, 1965), 74.

[6] Bainton, *Roly*, 85.

[7] Bainton, *Roly*, 58.

[8] Charles Donald O'Malley *Michael Servetus, a Translation of his Geographical, Medical and Astrological Writings* (Philadelphia: American Philosophical Society, 1953), 9-10.

[9] Henri Tollin, "Character-Portrait of Michael Servetus," trans. F. A. Short, *Christian Life*, 1 December 1877.

[10] Ephraim Emerton, "Calvin and Servetus," *Harvard Theological Review* 2 (1909), 145.

[11] Émile Edmond Saisset, "Doctrine philosophique et religieuse de Michel Servet," *Revue des deux mondes* 21 (15 February 1848), 593.

[12] Tollin, "Character-Portrait," 1 December 1877.

[13] Alexander Gordon, "Miguel Serveto-y-Reves," *Theological Review* 15 (1878), 415.

[14] Roland H. Bainton, "The Present State of Servetus Studies," *Journal of Modern History* 4 (1932), 73.

[15] Roland H. Bainton, "Burned Heretic: Michael Servetus," *Christian Century* 70 (28 October 1953), 1231.

Preface to the Revised Edition

When Blackstone Editions and the Unitarian Universalist Historical Society investigated the possibility of reprinting *Hunted Heretic*, we had to answer two questions. First, why reprint scholarship that is over 50 years old? And secondly, are there not enough copies of the 1953 original or the 1960 paperback edition available on the used-book market to satisfy any reasonable demand?

The answer to the first question is that *Hunted Heretic* has so far stood the test of time. Other books on Servetus have since been written, but none that so artfully combines depth of scholarship with introductory accessibility. Scholarship does indeed move on, but we have found that little that contradicts what Bainton wrote – merely much that acts as supplement. Of course *Hunted Heretic*, like every work of scholarship, contains a few errors, and a few questionable interpretations; these are discussed in the Introduction by the distinguished Spanish Servetus scholar Ángel Alcalá, who translated *Hunted Heretic* into Spanish in 1973. But on the whole, the book holds up remarkably well.

Though the basic scholarship remains sound, we found the apparatus in need of updating. Therefore we decided to make this volume, not a simple reprint, but a revised, updated, and enriched edition of *Hunted Heretic*. Like a DVD reissue of a beloved classic movie, it comes packaged with many "special features." We have revised the chronology, updated the notes and bibliography, and added two appendices: a rare, early, and hard-to-find primary document, and a short biography of Roland Bainton.

The text

The text of this edition is the same as that of the original 1953 edition, with the following exceptions:

Two paragraphs on Servetus's life in Vienne, written by Bainton for the Foreword of the 1960 paperback edition, have been incorporated into chapter 7. We have also included a small amount of additional material, mostly in chapters 4 and 8, from the 1973 Spanish edition. Square brackets are used to identify the new text. To avoid confusion, a few short notes of Bainton's, which were in square brackets in the earlier edition, have been changed to footnotes at the bottom of the page.

Personal names and a few other terms (such as "Qur'an" instead of "Koran") have been changed to conform the current Library of Congress authority file.

Notes and bibliography

Mindful that *Hunted Heretic* has served as an introduction to Servetus for generations of readers, we have made a special effort to make the notes as clear and accessible as possible. We have avoided the use of abbreviations for journals and standard works, used short forms sparingly, and cited each work in full the first time it is referenced in a chapter. The intention is that the reader without previous background in Reformation studies should be able to find the works readily in a library catalog.

In addition to source notes, Bainton's original endnotes included what may be described as suggestions for further reading on topics discussed in the book: Augustine's doctrine of the Trinity, the medieval scholastics, Anabaptism, what the Qur'an says about Jesus, and so on. Alcalá updated the notes in the 1973 Spanish edition, citing new scholarship on Servetus's family and adding references to Spanish sources for background on such topics as the Marranos, the Alumbrados, and the iconography of the Trinity in Spanish art. We have incorporated Alcalá's additions and also expanded the notes to include recent scholarship on many of the topics covered by the book. English-language sources are emphasized, but works in French, Spanish, and German have also been included. As in the main text, square brackets are used to identify the new material in the notes.

The bibliography in this book is a new one, prepared expressly for this edition. It does not aspire to be complete, but aims to include the most informative and historically important works on Servetus. Bainton began, in a small way, to annotate the bibliography in *Hunted Heretic*. The bibliography in this edition includes his notes and adds many other annotations – some of them mini-reviews – taken from various works by Bainton and other Servetus scholars, including Earl Morse Wilbur, Ángel Alcalá, Jerome Friedman, and Charles Dardier.

Illustrations

The illustrations in *Hunted Heretic* are among its most beloved features. Many readers retain fond memories of the representations of the Trinity or the string quartet of Plato, Aristotle, Galen, and Hippocrates. This edition includes the original illustrations where possible. A few, such as the view of Basel in chapter 2 and the map of the New World in chapter 5, were judged to be of insufficient quality to be reproduced. To compensate for the loss of these, we have added several new illustrations: the introduction and title page of the 1541 edition of Ptolemy's Geography; two sixteenth-century views of Geneva; Hermes Trismegistus, the mythical founder of the Hermetic tradition; and a figure of great personal significance for Servetus, his patron and namesake, the Archangel Michael.

Appendices

Appendix A contains the earliest known account of the execution of Servetus, an anonymous work known as *Historia Mortis Serveti*, which was written around 1554. This brief account has been preserved and made available over the centuries by including it in books on Servetus, including the Dutch edition of Sébastien Castellion's *Contra Libellum Calvini* (1612) and Johann von Mosheim's *Anderweitiger Versuch* (1748). It was translated into English in 1878 by the British Unitarian scholar Alexander Gordon and printed in that year in the Unitarian newspaper, *Christian Life*. As all of these works are now rare, hard-to-obtain documents found only in a handful of research libraries, we have included Gordon's translation here in order to make it available to a new generation of Servetus scholars.

Earlier editions of *Hunted Heretic* included an extremely brief biographical note about the author. Now, some fifty years after the original publication and twenty years after Bainton's death, it is possible to see *Hunted Heretic* in the context of the time in which it was written, and to assess its place in the life's work of its author. We have therefore included a short biography of Roland Bainton as Appendix B. We hope that it will give readers a greater appreciation both of Bainton's accomplishments in the field of religious history, and of the passions that drove him to make the effort. This edition of *Hunted Heretic* is, among other things, a memorial to a man who had a vision of scholarship as a tool for helping to break down the walls of cultural and linguistic isolation in the world, bringing humanity closer to understanding, harmony, and peace.

Acknowledgements

Many institutions and individuals have helped bring about this new edition.

This volume is part of a series of classics in liberal religious history sponsored and funded by the Unitarian Universalist Historical Society. Some of the funding for this program was donated by the New York State Convention of Universalists.

Herbert Bainton and the Bainton family gave kind permission to reprint Bainton's text. Ángel Alcalá allowed us to include material from his 1973 Spanish edition of *Hunted Heretic*. The Cleveland Museum of Art gave permission to use the engraving of the Archangel Michael.

The research for this edition was done with the assistance of the Brown University Libraries, the Houghton Library and Andover-Harvard Theological Library at Harvard University, and the Wiggin Memorial Library at Meadville/Lombard Theological School. Special thanks to Senior Library Assistant Joyce Meakin of the Harris Manchester College Library, Oxford, for locating the issues of *Christian Life* containing the translations of *Historia Mortis Serveti* and Tollin's "Character Portrait."

Jaume de Marcos and Sergio Baches Opi contributed to the bibliography, and Jaume helped with the translation of Spanish material. In addition to writing the introduction, Ángel Alcalá made helpful suggestions for improving the bibliography, arranged for books to be sent from Spain, and provided general advice and support. Lynn Gordon Hughes helped with text editing and with the revision of the notes, bibliography, and index.

We are indebted to Pat Falcon, Gwen Howard, Anthony David Steers, and Laurie Stearns; to members of the Unitarian Universalist Historical Society; and to the participants in the International Council of Unitarians and Universalists' 450th Anniversary Servetus Conference (held in Geneva in October 2003) for advice, assistance, and encouragement.

Introduction

Early in 1973 I offered Jesús Aguirre (later the Duke of Alba by marriage), then director of the prestigious Madrid publishing house Taurus, to translate *Hunted Heretic* into Spanish. I had come to the United States in September 1962 to pursue advanced studies in philosophy at New York University and then decided to stay as a professor of Spanish Language and Literature at Brooklyn College, part of the City University of New York. In my research I investigated the philosophical and theological constraints that shaped Spanish literature during the fifteenth through seventeenth centuries. The hierarchies governing Spanish society conditioned its peculiar characteristics: a publication permit by the State Council was required and books might also be suppressed or prohibited by the Inquisition tribunals. While immersed in these studies, I discovered Roland Bainton's book and instantly became an admirer of Servetus as well as of the author. In the spring of 1972 Bainton and I met in Hyde Park, New York at the house of a common friend. We afterwards corresponded frequently until the year of his death. I proudly possess a file of his letters and hand-written Christmas cards, all of them addressed with a friendly "*querido amigo.*"

I asked Bainton to allow me to write a prologue and an epilogue for the Spanish translation, updating the original 1953 edition. He contributed some material, drawn mainly from his foreword to the 1960 paperback reprint. As a title I preferred *Servet, el hereje perseguido* (the persecuted heretic) instead of *cazado* (hunted). I suggested to him that we supplement the new edition with a translation of the extremely useful and carefully researched "Bibliography of His [Servetus's] Works and Census of Known Copies" by Madeline Stanton. John. F. Fulton had appended this bibliography to his *Michael Servetus, Humanist and Martyr*, which appeared in 1953, the same year that Bainton's book was published. We also prepared a new bibliography, divided into sections, which facilitated finding appropriate materials for the study of any of the several scholarly fields cultivated by Servetus himself. Looking back over the last thirty years, I take satisfaction in noting that the Spanish edition of *Hunted Heretic* has been a formidable stimulus to serious Servetus studies by Spaniards. In both historical technique and sophistication, Bainton set a high standard for them.

It is, nevertheless, hard to understand why an accomplished researcher like Bainton paid no attention to any of the comprehensive Spanish studies of Servetus. Perhaps he held an *a priori* conviction that none was worthy. He mentions in footnotes only Eloy Bullón's not too reliable book on Servetus's edition of Ptolemy's *Geography*, José Castro y Calvo's confused study on the *Syruporum*, and Mariano de Pano's articles on Servetus's childhood. To these, in his bibliography, he adds negligible pamphlets such as those by Pompeyo Gener, José Izquierdo, and Antonio Martínez Tomas. It is difficult to comprehend the absence of the well-documented and detailed *Historia de los Heterodoxos Españoles*, a profound and epoch-making study by Marcelino Menéndez Pelayo, the most prolific and erudite Spanish historian. Bainton's failure to include this book is not excused by the fact that that Menéndez Pelayo, a strict Catholic, condemned Servetus doctrinally (though he admired him in many other respects). Thus, Bainton's book on Servetus has this one main weakness: lack of attention to the contributions of Spanish scholarship.

In my prologue to *Servet, el hereje perseguido*, I called Bainton "the supreme authority on issues of sixteenth-century religious history." His analysis of Servetus's theological doctrines is nearly unsurpassable. Needless to say, however, like all things human, his masterful work can be improved, even in his own area of theological research. *Hunted Heretic* needs clarification, especially to incorporate biographical details unearthed by research after Bainton's death. Such is my simple and modest task in the following pages.

The most important source of misunderstanding is the unfortunate title of Chapter 1, "Dog of a Marrano." Today, in studying the time of the Spanish Inquisition, we differentiate very carefully between a *converso* – a convert, or at least someone baptized, from Judaism or Islam, whether sincere or not – and a *marrano*, an adaptation from *marrar*, *marrado* (to mar, marred), a term applied to secret Judaizers. The term "marrano," which also means "pig" and "dirty," was hurled at conversos as an insult out of a popular slanderous belief that the members of both these groups had accepted baptism dishonestly. In my translation, *hijo* (son) — not *perro* (dog) — *de marrano* was chosen to tone down the offensive expression. The word "marrano," nevertheless, ought not to be admitted at all. In making "Dog of a Marrano" the title of the chapter on Servetus's birth and upbringing, Bainton appears to accept the insult and to imply that Servetus and his family not only had Jewish ancestors, but were practicing Judaism secretly in their hearts and in their home. No document exists, nor can any be found, which would support such a claim. Bainton did not actually say that Servetus was a marrano, only that French students might have insulted him this way simply because he was Spanish, but it is an impression that an unwary reader might easily carry away.

Servetus, nevertheless, did have some converso ancestry. In 1932 Castro y Calvo published documents relating to Servetus's family which, together with others already printed by de Pano at the turn of the century, reveal that a branch of Servetus's maternal ancestry descended from the Zaporta family, converts from Judaism. His mother's full name was Catalina Conesa Zaporta. The Zaportas had been rich Jewish merchants based in Monzón, not far from Servetus's native town, Villanueva de Sijena. Like dozens of rabbis and thousands of Jews, they accepted baptism around the time of the so-called "Tortosa Disputation" held from February 1413 to November 1414 in the presence of anti-pope Benedict XIII. It is understandable that these "new Christians" tried to deflect suspicion and to disguise their ancestry by marrying into families of ancient and undoubted orthodoxy. Conesa was a caballero from Barbastro. According to a document signed in 1327 and another in 1498, the Servetos belonged to the lesser nobility of Northern Aragón.[1]

Despite some recent controversy,[2] Bainton remains correct in saying that "there is no doubt" as to the identification of Villanueva de Sijena as Servetus's native town. The argument in favor of Tudela in Navarre is based only on Servetus's own false statements to the French when trying to disguise his real identity. The name Serveto does not appear in the rosters of the notarial and ecclesiastical archives in Tudela. Servetus's true place of origin is revealed by the subtitle of his first books, *Per Michaelem Serveto alias Reves, ab Aragonia Hispanum*; his adopted French name, Michel de Villeneuve (not "de Tudele"); his confession at the Geneva trial; and, definitively, in the text of his condemnation to death:

"against you, Michael Servetus from Villanueva of the Kingdom of Aragon in Spain." He could not confront the truth of his death without admitting the truth of his birth.[3]

Bainton held a too-optimistic view of the supposedly peaceful *convivencia* between the three religions and cultures of medieval Spain. This rosy and romantic perspective has been discredited by modern critical studies. Although officially tolerated, Jews and Muslims were never loved by "old Christians." Following Augustinian theory, legalized in Medieval practice, they did everything possible to make Jewish and Muslim lives miserable in order to force them to baptize. A minor detail: I am astonished to see that Bainton appears to believe the story of Torquemada comparing the Catholic Monarchs with Judas. He must have taken it from William H. Prescott or some other popular historian,[4] but it is spurious and legendary.[5]

It does not appear that Servetus developed a critical approach to the Trinity before he left Spain, nor was he inspired by having personally met descendants of Jews or Muslims. It is not known whether in his time there were any Jews in his native town. According to Mikel de Epalza and other scholars, there were no Muslims there. There is no basis for the thesis defended by Richard H. Popkin, that Jewish influence shaped Reformation anti-Trinitarian thinking.[6] In any case, Servetus's heterodoxy had other roots.

The years Servetus spent with his employer, Juan de Quintana, at the itinerant court introduced him to Spanish politics and world affairs. Quintana was not "a Franciscan Minorite," as Bainton called him (after Marcel Bataillon and others), but, as the documents tell us, a *clericus oscensis*, a cleric from Huesca. He was an elected member of the Aragonese Parliament, a royal counselor on national problems such as the Toledo alumbrados (the analysis of whose doctrines bears his signature), and a member of the committee that advised on the Granada moriscos. He attended the meeting convened in Valladolid to discuss the orthodoxy of the writings of Erasmus, who was better-known amongst intellectuals and politicians of Spain than in many other countries. Erasmus's purported anti-Trinitarian views were a subject of debate. Accordingly we cannot but suspect that Servetus was educated about alumbrados, moriscos, and anti-Trinitarianism before he left to study in Toulouse.

No doubt, Servetus "discovered" the Bible in Toulouse. It was odd of Bainton, however, to suppose that the edition Servetus likely read was the imposing, scarce, and outrageously expensive *Complutensis*.

There were many printed versions of the Bible at the time. The *Comma Johanneum*[7] was retained in all of them except in first edition of the New Testament of Erasmus.

In *Christianismi Restitutio* Servetus gave an empassioned first-hand account of the imperial coronation in Bologna, in February 1530.[8] He uttered no word, however, about his probable presence at the Diet of Augsburg that summer. His presence at Augsburg would explain his familiarity with Melanchthon and why he felt it necessary to write *Apology to Melanchthon*, perhaps his best writing. It is well known that Alfonso de Valdés (ca.1492-1532), one of the Emperor's secretaries, had important discussions with Luther's emissary at Augsburg, and that they nearly reached a tentative agreement between Catholics and Protestants. Alfonso and his brother Juan were leading forces behind Spanish Erasmianism. Juan de Valdés (ca.1494-1541) was persecuted and forced to flee Spain after writing *Catechism of the Christian Doctrine* (1529).[9] He taught spiritual and theological doctrines (though not anti-Trinitarian ones) similar to those later adopted by Servetus. In fact, Servetus's spiritual, pacifist, and Paulinian ideology, including some of the terminology he used in *Christianismi Restitutio*, appear to be more Valdesian than Erasmian.[10] This point deserves further investigation.

The more I study Servetus the more I am convinced that, although he was introduced to the religious and political situation by Quintana, it was not until he studied under Oecolampadius at Basel that he began to learn theology and Biblical languages. He must have learned Latin along with other Humanities disciplines from his father, who was a notary at the rich and noble convent in his native town, and also perhaps as a student at Montearagón, an Augustinian monastery on the outskirts of Huesca. There is no evidence that Servetus read Greek or Hebrew before he prepared to write *De Trinitatis Erroribus* in 1531. None of Servetus's three classical languages was a model of perfection. His Latin style was lexically poor and, at times, unnecessarily convoluted, for he was struggling to express difficult thoughts which were not common in current philosophical and theological treatises. On the other hand, the fact that in his early works he employed a dialogue format, constantly addressing a second person, suggests that not only *Dialogorum de Trinitate*, but also *De Trinitatis Erroribus*, and most importantly, the newly-edited *Declarationis Iesu Christi Filii Dei Libri Cinque*, were written as a result of heated discussions between Servetus and Oecolampadius.

Bainton did not know of *Declarationis* (the Stuttgart Manuscript) when writing *Hunted Heretic*. Notice of *Declarationis* was first given in 1953 by its discoverer, Stanislas Kot, in the important compilation of articles edited by Bruno Becker, *Autour de Michel Servet et de Sébastien Castellion*.[11] Bainton saw the galleys of Kot's article and discussed it in his bibliography. A more extended analysis was prepared for the 1973 Spanish translation.[12] Contrary to Kot's opinion, and as Bainton anticipated years ago in our epilogue after studying the *Declarationis* manuscript (a copy of which he sent to me), everything in this important text indicates that it is "a draft less mature than *De Trinitatis*." Although its structure is similar to *De Trinitatis* and most of the Biblical texts analyzed are the same, it contains textual repetition, showing that it was conceived as a provisional draft and not intended to be a definitive text meant to see public light. The paucity of Patristic quotations – none in any other language than Latin – and the lack of any reference to Scholastic theologians, demonstrate that Servetus wrote *Declarationis* not as an epitome of his developed thought, but as a summary of his discussions with Oecolampadius and as a record of the process of his own private learning.

It is perhaps indicative of the not too high "present state of Servetus studies" (to borrow the title of a famous Bainton article) that this important manuscript has not been studied, much less published, in the more than fifty years since it was discovered. Marian Hillar and I have finally transcribed *Declarationis*, and I have translated it into Spanish. The translation, together with the original Latin, preceded by a detailed introduction, is now available in volume 2 of Miguel Servet, *Obras Completas* (2004).

The identification of "Alphonsus Lyncurius Tarraconensis," who signed the preface to *Declarationis*, with Celio Secondo Curione, Matteo Gribaldi, Martin Borrhaus, or others, should be abandoned. There is no reason to doubt Lyncurius's confession that he is a compatriot of Servetus, a "Tarraconensis." This can be interpreted either in the classical and humanistic sense of belonging to the Roman Empire province of Tarraco (now Tarragona, in Catalonia) or in the ecclesiastical sense of belonging to the archbishopric of that city, of which the diocese of Lérida, or Lleida, and the parish of Villanueva de Sijena were a part. Lyncurius, perhaps a Spanish student in France, must have met Servetus at an early age, but after *De Trinitatis*, most likely in Paris. He was not only given the *Declarationis* text, but also had been informed of the titles of several of Servetus's planned treatises. Some of these had been published as parts of *De Trinitatis Erroribus* or later appeared as sections of *Christianismi Restitutio*. The two Spaniards must have lost touch with each other after Servetus changed his name to Michel de Villeneuve and moved to Lyons. Lyncurius, writing his preface after learning of Servetus's death, seems not to have known of Servetus's medical profession or of his later works, including the almost totally suppressed *Restitutio*.

Only a few other details in Bainton's book require clarification. I have ascertained that just four of the scholia to Ptolemy's *Geography* may be attributed to Servetus. Also by Servetus are: 1) the patriotic sentence about the name of America, that it should have been Columbia; 2) the short passage, afterwards tempered, about the curing power of the king of France; and 3) the chapter on the Ottomans, which was mostly cribbed from a contemporary Italian historian whom he mentioned. The rest he reproduced unaltered from Fries's and Pirckheimer's editions.[13] Analyses which I included in the introductions to the relevant volumes of *Obras Completas* show that there is no serious basis for the claims that Servetus wrote any of the works recently attributed to him.[14] The bibliography of Servetus's writings, therefore, remains the one recognized traditionally, plus *Declarationis*.[15]

Bainton's book concludes by urging us to learn from John Calvin's intolerance the lesson of freedom of conscience that Servetus himself taught from his earliest writings, and that Castellio and others developed in their controversy against Calvin and Beza.[16] Following Bainton's lead, I am convinced that, despite Servetus's philosophical, theological, Biblical, medical, and reformist contributions, the idea of religious tolerance is his most enduring legacy. There is no doctrine we need more urgently in our chaotic new century than respect for our neighbor's conscience, which ought never to be repressed by the power of the sword or the magistrate. Moreover, we ought to adopt the practice of mutual tolerance between states, religions, and cultures. It is my absolute conviction that, as I said in the title of a recent article, these are "Servetus's Two Great Legacies: Radicalism as Intellectual Method and the Right to Freedom of Conscience."[17]

I would like to express my gratitude to the editor and the publisher of this book for giving me the opportunity to offer a modest scholarly introduction and update to readers of this new edition of the great Yale professor Roland Bainton's *Hunted Heretic*, the starting point of modern Servetian scholarship. We all hope that this book not only stimulates fresh studies of the theological ideas of the heroic radical defender of religious liberty, but helps to spread in the world the rights of freedom of conscience for which Servetus died.

Ángel Alcalá
New York, October 15, 2004

Notes

[1] José Barón Fernández, *Miguel Servet: su vida y su obra* (Madrid: Espasa-Calpe, 1970), 26, 309; Ángel Alcalá, ed., *Miguel Servet: Obras Completas,* vol. 1 (Zaragoza: Larumbe, 2003), xxx-xxxi, 5-6.

[2] For further discussion of the controversy over Servetus's birthplace, see chapter 1, note 2 (pp. 171-172).

[3] The basic documents regarding birth, family and place have been published in *Obras Completas,* vol. 1.

[4] William H. Prescott, *The History of the Reign of Ferdinand and Isabella* (Philadelphia, 1837), 2:136-137; Rafael Sabatini, *Torquemada and the Spanish Inquisition* (London, 1913), 364-366.

[5] David A. Boruchoff, "Instructions for Sainthood and other Feminine Wiles in the Historiography of Isabel I," in Boruchoff, ed., *Isabel La Católica, Queen of Castille* (New York: Macmillan, 2003), 21-22, n. 38.

[6] Richard H. Popkin, "Marranos, New Christians and the Beginning of Modern Anti-Trinitarianism," in Yom Tob Assis and Yosef Kaplan, ed., *Jews and Conversos at the Time of the Expulsion* (Jerusalem: Zalman Shazar Center for Jewish History, 1999), 143-161.

[7] 1 John 5:8; see p. 6.

[8] *Christianismi Restitutio,* 462; see p. 11.

[9] Juan de Valdés, *Diálogo de Doctrina Cristiana,* trans. Ángel M. Mergal, in Ángel M. Mergal and George Huntston Williams, *Spiritual and Anabaptist Writers* (Philadelphia, 1957).

[10] Alfonso de Valdés, *Obra Completa,* ed. Ángel Alcalá (Madrid: Biblioteca Castro, 1996); Juan de Valdés, *Obras Completas,* vol. 1, ed. Ángel Alcalá (Madrid: Biblioteca Castro, 1997).

[11] Stanislas Kot, "L'influence de Michel Servet sur le Mouvement Anti-trinitarien en Pologne et en Transylvanie," in Bruno Becker, ed., *Autour de Michel Servet et de Sébastien Castellion* (Haarlem: Willink & Zoon, 1953).

[12] See pp. 228-229.

[13] See *Obras Completas*, vol. 3.

[14] See pp. 210-211.

[15] See pp. 200-202.

[16] See the recent translation into English of Guggisberg's magisterial work: Hans Guggisberg, *Sebastian Castellio, 1515-1563: Humanist and Defender of Religious Toleration in a Confessional Age*, trans. and ed. Bruce Gordon (Burlington, Vermont: Ashgate, 2003); and the translation into French of Castellio's *Contra libellum Calvini*: Sébastien Castellion, *Contre le Libelle de Calvin*, trans. Étienne Barilier (Geneva: Carouge, 1998). Part of *Contra libellum Calvini* is translated into Spanish in *Obras Completas*, vol. 1.

[17] Ángel Alcalá, "Servetus's Two Great Legacies: Radicalism as Intellectual Method and the Right to Freedom of Conscience," trans. Javier Miranda, in *The Role of the Dissenter In Western Christianity: From Jesus through the 16th Century* (Berkeley: Starr King School for the Ministry, 2004). See also the remarkable articles and crusading books by Marian Hillar, listed in the bibliography, p. 212 .

HUNTED HERETIC

The Life and Death of Michael Servetus, 1511-1553

Chapter 1

Dog of a Marrano

Michael Servetus has the singular distinction of having been burned by the Catholics in effigy and by the Protestants in actuality. This coincidence of itself would have secured for him no more than a niche in the hall of eccentrics were it not that his martyrdom came to have a significance exceeding that of perhaps any other in his century — because it served as the occasion for the rise in volume and intensity of the toleration controversy within Protestantism. This is the essential reason for recounting again — just four hundred years after his execution — the story of his life and death.

Some there are who resent the prominence thus given to one single burning. "Were there not," they ask, "thousands of victims of the Inquisition? Did not hundreds and even thousands of Anabaptists suffer at the hands of the Catholics and the Protestants alike? Why, then, select the Servetus episode for special notice unless it be to cast opprobrium upon the memory of John Calvin?" With some, and at certain times, this may indeed have been the motive — but it is not so here. John Calvin is the granite block from which we of the Puritan tradition have been carved, and precisely because of our loyalty to the rock from which we are hewn, we would not disguise the flaws. To point them out is not so much to reproach a spiritual ancestor as to engage in searching of heart lest we perpetuate only the vices of our forebears. In this our day, religious liberty is in peril. This study may be revealing as to the reasons why men persecute and the reasons why, as Christians, they should not.

Apart from his dramatic death and the ensuing controversy, Servetus is a fascinating figure because he brought together in a single person the Renaissance and the left wing of the Reformation. He was at once a disciple of the Neoplatonic Academy at Florence and of the Anabaptists. The scope of his interests and accomplishments exhibits the type of the "universal man" of the Renaissance, for Servetus was proficient in medicine, geography, Biblical scholarship, and theology. In him the most diverse tendencies of the Renaissance and the Reformation were blended. His clash with Calvin was more than personal. It was the conflict of the Reformation with the Renaissance, and of the right wing of the Reformation with the left. Without going beyond Servetus and Calvin, one meets most of the significant currents of the sixteenth century.

We do not know precisely when Servetus was born.[1] The discrepancies in his testimony on this score may be noted here because they are typical of discordant statements on several points. What we know of his life is derived almost exclusively from his own answers to questions on two occasions, both in 1553 – first in France and then at Geneva. In both instances he was on trial for his life and was not above dissembling in order to mislead his inquisitors. He had the greater reason in France, where his identity was unknown, than at Geneva, where he had already been exposed. Yet, as to his birth, the testimony given in France is the better corroborated. At Geneva he claimed to be forty-four, of the same age as Calvin, and in France to be forty-two. If the former was true, he was born in 1509; if the latter, in 1511. The later date appears to be correct, because of another statement – that on the appearance of his first book in 1531, he was of the age of twenty.

As to the place, there is no doubt.[2] He was a Spaniard, from a family noble in blood and devout in religion. Documentary evidence lately come to light identifies the town as Villanueva – whence Servetus later took the pseudonym *Villanovanus*, or in French *de Villeneuve* – a hamlet in the province of Huesca and the diocese of Lérida on the Alcanadre some sixty miles above Zaragoza (Saragossa). The father, who called himself "Antonio Serveto alias Revés," was a notary. The parish church has an altarpiece to Santa Lucía erected by his widow, Catalina Conesa, and her son, "Mosén Juan Serveto de Revés clérigo infanzón rector de Poleñino."[3] The brother of Michael Servetus, then, was a priest.

Where Servetus received his early training we do not know, but a great deal we do know about the Spain of his formative years. Many of the tendencies apparent in his subsequent work may have been derived from currents then flowing through the Iberian peninsula. Spain, like the rest of Europe, was enjoying an interlude between eras of intense intolerance. The reason was primarily that the Catholic Church no longer felt itself to be seriously menaced: the force of medieval sectarianism was spent and the Protestant Reformation had not yet arisen. In this genial interval a movement called Evangelism flourished in Catholic lands, in the circle of Valdés at Naples, of Marguerite of Navarre and Bishop Briçonnet in France, of Colet and More in England and of Erasmus in the Low Countries. For Spain the altered temper was more marked because the contrast was more glaring, inasmuch as Spain had been notorious for the rigors of the Inquisition.

The situation of Spain had been peculiar. Before the crusades, under the Moors, she had been the bridge between Christendom and Islam. And at the court of the caliphs the Jews had found a welcome. The three religions, like the three rings of Boccaccio and Lessing, accorded each other a genuine recognition. The crusades terminated this earlier period of latitude and injected such a temper of intolerance that Spain was confronted with the choice of lining up either with Christendom beyond the Pyrenees or with Islam beyond the Straits.

Spain decided for Europe and the Christian faith. Then war was prosecuted against the Moors and pressures were applied to the Jews. There was nothing racial in all this and the Moors and the Jews alike were acceptable if they would submit to baptism. Thousands of Jews complied and thereby gained entree to the highest offices not only of the state but also of the Christian Church. Pablo de Santa María, bishop of Burgos, for example, was Jewish; incidentally from him Servetus appears to have derived most of his Hebraic erudition. But many of the *conversos* retained some of the practices of Judaism such as the observation of the seventh day as the Sabbath and the kosher regulations. In such cases they were regarded as relapsed heretics to be sent to the stake. The great inquisitor, Torquemada, was convinced that such retrogression on the part of the converts could not be avoided so long as Jews were at hand to subvert the *conversos*. The Jews therefore must be expelled from Spain. When they sought by presents to insure immunity, the Grand Inquisitor strode before Their Majesties and, flinging his crucifix upon the table, exclaimed, "For thirty pieces of silver, Judas betrayed his Master and would you sell Him for thirty thousand?" Ferdinand and Isabella succumbed to this importunity and the vessels of Columbus, embarking for the western route to India, saw the sails unfurled to take the Jews into exile. Only *conversos* remained in Spain, and only under surveillance. In that same year, 1492, Granada fell and then the same problem arose with regard to the Moors. Baptism or banishment was the choice. Contempt was expressed for these dubious Christians through the opprobrious epithet, *Marranos*.[4] All of this had taken place within the memory of the father of Servetus, and in Michael's youth the Inquisition was by no means in abeyance. Yet the convulsive period had subsided.

During the first ten years of Servetus's life, the dominant figure in Spain was the great Cardinal Jiménez de Cisneros, an amazing combination of the old and of the new. A medieval figure was he, a Franciscan who took pains to let his hair shirt protrude at the neck when he wore the robes of his exalted office, a disciple of Lady Poverty who would tramp Spain barefoot, and equally medieval in that as Chancellor of the Realm he would employ the wealth of the State to extend the crusade against Islam beyond the Straits. Withal he was committed to an appropriation of the new Renaissance learning for the service of the Church. He it was who organized the University of Alcalá and encouraged discussion within the framework of scholastic tradition. One chair in the university was given to the Thomists, one to the Scotists, and one to the Ockhamists, called in that epoch the Moderni. The University of Salamanca thereupon, not to be outdone, founded three chairs for the Moderni. Jiménez was responsible for the first publication of the Bible, including both of the testaments, in the original tongues. The Jews had anticipated him with the Old Testament in Hebrew and Erasmus with the New Testament in Greek, but he first achieved the publication of the whole, executed in accord with the best critical tools and principles then available. The completed edition, called the Complutensian Polyglot, appeared in the year 1522.

At the same time, with the favor of the Cardinal, the mystical movement of the Alumbrados flourished in Spain. Francisco de Osuna aspired to the sweetness of ecstasy, the raptures of spiritual exaltation. The knowledge of God, he said, is the knowledge of the intense love of the soul purified by the moral virtues, illuminated by the theological virtues, made perfect by the gifts of the spirit and the beatitudes of the gospel. It is the heart that counts more than the head, the hands, the eyes, or the feet. Outward ceremonies without inward dispositions profit nothing. The way is through groanings unutterable.[5] Some of the Alumbrados indulged also in apocalyptic dreams of a Christendom renewed, extending from Jerusalem to the ends of the earth, a marvelous reform of the Church by men of the spirit in the power of the Most High. The young men of Spain were dreaming dreams and the old men were seeing visions.[6]

Then came new currents from the north, during the second decade of the life of Servetus. Charles, King of Spain and Holy Roman Emperor, in the year 1522 regained control of Castille and commenced thereupon in Spain the longest residence of his career. He had been educated in the Netherlands and brought with him in his entourage many courtiers of the Low Countries. They were admirers of Erasmus of Rotterdam, who came to enjoy an unparalleled vogue in Spain during the years 1522 to 1532. Many of his works were rendered into the vernacular; Spain became imbued with his ideal of a simple nondogmatic piety dedicated to lofty living, charity, concord, and peace, eschewing all wrangling over the refined distinctions of theology. Erasmus trusted, much more exclusively than Jiménez, the power of the gospel to take captive the minds of men without any exterior constraint. Like Jiménez he dreamed, with a well-nigh apocalyptic fervor, of the restoration of Christianity in its primitive purity, according to the pattern of the unadulterated word of God in the ancient tongues.

The popularity of Erasmus does not mean, however, that Spaniards had ceased to be very jealous for the Lord God of Hosts. There was one point in particular at which dogmatic rectitude became a matter of national honor, and that was the doctrine of the Trinity and of the deity of Christ. The reason was that abroad all Spaniards were regarded as Marranos and suspect as to faith in the doctrine of the Trinity, the Christian tenet most difficult for them to accept and easiest to attenuate. In Italy the current estimate deemed every Spaniard to be tainted with heresy. A character in an Italian comedy says, "You Spaniards do not believe in Christ." Ariosto reports that Spaniards do not believe in *unità di Spirito il Padre e il figlio* and another comedy represents a Spaniard, having received absolution from all his sins, returning to his confessor to report that he had overlooked a *peccadiglio*: he did not believe in God.[7]

In France and Germany the Spanish reputation was no better and Luther declared that he would rather have a Turk for an enemy than a Spaniard for a protector. "The Spaniards," said he, "are all Marranos and, whereas other heretics defend their opinions obstinately, the Marranos shrug their shoulders and hold nothing for certain."[8]

The Spaniards, in view of these jibes, were peculiarly sensitive to any imputation of deviation from orthodoxy in the doctrine of the three in one. Erasmus, despite his immense reputation, was subject to a hefty attack from the Spaniard, Zuñiga, because of passages in his edition of the Greek New Testament which might be construed as undercutting the doctrine. Erasmus left out the so-called *Comma Johanneum*. The genuine text of 1 John 5:8 reads: "There are three on earth that bear witness, the Spirit, the water and the blood, and these three agree in One." The spurious portion adds: "There are three that bear record in Heaven, the Father, the Word and the Holy Spirit, and these three are One." This addendum was not discovered by Erasmus in any Greek manuscript nor was it known to the early fathers of the Church who, had they been acquainted with it, would undoubtedly have availed themselves of so devastating a response to the Arians. Erasmus, therefore, expunged the verse so long current in the Vulgate translation. In commenting also on the Gospel of John, Erasmus observed that the term God is applied in the New Testament almost exclusively to the Father. Erasmus attacked no doctrines. He merely stated facts. But he was nevertheless subject to vehement remonstrance and that in Spain.[9]

Whether Servetus, at that time only in his early teens, was acquainted with all this discussion may well be doubted. At any rate he did not employ the observations of Erasmus to bolster his own later critique of the doctrine of the Trinity. Instead of rejecting the spurious verse in the First Epistle of John he sought, rather, to place upon it an acceptable interpretation.[10] But that Servetus was altogether unaffected by the liberal climate is even more improbable, since at the age of fourteen he became attached to the service of Juan de Quintana, a Franciscan Minorite, a doctor at the University of Paris and an eminent member of the Cortes of Aragón. This Quintana was a man of Erasmian spirit and irenic temper who told Melanchthon at the Diet of Augsburg that he could not understand why the Lutheran doctrine of justification by faith should have aroused such a storm.[11] How well Servetus came to know Quintana we cannot tell. We do know that the service, whatever its nature, involved personal acquaintance. In this entourage Servetus could scarcely fail, with his avid mind and precocious development, to absorb much.

The service with this churchman was neither exacting nor confining. Quintana released Servetus for two years to pursue the study of law at the University of Toulouse.[12] Quite possibly this university was selected by Servetus's parents because of its reputation as a citadel of orthodoxy in the very territory once dominated by the Albigensian heretics. A Protestant considered this city to be "very superstitious, being full of relics and other instruments of idolatry, so that one would be condemned as a heretic if one did not raise the hat before an image or bend the knee and ring the bell called *Ave Maria*, or if one tasted a single morsel of meat on a saint's day. And there was no one who delighted in languages and letters, who was not watched and suspected of heresy."[13] This account refers to a somewhat later time; but in the early 1530s banishments and burning began, and in the late 1520s the University had been no less devoted to the faith.[14]

Quite possibly, on the other hand, the reputation of the University in the field of religion had nothing whatever to do with the choice. Servetus was desirous of studying law and, in this field, Toulouse was pre-eminent. The University numbered some 10,000 students and 600 professors. Of the four faculties, theology, medicine, and letters could not vie with jurisprudence.[15] But even law did not exclude theology. When Servetus opened the Codex of Justinian, the great textbook of the Roman law, his eye might fall upon the section dealing with the penalties for ecclesiastical offenses. He would discover that for the repetition of baptism and for a denial of the doctrine of the Trinity, the penalty was death.

Toulouse, despite the measures taken to prevent any recurrence of the Albigensian heresy, was not a stranger to the new currents of reform. The Franciscans in particular were rallying here for the purification of the Church and the conversion of the new world. Student groups were poring over "the oracles of scripture" from which, Servetus later testified, "the Holy Spirit enters us as a stream of living water."[16]

"I beg you," he said, "read the Bible a thousand times. If you have no taste for it you have lost the key to knowledge."[17] So great was his own enthusiasm that Justinian was never opened again.[18] Was there anything in the particular edition of the Bible used by Servetus to evoke such passionate devotion? Apparently it was not the New Testament of Erasmus which he used, for in that case he would presumably have noticed the omission of the Trinitarian passage in 1 John. Probably he was delving in the massive tomes, Hebrew, Greek, and Latin – given to the world in 1522 by his great compatriot, Jiménez – the Complutensian Polyglot.

The edition really did not matter. Any edition contained explosives enough. Servetus was a Spaniard and may well have been riled by the ribbing of fellow students who would call him *chien espagnol de Marrane*. And apart from all such jibes, a sensitive and inquiring Spaniard could scarcely escape a concern for the problem of the Moors and the Jews. Why, if the Christian religion were a revelation of God on High, did these peoples, one of them once the chosen of the Lord, so obstinately refuse to believe? The great stone of stumbling was the doctrine of the Trinity. To them it spelled simply tritheism and conflicted obviously with the great affirmation "Hear, O Israel, the Lord Thy God is One." The interpretation placed on the doctrine by the Moors and the Jews was certainly not perverse when one recalls that pictorial representations showed the Trinity sometimes as three identical old men, sometimes as distinguished in that the Father wore a tiara, the Son carried a cross, and the Spirit a dove. Or, again, one body was shown with three heads or one head with three faces.[19] Muhammad, according to Servetus, was ready to admit that Christ was the greatest of the prophets, the Spirit of God, the power of God, the breath of God, the very soul of God, the Word born by the inbreathing of God from the Ever-virgin; but God alone knew what a laughingstock this doctrine of the Trinity had been to the Muslims.[20] As for the Jews, said Servetus, "I am constrained to weep when I see the blind responses which have been adduced against Rabbi Kimhi's criticism of the Christians on this point."[21]

What, then, was the amazement of Servetus when he delved in the sacred word to find nothing whatever about the Trinity. The expression itself is not there – nor any mention of the one substance and the three persons. The key word, *homoousios*, describing the relation of the Son and the Father, is absent. There is something about the Father, something about the Son, something about the Holy Ghost. They are never declared to be three in one. Should we then, thought Servetus, require of the Moors and the Jews adherence to a doctrine not enunciated in the word of God? If they accept baptism and afterwards err on this tenet of the three in one, shall we, then, send them to the stake? And if the doctrine is not Biblical when and where did it arise? Servetus set himself to find out. He may have progressed far with the subject while still at Toulouse, but on this score we possess no definite information.

His studies were interrupted when he was recalled to the service of Quintana. The reason was that Quintana himself had been summoned to fill his office of Confessor to His Imperial Majesty, and with him to go to Italy for the coronation and then to Germany in the hope of a settlement of the Lutheran affair. Charles V, after a residence of seven years in Spain, was ready now to devote himself to Europe. He realized that if Christendom were to be saved and the Turks repelled, dissensions in Europe must first be allayed. He had had his own quarrel for some time with the Pope because His Holiness, constantly endeavoring to maintain a balance of power, had veered toward support of France. The reason was that Charles all too heavily tipped the scales by his election as Holy Roman Emperor in Germany, at a time when he already controlled Spain, Burgundy, the Netherlands, and Austria.

In the ensuing conflict the imperial troops sacked Rome and made the Pope a prisoner. This was in 1527. The Emperor had the discernment to perceive that a captive pope so lost prestige as to be a useless tool. Some measure of freedom must be restored. For that reason the Emperor resolved to journey to Italy and accept coronation at papal hands. This was not otherwise strictly necessary. Charles had already been crowned by the Estates in 1520. The Pope's blessing was like a church wedding after a civil ceremony. Some of Charles's predecessors had dispensed with it. But to restore the ancient custom would be a gesture of reconciliation and a device for restoring the harmony of the two great powers of the medieval world, corresponding to the sun and the moon in the firmament of heaven, the Emperor and the Pope. When that was done Charles would then proceed to Germany and, through a moderate churchman like Quintana, might be able to pacify the Lutherans.

The Emperor left Spain on the flagship of Admiral Doria in July of 1529. The court came with him. This meant that the Netherlanders, who had disseminated the cult of Erasmus, were withdrawn from Spain, and the Erasmian vogue declined. But this event alone was not responsible. The shades were deepening all over Europe. In Italy the sack of Rome marked the end of the period of the Renaissance at the Vatican. The year in which Charles left Spain was the year in which religious war flared in Switzerland. Bigotry, dogmatism, fanaticism, and atrocities were in store.

Charles landed at Genoa in August to make his peace with the Pope. The imperialists looked askance. They had just been on the point of enlisting Erasmus to edit Dante's *De Monarchia* in order to support the claims of the Empire against the Church. But now, behold the Emperor reverting to the kissing of the papal toe.[22] Charles knew what he was about. A little pageantry was a paltry price for peace and power. The Pope in turn compensated for his actual weakness by staging one of the most magnificent spectacles, exceeding the brilliance of medieval pageantry. Rome would have been the natural stage but there were reasons for choosing Bologna, and as the proverb has it, "Where the pope is, there is Rome."[23]

The occasion was gorgeous. Private and public munificence erected triumphal arches and golden inscriptions on every comer to celebrate the Emperor's victories and the discovery of the isles at the Antipodes. From the gaping throats of sculptured lions spurted red wine, and white from eagles' beaks. On the dwellings golden and purple gewgaws fluttered and sparkled. Fife and drum, trumpet and trombone sounded like the Judgment Day. Dogs raced about and horses pranced. A concourse of a hundred thousand of all ages thronged the streets and perched on walls, windows, and gables to see the Emperor and the Pope, the dignitaries from Britain and from the Isles of the Levant, princes and peers, cardinals and canons in resplendent attire. The Most Holy Father, Clement VII, rode in the midst of four cardinals on foot. On his head was a triple crown. Beneath a golden canopy he sat in a

The Pope and the Emperor in the Procession after the Coronation at Bologna

golden chair. When the Pope and the Emperor met, His Majesty kissed the feet of His Holiness, and begged to be received as his son.[24]

The imperialists shrugged. Servetus glowered. A quarter of a century later he wrote, "With these very eyes we have seen him[a] borne in pomp on the necks of princes, making with his hand the sign of the cross, and adored in the open streets by all the people on bended knee, so that those who were able to kiss his feet or slippers counted themselves more fortunate than the rest, and declared that they had obtained many indulgences, and that on this account the infernal pains would be remitted for many years. O vilest of all beasts, most brazen of harlots!"[25]

What had happened to Servetus? This is not the language of a frustrated imperialist. These are the words of medieval sectaries or Protestant reformers. This is the language of a Wycliffe, who scornfully contrasted the poverty of Christ and the luxuriance of the pope. This is the language of a John Hus, who pictured Christ the lowly riding upon an ass while the pope traveled upon a charger with a golden bit and tassels streaming to the ground. It is the language of a Melanchthon and of a Luther, who issued a book of woodcuts displaying on one side Christ barefoot and on the other the pope carried in a palanquin; on one side Christ extracting a coin from the fish's belly, on the other the pope raking in the proceeds of indulgences; in the end, Christ ascending to heaven and the pope as antichrist descending to hell.

Somewhere along the line Servetus had imbibed, if not the virus of the Protestants, then the scathing apocalypticism of the Spiritual Franciscans, who foretold the doom of the papacy as the prelude to the restoration of Christianity in the great age of the Spirit.

---

[a] i.e. the Pope.

Three identical men

Three men distinguished

One head with three faces

One body with three heads

Representations of the Trinity

Chapter 2

The Errors of the Trinity

Servetus discreetly slipped away from the service of Quintana and the imperial court. Just what was in the mind of the young man at this juncture cannot be determined with precision. A year and one half later he was to publish a book *On the Errors of the Trinity*, which contains both an assault upon the traditional view and a reconstruction of his own position. The former necessitated his withdrawal from Catholic lands; the latter was to make his residence untenable also on Protestant soil. Though, no doubt, the negative and the positive aspects of his thinking matured together, they will for purposes of presentation be here divided. His attempt to demolish the doctrine of the Trinity will be described in this chapter, and his own emergent view in the next. This division may not be altogether arbitrary, because the books which undermined his confidence in the scholastic view of the Trinity were readily accessible in France,[1] whereas the early Fathers, from whom he drew his own solution, were just being printed in Basel.

Before dealing, however, with the views of Servetus, a little excursus is needful on the doctrine of the Trinity as it had been evolved and defended throughout the centuries. Initially, it was adopted as a formula to express all that the doctrine of the incarnation implied with regard to the being of God himself. If God actually and uniquely became flesh in Christ, what does this mean for the nature of God? That he was one God was the tradition of Judaism from which the Church had no mind to diverge, but if there was a distinction between God and Christ, and yet Christ was God, would there not be two gods? Or if Christ was not really distinct, but only a mode of the Divine behavior, then God would indeed be one, but Christ could hardly be regarded as genuinely human; and when the Spirit was personalized, then the problem of the two became the problem of the three. The solution was to posit both a oneness and a threeness in God, a diversity within unity, a pluralism within monism. The word chosen in Latin to express the oneness was *substance,* and the word for the threeness was *person.* There are, then, three persons who share or participate uniquely in the substance or being of God. On the side of Christology, Christ was declared to be of one substance with God as to His divinity and with man as to His humanity. This was the doctrine formulated at Nicaea in A.D. 325 and more precisely at Chalcedon in A.D. 450.

Thereafter the doctrine was assumed. Western speculation then concerned itself with the question as to how the doctrine of the Trinity could be known, whether it could be proved, and whether it could be explained. Broadly speaking, three schools of thought developed. The first was associated with the name of St. Augustine in the fourth and fifth centuries and claimed that the doctrine cannot be proved, but may be illustrated; the second, stemming from Richard of St. Victor in the twelfth century, averred that the doctrine can be demonstrated; and the third, originating with William of Ockham in the fourteenth century, claimed that it can neither be demonstrated nor illustrated, but can only be believed. The first view may be called the illustrative, the second, the demonstrative, and the third, the fideist – the term used to describe a blind faith without rational support.[2]

Augustine, who formulated the first position, conceded that the doctrine never would have been attained apart from revelation. It is, indeed, implicit in Scripture and the Nicene elucidation of the purport of Scripture is sound. Yet no deductions would lead anywhere if revelation had not provided the premise. The doctrine, therefore, must be received on faith, since we see only in a glass darkly. At the same time faith need not be blind and we should endeavor to understand insofar as we are able. Some questions, to be sure, are completely beyond our ken: as, for example, the difference between the generation of the Son and the procession of the Holy Spirit. The creed says that the Son was *generated* by the Father but the Spirit *proceeds* from the Father and the Son. At other points, however, we aspire to understand and the way lies through analogy, by which the doctrine, though undemonstrable, can nevertheless be illustrated.[3]

Augustine discovered a comparison in the constitution of man, in whom there is a psychological trinity of memory, intellect, and will. Inasmuch as these, being three, are yet inseparable in action, they offer a clue to the understanding of the inner trinitarian relationship within the Being of God. The similitude is only an illustration; yet it has some demonstrative value since man was created in the image of God, and that image has not been wholly obliterated by the Fall. Just as one may infer the presence of a cow from tracks in a meadow, so one may reach out from the structure of man to the structure of God. This approach by way of analogy and illustration was to dominate a long line of theologians in the West, including Aquinas. Servetus did not consider it worthy of mention. Since the doctrine itself was under dispute, an illustration falling short of demonstration was naturally of no help. Servetus would cite Augustine only in case he propounded some insoluble conundrum in the doctrine.

Among the theologians in the succession of St. Augustine was Peter Lombard (died 1160), whose book *The Sentences* was the great text for medieval theology.[4] He was brash enough to assert that the doctrine of the Trinity could be found on every page of Holy Writ. Servetus gasped. "To me," he exclaimed, "not only the syllables but all the letters and the mouths of babes and sucklings, even the very stones themselves, cry out that there is one God the Father and His Christ, the Lord Jesus."[5] "Not one word," he affirmed, "is found in the whole Bible about the Trinity nor about its persons, nor about the essence nor the unity of substance nor of the one nature of the several beings nor about any of the rest of their ravings and logic chopping."[6]

The Lombard, fortified by his blithe confidence, grappled resolutely with the problem raised by the Arians – ancient opponents of the Nicene position – that, if the Father is ungenerated and the Son generated, there must be more than one substance. Augustine had contented himself with saying that the terms *generated* and *ungenerated* are not to be understood according to substance. The Lombard went further and roundly declared that the substance neither generates nor is generated. Joachim of Fiore in the late twelfth century pointed out that if the Lombard were right, and the substance were aloof from the process, then the substance would constitute a fourth entity and there would be a quaternity. "Precisely!" ejaculated Servetus.[7] To obviate this conclusion Joachim reduced the one substance to such a wraith that nothing remained to hold the three persons in unity and, in consequence, they became three gods.[8] This conclusion also appeared to Servetus to be inescapable. The Church, of course, would not have it so; and the Fourth Lateran Council in the year 1215 ratified the position of Peter Lombard, which thereafter became the authoritative teaching enshrined in the Canon Law.

The second attitude toward the problem of the Trinity in the Middle Ages was inaugurated by Richard of St. Victor, who held that the doctrine is susceptible not only of illustration, but also of demonstration. His assurance was derived from Neoplatonic thinking which conceived of God in terms of dynamic Being, self-diffusive and expansive. God is not static and quiescent, but ebullient and uncontained. The problem then was to explain why the process of expansion should have been arrested at three. And here Richard had recourse to another picture of deity. Essentially he employed the Hebrew view of God to control the Greek. The God of the Old Testament was a single person, willing, acting, commanding, loving. This quality of love, according to Richard, restrained the process of diffusion from exceeding three. God is love and love requires an object to love distinct from and equal to the lover; hence God must have God to love. So far, however, this requires only two. Why then must there be three and only three? Because perfect love is without jealousy and must have a third with whom to share this love. Thus personality operative through love imposes limitations upon the diffusion of being.[9]

Another variant of the argument may be mentioned because cited by Servetus. The author was the scholastic, Henry of Ghent (Henri de Gand), who died in 1293. In his judgment, the Trinitarian structure of God was necessary to account for the creation of the world because creation is the work of wisdom and will. But wisdom and will are inoperative so long as they are dormant in God. They must first be projected — that is, personalized as the second and third persons of the Trinity — if they are to achieve the work of the creation. Behind this thinking lay the old Stoic picture of the Logos first as immanent in God, then as projected in the form of reason and expression.[10]

This entire approach was to Servetus sheer nonsense, unworthy even of a refutation. For one thing, he did not understand it and supposed that Henry was marrying wisdom and will, that they might copulate and beget. The comment of Servetus was simply: "More of this stuff I pass over!"[11]

The third school on this problem of the Trinity in the Middle Ages despaired alike of demonstration and of illustration and resorted, therefore, to an appeal to the authority of the Church in an attitude of fideism. This was the school known as the Moderni, stemming from

William of Ockham.[12] The reason for the altered attitude to the doctrine of the Trinity was a shift to Nominalism, which is the philosophy of stark individualism. Reality, in this view, is held to consist of individuals, related only in the sense that they stand side by side in space and time. The concepts into which they are classified by men are nothing but concepts, mere names – whence the term *Nominalism*. According to this view, the State is not an entity in and of itself but is only the aggregate of its citizens. The Church again is not an entity in the mind of God, but simply the sum of individual church members. In the technical terminology of the time, there is no "universal," no entity embracing the individuals.

If the Nominalist position were true, how then could the members of the Trinity be held together? They would not be related even in the sense of being side by side in space and time since they are beyond space and time. The orthodox dogma regarded *substance* as the entity holding the three in unity. But for Ockham this substance was not a "universal." It was, indeed, nothing but a descriptive term applicable to that which the three actually have in common. This they do have in common: that all three are *called* persons. But, to use Ockham's own words, "The community lies only in words and concepts in the same way that many may be said to constitute a whole." If, then, no real bond exists and there are three persons in the godhead, what other conclusion can there be, if not that the three persons are three gods? Ockham did not voice this position in terms so blunt, but he did say that there are in the godhead three absolutes.

He was perfectly aware that he had reached an impasse. From the point of view of logic he conceded the syllogism to be sound: God is a Trinity, the Father is God, therefore, the Father is a Trinity. Yet this is fallacious from the point of view of faith. The doctrine of the Trinity, therefore, cannot be demonstrated. It cannot even be illustrated. One would not know that a statue was of Hercules any more than of Socrates if one had never seen Hercules. Nor from the tracks in a meadow could one infer a cow any more than a donkey, if one had never seen a cow. If then the doctrine of the Trinity were retained the only basis could be fideism.

Among the followers of Ockham, there were four expressly cited by Servetus: Robert Holkot, who died in 1349; Gregory of Rimini, who lectured in Paris in 1344; Pierre d'Ailly (1350-1420?), the great Cardinal, whose *Imago Mundi* stimulated Columbus to make the vast adventure; and John Major (1469-1550), a Scot active in Paris.[13] Their general point of view was so similar that one may wonder whether they need be pursued individually. There is, however, a reason beyond the point of elucidating fully the sources of Servetus. These four names with that of Ockham are a clue to the role of Servetus as the bridge between the late scholastic critics of the Trinity and the Antitrinitarians of the sixteenth century, who did not themselves delve in scholastic lore. When, then, we find them citing precisely these five authors we may be sure that their source is Michael Servetus.

Robert Holkot reveled in conundrums, enumerating sixteen contrarieties in the doctrine of the Trinity, as for example: that God cannot be three persons because three persons constitute three gods. Again, if the three persons be distinguished finitely there will be finitude in God; if infinitely, the three will differ as much as God and the Devil or man and an ass. Again, the Divine Essence generates. It must generate another God. In that case there would be two gods. The fourteenth problem was that the Trinity is a unity, yet it is not the Father, nor the Son, nor the Spirit, so consequently there must be a fourth element in Divinity. Holkot concluded that to seek to establish the Catholic faith by way of reason is not only presumptuous but fatuous. One may humbly seek a rational explanation. If it be given, then let God be praised; but if not, the seeker should not brandish his horns but bow his head. Let him recognize that natural logic is deficient in the area of faith. Aristotle realized that each discipline has a logic peculiar to itself. And why, then, should there not be a special logic peculiar to faith? Holkot did his best to discover answers but the emphasis was upon the incomprehensibility if not, indeed, the irrationality of the doctrine of the Trinity.

Gregory of Rimini was troubled by the old difference, noted by Augustine, that the Son is *begotten* of the Father but the Spirit *proceeds* from the Father and the Son. Why should there be any difference in the manner of the process of derivation? If it be answered that the Son is derived from one, but the Spirit from two, the reply is that the origin of a flame is not different if it be kindled from two rather than from one fire. We are driven, therefore, to admit that the differentiation transcends our faculties because the derivation of the Son and of the Spirit is ineffable and incomprehensible.

Pierre d'Ailly concluded like the others that the Trinity can neither be demonstrated nor illustrated. "But God desired that such truths be believed by Catholics and, for that reason, he revealed them to the

Church and caused them to be settled by Her authority. Wherefore some of the determinations of the Church do not proceed according to evident deduction from Scripture but according to spiritual revelation made to Catholics. If anyone inquires as to the manner of this revelation, I answer that it is difficult to declare save to those to whom the revelation is given. It is a special gift of God to believe correctly." At the same time d'Ailly felt that the scholar must be very guarded in the expressions which he employs in the presence of the uninstructed. If we speak *personaliter,* that is, with reference to the persons, we may say that there are three gods. "But such an expression, though true and appropriate among experts, is nevertheless not customary and should be avoided for the sake of ordinary believers."

John Major, a contemporary of Servetus, put the matter much more bluntly when he said, "On account of the infidels the saints did not admit a plurality of gods. Yet the case may be so understood among experts." Even less guarded was the statement of Erasmus – which Servetus may or may not have known – that "According to dialectical logic it is possible to say there are three gods. But to announce this to the untutored would give offense."

With this whole line of authors Servetus was acquainted. The range of his reading, when he was only eighteen or nineteen years of age, was astounding. He cited all of the authorities: St. Victor, Ockham, Holkot, d'Ailly, Gregory of Rimini, and John Major. (It is rather odd that he made no mention of Aquinas, whom later he was to edit in Spanish.) Servetus was in a position to subject them all to the touchstone of Biblical authority in the original tongues, Hebrew and Greek.

He appears to have attacked the course of Trinitarian speculation by contrasting the late scholastic theories with the earliest Biblical formulations. The discrepancy between them was the measure of the corruption which had invaded the Church. This divergence was exaggerated because the conundrums of the scholastics were by Servetus deemed to be insoluble. His skepticism far exceeded theirs, because they at least did seek solutions; but what they called unfathomable he considered untenable and their ineffable was his incredible. After reading all of their questions, objections, and reconciliations he came away convinced that the doctrine of the Trinity is riddled with fallacies. With devastating avidity he despoiled their arsenal in order to demolish their rampart.

One wonders why Servetus found their syllogisms so cogent. Was it because he shared their Nominalist philosophy? Perhaps. Or was it because he was no metaphysician at all, but simply a student of the Bible? This appears more probable.

In a word, then, the doctrine of the Trinity for Servetus could be defended only by sheer sophistry. Its origin at the Council of Nicaea in 325 A.D. constituted the fall of the Church — that in conjunction with another abomination, namely, the rise of the temporal power of the papacy in the very same period. Servetus evidently still accepted as genuine the legend that Constantine had conferred temporal sovereignty upon the pope. When, then, Servetus saw the vicar of Him, who had not where to lay His head, receiving homage like a lord of the Gentiles, when this same vicar sent to the stake those who refused to transmute the Son of Mary into a metaphysical abstraction, he could not but exclaim, "O vilest of all beasts, most brazen of harlots!"

A young man who entertained these views was not well situated in the service of the Confessor to the Emperor. Servetus is next discovered on Protestant soil. By July, 1530, he was in Basel. By what route he went we do not know. On one occasion he testified that he accompanied Quintana to Germany. In that case he might have gone to the Diet of Augsburg and he might have seen Melanchthon and he might have seen Bucer and he might have been taken by them to the fortress of the Coburg to see Luther. All of this has been conjectured, but we do not know that he ever went to Augsburg. On another occasion he asserted that he had gone by way of Lyons and Geneva to Basel. It doesn't matter much except that we must not indulge in a riot of conjectures.[14]

More interesting would be to know why Servetus went to Basel. Perhaps he supposed that Erasmus was still there. To him Servetus may well have owed his first religious awakening. Even if he did not know the dubious passages in the edition of the New Testament with regard to the doctrine of the Trinity, he could scarcely have failed to read the preface of Erasmus to the edition of Hilary in 1523[15] — the very edition which Servetus himself had employed — where Erasmus said:

> The ancients philosophized very little about divine things … The curious subtlety of the Arians drove the orthodox to greater necessity … Let the ancients be pardoned … but what excuse is there for us, who raise so many curious, not to say impious, questions about matters far removed from our nature? We define so many things which may be left in ignorance or in doubt without loss of salvation. Is it not possible to have fellowship with the Father,

Son, and Holy Spirit without being able to explain philosophically the distinction between them and between the nativity of the Son and the procession of the Holy Ghost? If I believe the tradition that there are three of one nature, what is the use of labored disputation? If I do not believe, I shall not be persuaded by any human reasons ... You will not be damned if you do not know whether the Spirit proceeding from the Father and the Son has one or two beginnings, but you will not escape damnation, if you do not cultivate the fruits of the Spirit which are love, joy, peace, patience, kindness, goodness, long-suffering, mercy, faith, modesty, continence, and chastity ... The sum of our religion is peace and unanimity, but these can scarcely stand unless we define as little as possible, and in many things leave each one free to follow his own judgment, because there is great obscurity in many matters, and man suffers from this almost congenital disease that he will not give in when once a controversy is started, and after he is heated he regards as absolutely true that which he began to sponsor quite casually ... Many problems are now reserved for an ecumenical council. It would be better to defer questions of this sort to the time when, no longer in a glass darkly, we see God face to face ... Formerly, faith was in life rather than in the profession of creeds. Presently, necessity required that articles be drawn up, but only a few with apostolic sobriety. Then the depravity of the heretics exacted a more precise scrutiny of the divine books ... When faith came to be in writings rather than in hearts, then there were almost as many faiths as men. Articles increased and sincerity decreased. Contention grew hot and love grew cold. The doctrine of Christ, which at first knew no hairsplitting, came to depend on the aid of philosophy. This was the first stage in the decline of the Church ...The injection of the authority of the emperor into this affair did not greatly aid the sincerity of faith ... When faith is in the mouth rather than in the heart, when the solid knowledge of Sacred Scripture fails us, nevertheless by terrorization we drive men to believe what they do not believe, to love what they do not love, to know what they do not know. That which is forced cannot be sincere, and that which is not voluntary cannot please Christ.

Surely a man who talked in this fashion would be willing to listen to the doubts of a Servetus. And he who had so passionately proclaimed the restoration of Christianity would be happy to join in a crusade to eliminate corruption.

Servetus failed to realize that Erasmus was not commending denial but only condemning *debate* about that which we are not in a position to settle. The point of Servetus was rather that we should not *demand* as an essential of the faith that which we do not know. Much less should we make into a cardinal tenet that which can be demonstrated from Scripture to be a palpable error. But there was no opportunity to discuss the matter with Erasmus, for he had already been gone from Basel over a year. Servetus was to find a Basel very different from the one to which Erasmus had come in 1522 when he left the Low Countries rather than be turned into an inquisitor. Basel, in the meantime, like a swimmer sucked into the Rhine, had been swept tumultuously into the swirl of the Reformation.[16]

The reformer of Basel was Oecolampadius.[17] He is described as of sallow complexion, emaciated body, long nose, and thin quavering voice. Between the years of 1515 and 1518 he had been active in Basel as a preacher and editor and had assisted Erasmus with his edition of the New Testament. Gripped by the Lutheran agitation, Oecolampadius attested his faith by marriage in March of the year 1528. Erasmus commented, "A few days ago Oecolampadius married a girl who is not bad looking. He means to crucify his flesh during Lent."[18]

Having taken the step, Oecolampadius was for no sitting on two stools; he deplored the repeated decree of the Town Council that everyone should be free in faith, that no one should be compelled to go to Mass or to preaching but each be left to his own conscience. "A badly educated conscience they have," retorted Oecolampadius, "who, after five years of preaching, still hold to Mass and to the worship of images, which are a worse abomination than adultery. Is adultery against God to be tolerated more than adultery against man?" The Mass must go. The Evangelicals gained possession of five of the city churches and the magistrates thereupon removed the images in these edifices. But this did not suffice. The Mass must go – everywhere, utterly. The Evangelical movement grew stronger through the accession of refugees, monks and nuns escaped from cloisters, and also through a coalition with the socially disaffected. The whole city seethed. Erasmus, translating Chrysostom, was annoyed by the vilification which neighbors heaped upon workmen singing psalms in a neighboring vineyard. Pestilence and rumors of war excited the populace. There were riots, parleys with the Town Council, negotiations and concessions. In January, 1529, the Mass was restricted to three celebrations a day in Basel, until the month of May, that discussion might continue. But this did not suffice. The Mass must go.

On the 8th of February, 1529, before daylight, eight hundred men assembled in the Church of the Franciscans and from there submitted to the Council a demand for the complete abolition of the Mass, the retirement of the Catholic members from the government, and the drafting of a new constitution. The Council deliberated all day. At nine o'clock in the evening the petitioners took arms and possessed themselves of the market place. The Council made indefinite promises and went to bed. The next day the deliberations were resumed. Thousands assembled in the market place. When by noon no decision had been reached and the populace was stomping in the cold, someone proposed that they employ the time in smashing the remaining images. The mob surged up the hill to the Muenster and then to the other churches of greater Basel, smashing with hammers and hewing with axes all the graven and the carved images. Still the Council deliberated; but at length it capitulated and agreed that the Mass should go. This was on the 9th of February, 1529.

In the morning Basel surveyed the debris: torsos, heads, arms, and legs in stone and wood, shreds of painted canvas, stained glass, and glittering decorations, all in heaps of rubbish. The Council gave the wood to the poor for fuel, and when they quarreled, decreed that all of it should be burned. The fires flared for two days and two nights, consuming the works of generations of piety. Two only survived. The St. George high up on the façade of the Muenster had been too high to reach – the Saint still tilts against the dragon. And the Virgin on the city gate may have been too remote. To this day she smiles down upon the babe in her arms and on the passers-by through the portal beneath.

Erasmus announced to Oecolampadius his intention of leaving. Oecolampadius was aghast and besought him to remain. But Erasmus replied that he had already sent on his silver by one messenger and his bedding by another to Freiburg and really he must follow.

The Mass was gone. Next the sectaries were to be treated with diminishing leniency. The Anabaptists – who rejected infant baptism, the oath, the paid ministry, legal suits, military service, and the union of Church and State – were regarded as a menace to society, both ecclesiastical and political. The Town Council had repeatedly banished them on pain of death, but so far had never executed the penalty. Oecolampadius wrote to Zwingli, the reformer of Zurich, that the government was too cool in repression.[19] Such was the temper when Servetus passed beneath the smiling Virgin on Basel's city gate.

Basel's Spalentor
From a drawing by Roland H. Bainton

Chapter 3

The Eternal Word

Servetus at Basel was the guest of Oecolampadius. There was nothing significant about that. The entertainment of refugees was a recognized ministerial function and any day one might come, having barely escaped with his life, slipping over the border with only a pack on his back. At the beginning of the Reformation there was no disposition to subject every new arrival to a theological quiz before allowing him to sit at one's table. Oecolampadius, himself, some five or six years before, had been addicted to entertaining the dubious, but in the meantime he had grown more chary of subversive strangers. Under the circumstances he was singularly forbearant to suffer Servetus to continue in his house *"pour longtemps,"* perhaps for the full ten months of his residence.[1] How Servetus supported himself we do not know; in all likelihood he corrected proof for the publishing houses.

Adequate time remained for his own studies, and Servetus had still much that he desired to explore and elaborate. One is tempted to assign the negative development of his thought with regard to the Trinity to the residence in Toulouse and the positive reconstruction to the Basel period. So sharp a demarcation would, of course, be untenable. Yet there is a positive point already noted with regard to the books available. The late scholastics, in addition to the Bible, were most responsible for shaking the confidence of Servetus in the traditional formula; and these all were available in Toulouse. The early Church Fathers of the second century contributed most to his own reconstruction; and those which chiefly influenced his thinking – Tertullian and Irenaeus – had only lately been issued from the presses of Basel. These are not the only ante-Nicene fathers whom he quotes and some of the others he could have seen earlier. Cyprian and Lactantius had been issued in the late fifteenth century. The epistles of Ignatius, both the spurious and the genuine, had been brought out in Latin translation in 1512 by Symphorien Champier of Lyons, later to be a patron of Servetus. Origen in Latin was published by Badius in Paris in the same year. To these authors Servetus has but occasional references.

Some works he would gladly have used but they were not yet in print. Clement of Alexandria came out in Greek only in 1550 and in Latin in 1551. Servetus especially regretted his inability to consult him.[2] Justin Martyr appeared in Greek in 1551. At this period Servetus knew him only through a citation in Irenaeus.[3]

This enumeration, together with the sources previously mentioned, does not exhaust the list. He was acquainted likewise with writers of the Nicene period itself and of the theological controversies following. But they were not important either negatively or positively for his thinking. The authors who affected him most in the reconstruction of his thought were those closest to the New Testament and, among them pre-eminently, as already noted, were two: Tertullian and Irenaeus. The former, edited by Beatus Rhenanus, appeared in 1528. At the close was a discussion of those passages in which Tertullian appeared to diverge from later orthodoxy. A section of this appendix dealt with his views on the Trinity. The editor contended that the discrepancies were verbal, and that a proper equation of the terminology of Tertullian with that of the late scholastics would effect a reconciliation. But for Servetus any concession of deviation was grist which he commenced avidly to grind. If the Council of Nicaea in 325 marked the fall of the Church, if all the authors thereafter were perverted and those before were relatively sound, differences between the two periods became highly significant.

Irenaeus came out in a Latin translation, the work of Erasmus, first in 1526 and again in 1528. The preface pointed out that the name Irenaeus is derived from the Greek word meaning peace. The saint was well named, said Erasmus, for he was a man of irenic temper laboring in his own day to allay dissension and foster concord in the Church. Would that in our own time, sighed Erasmus, there might be more *Irenaei!* Servetus really hoped that his own work by dispelling error would promote peace.

But ironically his view, when proclaimed, promptly precipitated controversy, for his hearers at once identified him with the ancient heretics Paul of Samosata, Marcellus of Ancyra, and Photinus. A word about their views. Their problems centered partly on the being of God, but even more on the person of Christ. If Christ were God the two questions could not be separated. Paul of Samosata was of the Syrian school, which was very insistent on the oneness of the godhead and the real humanity of Jesus. Yet Jesus was no ordinary man, for he had done what no ordinary man can do. On behalf of his followers he had made possible the forgiveness of sins, newness of life, and triumph over death in a blessed immortality. To have done all this, he must have been in some sense God, yet not in a sense that would make two gods.

One way out was to conceive of Christ simply as a mode of the Divine activity, so that God acts now as the Father, now as the Son, now as the Spirit. The unity of the godhead was thus conserved, but the humanity of Jesus was irretrievably lost. Another solution was to separate Christ from God so that, although more than man, he was still distinctly less than God. The trinitarian formula avoided both extremes by positing enough of unity in God to save him from division and enough differentiation to save Christ and the Spirit from absorption.

A different solution was offered by Paul of Samosata and later Marcellus and Photinus. The essence of it was to divide Christ, or at any rate to make a distinction between the Word and Jesus. The Word was simply a phase of God's activity. "In the beginning was the Word, and the Word was with God, and the Word was God." With regard to the Word the famous term *homoousios,* meaning of one substance or essence, may be used to describe the relationship to God. The Word is not to be equated with the man Jesus. Rather the Word was conjoined to him, became incarnate in him, and then Jesus became the Son of God. The Word, then, was eternal. The Son of God was not eternal. What this solution really adds up to is a theory of modalism as to the relationship of the Word to God, and of subordinationism in the relationship of the Son to the Father.[4]

The similarity of the view of Servetus to this position is quite striking. Yet he stoutly repudiated any dependence and as a matter of fact he arrived at the same conclusion by pursuing the same course. He started where Paul of Samosata had commenced and quite unwittingly emerged with a very similar position. Back of Paul of Samosata was Ignatius of Antioch, the father of the Syrian tradition, with his great emphasis upon the unity of God and his suggestion that Christ is God manifest, whereas the Father is God recessive in ineffable silence. The letters of Ignatius lay before Servetus. Before him, too, were Tertullian and Irenaeus. The latter in one passage equated Logos or mind with the Father.[5] This certainly sounds modalistic.

In Tertullian one finds, to be sure, the clearest anticipation of the Nicene view, for he has the word Trinity and the doctrine of the one substance and the three persons. Nevertheless there are subordinationist suggestions and even hints which could lead in the direction of Paul of Samosata. Tertullian regarded the Logos as eternal with God, but the Son as a historical emergence when the Logos became flesh in Jesus; hence, the Son is not eternal and is therefore subordinate. But Tertullian verged on modalism when he spoke of the Father, the Son, and the Spirit as dispensations or administrations, even almost as temporal manifestations. For, said he, the administrations shall cease when the Son subjects all things to the Father and God is all-in-all.[6]

Servetus, ruminating on all of these passages, tried to find his way to some clarity. One thing to him was perfectly plain: Jesus was a man. The Scriptures over and over again refer to him as a man. He is also called the Son of God and even God. But if he were God, he could be God only in a sense in which man is capable of being God. We must bear in mind, said Servetus, that there are different ways of being God; here he availed himself of the several names for the deity in Hebrew which to him connoted varying degrees of divinity. The term *Jehovah,* he said, is applied to God as the Creator of the Heavens and the Earth. This term is never applied to angels or to men. But the term *Elohim,* indicating a lesser grade, is employed with reference to mortals. This actually invalid distinction in the Hebrew words was designed to conserve at once the unity of God and the humanity of Christ, and likewise to recognize in a meaningful sense the divinity of Christ.

Fundamentally, of course, Servetus's view of the person of Christ was conditioned by his conception of man and of the relation of man to God. He had appropriated from Ignatius and Irenaeus in particular something more than a new formula to describe the godhead. He had imbibed their own profound sense that the new life in Christ is a life in which we no longer live but Christ lives in us. One may even say that God lives in us.[7] Those who make a sharp demarcation between humanity and divinity, said Servetus, "do not understand the nature of humanity, which is of such a character that God can communicate to it divinity,"[8] "not indeed by a degradation of divinity but by an exaltation of humanity."[9] "God sends to us his light and this is God himself."[10]

I say, therefore, that God himself is our spirit dwelling in us, and this is the Holy Spirit within us. In this we testify that there is in our spirit a certain working latent energy, a certain heavenly sense, a latent divinity and it bloweth where it listeth and I hear its voice and I know not whence it comes nor whither it goes. So is everyone that is born of the spirit of God.[11]

Christ prayed the Father for the apostles that they might all be one "as Thou, Father, in me and I in Thee that they also may be one in us, that they may be one as we also are one," thus repeating the word that they might be one. Whence it follows that we are one after the same manner as they, constituting one nature. Certain it is that we are united, conserving the unity of the Spirit in the bond of peace.[12]

We are not on this account to infer that Christ has no pre-eminence.

If you say that you can see no difference between Christ and others, since we are all called sons of God, I answer that if we are called sons of God it is simply through His gift and grace, for He is the author of our sonship, and so is called Son in a more excellent way. That is why the article is used and Christ is called the son of God, to show that he is not a son in the general sense as we are, but in a very special and peculiar sense. He is a natural Son. Others are not born but become sons of God. By faith in Christ we are made sons of God, therefore by adoption we are called sons.[13]

Divinity and humanity, then, are not mutually exclusive and Jesus could be God without ceasing to be man. His relationship to God, since it was not that of other men, remained to be more precisely defined. For Servetus the Word was eternal, a mode of God's self-expression, ever-latent in the Being of God. This Word became flesh.

Let them leave off who contend that the Son was sent from the Father in any other way than as one of the Prophets. For he who was aforetime the hidden God of Israel, when his countenance lay concealed in the shadow of the Father, as he dwelt in the secret place of the Most High, and abode under the shadow of the Almighty, this One was the Son; this One was made manifest and this is the appearance of our Saviour, Christ.[14]

Before His incarnation He was called the Word. After His union with the man Jesus, He was called the Son. The Word, therefore, was eternal. The Son was not eternal.[15] With regard to the Trinity one may concede, with Tertullian, a Trinity of dispensations or administrations.[16] For Servetus these were simply phases or modes of God's activity. The Spirit is simply God's spirit moving within our hearts. "The *Holy Spirit* is not a distinct Being," says Servetus.[17] "Just as God is called the source of all being, so is He called also the source of light. He is called the Father of lights. I do not understand this light as the predication of a quality. He sends His light to us, and this is God himself. He sends His spirit to us, and this is God Himself."[18] "Apart then from God's spirit in us there is no Holy Spirit."[19]

Thus far the thought of Servetus seems clear enough. There is one God who manifests himself in diverse ways. His spirit enters into the hearts of men and they are capable of union with him. This was true in a unique measure of Jesus Christ in Whom God's Spirit or Logos or Word was pre-eminently manifest.

But ambiguity enters, in that the term *Christ* is applied both to the man Jesus, the Son, and also to the pre-existent Logos, the Word. The reason may well be that for Servetus the man Jesus became so identified with the Word that thereafter no distinction could be drawn.

> I do not separate Christ from God any more than a voice from the speaker or a ray from the sun. Christ is in the Father as a voice from the speaker. He and the Father are one as the ray and the sun are one light. An amazing mystery it is that God can thus be conjoined with man and man with God. A great wonder that God has taken to himself the body of Christ that it should be his peculiar dwelling place.[20]

> And because His Spirit was wholly God He is called God just as from His flesh He is called man. Do not marvel that what you call the humanity I adore as God, for you talk of humanity as if it were devoid of spirit and you think of flesh after the flesh. You are not able to recognize the quality of Christ's Spirit which confers being upon matter. He it is who makes alive when the flesh profiteth nothing.[21]

Such passages make abundantly plain that Servetus in all this was concerned with vastly more than refuting abstrusities. He was grappling with more than the problem of the Moors and the Jews. He was wrestling with the immensities and seeking to understand man's relation to the eternal. The question was not how Servetus should find enough to eat at Basel but how he should stand for all eternity before the ineffable splendor of the Divine Majesty. By means of Christ, was his answer, because Christ has demonstrated that man can be taken up into God and share with Him the life eternal.

Servetus grew lyrical as he contemplated the divine economy, the unrolling of the plan of the ages.

> See how gloriously God brought forth the Son whom He had decreed to beget as His only begotten. It was meet that He should so gloriously beget Him who was ordained to be the judge of the living and the dead. When I raise my eyes to Him who sits on the right hand of the Father in Heaven I tremble when I hear you refer to Him as the human nature. Do you not see

that it is He who governs all things? This alone suffices, if you will but look above, that He should be called not only the Son of God but God and the Lord of the world.[22]

One no longer knows, one no longer cares whether it be Jesus or the Word of whom one speaks. "With Daniel," exclaims Servetus, "I see Jesus Christ coming on the clouds of heaven. I see Him in the chariot of Ezekiel and riding amid the myrtles of Zechariah. I see Him on the throne of Isaiah."[23]

> He is the soul of the world, yea, more than the soul, for through Him we live not only in the temporal but also in the eternal life. The temporal He has given us in the Word and the eternal He has gained in His flesh. I would call Him more than the splendor of glory, for Paul speaks of the Lord of Glory crucified. He is the glorious star of the morning. There are those who have so misconceived His humanity that they blush to speak of the splendor of His glory, for He Himself said I am the Light of the World. Much greater things are to be said of Him. He is the Light of God, the Light of the Gentiles; the splendor of His countenance illumines the whole Heaven and will illumine the worlds in generations to come. He is the power of God by which the worlds were made and although the word of the cross is to some foolishness, to others it is the power of God. For, with marvelous power he has subjected the world to His sway and will subdue it. Without clamor of arms He leads captive the minds of men.[24]

By the Holy Spirit likewise we are vitalized during this our earthly pilgrimage.

> In that which is inhaled and exhaled there is an energy, a vivifying spirit of deity, for He by his Spirit sustains in us the breath of life, giving breath to the people that are on the earth and spirit to those that walk therein. He alone shakes the heavens and brings forth the winds from His treasures. He binds up the waters in the clouds and gives rain in His season. He alone doeth all these things. He alone worketh miracles everlastingly.[25]

And He alone shall be All-in-all:

> The Kingdom of Christ is a thousand times called eternal. Yet in the consummation of the ages He shall restore it to God. Not that the glory of Christ is thereby diminished, for it is His highest glory to have ruled all things well, even to the end, and to have subjected them all as He intended to the Father. This it is to deliver up the Kingdom to God, just as the general of the universal army renders up the palm of victory to the emperor. In the same way, inasmuch as all reason for ruling will then end, all power and authority shall be abolished, every ministry of the Holy Spirit shall cease since we shall no longer need an advocate or a mediator because God will be All-in-all. Then, also, the Trinity of dispensation will terminate.[26]

But that was precisely what Oecolampadius and others among the reformers feared. They were not prepared to concede that we shall no longer need an advocate or a mediator – for they were less optimistic with regard to human nature. And they inferred that if God's plan of salvation were not rooted in the very structure of his Being, enduring from eternity to eternity, man's everlasting salvation would in that case be imperiled. Oecolampadius declared his mind in writing to Servetus.

Johannes Oecolampadius

You complain that I am too harsh. I have good reason. You contend that the Church of Christ for a great span has departed from the foundation of her faith. You accord more honor to Tertullian than to the whole Church. You deny the one person in two natures. By denying that the Son is eternal you deny of necessity also that the Father is eternal. You have submitted a confession of faith which the simple and unsuspecting might approve, but I abominate your subterfuges ... I will be patient in other matters but when Christ is blasphemed, No!

Oecolampadius then set forth at some length the errors of Servetus and concluded, "I write this not in heat but because I desire to serve my God. May He so enlighten your eyes that you may confess in truth Christ the Son of God."

There was a second letter commencing with a tone of greater asperity, "To Servetus the Spaniard who denies that Christ is the con-substantial Son of God from Johannes Oecolampadius." This time the attempt was made to show that Servetus misinterpreted Irenaeus. The conclusion was:

As for your promise to persevere in the confession that Jesus is the Son of God, I call upon you to confess that He is the Son of God consubstantial and co-eternal because of the union with the Word. This you must do if we are to hold you for a Christian. *Vale!*[27]

Some twenty-five years after this event Heinrich Bullinger, who in 1530 was a junior colleague of Zwingli at Zurich, reported a conference of theologians in that city. Among others present were Bucer and Capito from Strassburg, Zwingli and Bullinger himself of Zurich, and Oeco-lampadius from Basel. Oecolampadius expressed to his colleagues his fear that in his city a Spaniard, Michael Servetus by name, of belligerent and persistent temper, an Arian, was disseminating his abominations. Zwingli advised the utmost vigilance lest the whole Christian religion be undermined. Oecolampadius should try to convert Servetus. To this the answer was that every effort had already been made but Servetus had such an unsoothed itch for controversy that one could do nothing with him. Zwingli then counseled any means possible lest these horrible blasphemies break out to the prejudice of the whole Christian religion. Bullinger concluded his report by saying, "Not long after Servetus, or rather *Perdetus,* left Basel."[28]

Servetus had good reason to fear that the tolerance which he had thus far enjoyed would not be extended indefinitely. The city ordinance of 1529 contained severe regulations against Anabaptists, despisers of the sacrament and deniers of the divinity of Jesus. On August 11, 1530, presumably about a month after Servetus came to Basel, Konrad in der Gassen had been brought to trial because he could not believe that Jesus was true God and true man. He affirmed also that spoken prayer is useless. When reminded that Jesus prayed audibly in Gethsemane he retorted, "On what evidence do you know that? The disciples were asleep." Konrad was executed.[29]

Servetus went to Strassburg. He must have expected to find there a milder regime. He had reason to look for a kindly reception from Bucer, the leading reformer of that city, who, having previously passed through Basel, had formed a sufficiently favorable opinion of Servetus to intercede on his behalf with Oecolampadius.[30]

A better choice than Strassburg at that moment was not available. Of all the cities to break with Rome, Strassburg had moved most slowly in invoking the arm of the magistrate to curb sectarian movements.[31] A town ordinance of 1527 warned the citizens against the Anabaptists but specified no penalty. When at length, in 1538, severer measures were taken, reference was made to the previous unwillingness to implement the imperial edict of the Diet of Speier of 1529, which had subjected the Anabaptists to the penalty of death. Up to the year 1538 only two executions had taken place in Strassburg and those for offenses which might easily be construed as other than heresy. Thomas Salzmann suffered for crazed utterances to the effect that Christ was an impostor[32] and Claus Frey because he would not abandon his spiritual sister and return to his wife and eight children.[33]

The ministers in their counsels were less mild than the magistrates. But Bucer, the most rigorous, would permit private assemblies of the sectaries so long as they did not disturb the peace nor attack the established Church. At first he was not altogether averse to the Anabaptist position, for he agreed that what really matters is the baptism of the spirit and he was willing to have water baptism deferred. He came to distrust the Anabaptists rather because of their exaltation of the inner word above the written Scripture, because of their advocacy of the separation of Church and State, and because of their addiction to chiliastic predictions.[34]

His associate, Capito, was so prone to entertain strange guests that he himself fell under suspicion. When Michael Sattler had been burned at Rothenburg in 1526 and others were imperiled, Capito addressed a petition to the magistrates in that region declaring that only blasphemy should be punished by the State. These folk were not guilty on that score, said he, "unless it were blasphemy to abstain from unseemly amusements, drunkenness, gluttony, adultery, war, murder, slander and all lusts of the flesh."[35] Again in 1528, he said that "Anabaptists start with the word of the cross for the mortification of the flesh and they relish the word of life in Christ risen and reigning. Baptism to them is a symbol of dying with Christ. Therefore I think we should look into their hearts and recognize candidly there the gift of God."[36]

And then there were the Zells, Mathias and his wife Catherine, the intrepid. The husband declared, "He who accepts Christ as his Lord and Saviour shall have a place at my table and I will have a place with him in heaven."[37] As for Catherine, she was never to be intimidated in her devotion to religious liberty. Some twenty-five years later when her husband was dead and all the leading reformers had gone the way of repression, she declared:

> Some rage against the poor Anabaptists and incite the magistrates against them as a hunter eggs on the dogs against rabbits or boars. Yet these poor folk accept the Lord Jesus with us and agree in all the essentials over which we separated from the papacy. As to salvation in Christ, they are in accord with us. But because they differ at other points, are they then to be persecuted and Christ in them, though they make a brave confession and many endure privation, imprisonment, fire and water?[38]

Inasmuch as the magistrates were lenient and the ministers were patient, sectaries flocked into Strassburg. There was Sebastian Franck, who believed only in a church of the spirit and would reverse the whole scale of values in church history, giving the heretics a preferred place. There was the stately Caspar Schwenckfeld, of patrician demeanor, committed to the restitution of the Church of the Apostles. There were Anabaptists, among them Melchior Hofmann, surging with apocalyptic dreams that in the coming days 144,000 apostles would assemble in Strassburg and thence go out with signs and wonders and such power of the spirit that none could withstand them.[39] Servetus would feel himself again in the atmosphere of the Alumbrados. Among this fervent, questing throng his own spirit was quickened with fervor for the coming of the great day of the Lord.

DE TRINITA·

TIS ERRORIBVS,

LIBER PRIMVS.

INSCRV=
tandis diui=
ne Triadis,
sanctis arca=
nis, ab homi=
ne exordien=
dum eo du=
xi, quia ad
Verbi spe=
culationem,
sine funda=

mento CHRISTI, ascendentes, quàm plurimos
cerno, qui parum aut nihil homini tribuunt, & ue=
rùm CHRISTVM obliuioni penitus tradunt:
quibus ego ad memoriã, quis sit ille CHRISTVS,
reducere curabo.   Ceterum, quid, quantumq; sit
CHRISTO tribuendum, iudicabit ecclesia.   Tria hæc in

  Pronomine demonstrante hominem, quem hu= homine cog=
manitatem appellant, concedam hæc tria. Primo noscenda, an
hic est IESVS CHRISTVS. Secundò, hic est teq de Verbo
filius Dei· Tertio, hic est Deus·   loquamur·

Initial Letter in the De Trinitatis Erroribus, 1531

Chapter 4

Nineveh Unrepentant

In the meantime men must bear witness to the truth. Servetus sought a publisher for the work he had composed entitled *On the Errors of the Trinity,* setting forth the views already expounded. Through a Basler well versed in the world of books, by name Roesch, Servetus was put in touch with Johannes Setzer of Hagenau, a village near Strassburg. Setzer was a very active printer, who in nine years issued some one hundred and fifty titles. Some of these were works by the Humanists and others by the Protestant reformers, particularly the Lutherans, with whom he sided in the sacramentarian controversy. His opponents, the Swiss Oecolampadius and Zwingli, contended that Christ's body cannot be in the bread and wine upon the altar because Christ has already ascended to the right hand of the Father and his body is there localized in heaven. Luther, on the contrary, asserted that Christ, who is God, must, like God, pervade all reality, including the physical. Setzer had been disseminating the Lutheran view and had thereby alienated the Swiss. The position of Servetus on the Lord's Supper was closer to that of the Lutherans, but one may doubt whether Setzer printed the book *On the Errors of the Trinity* to please Luther, since at the end of the book Luther was attacked on another count. The motive was more probably to irritate the Swiss – at least so contemporaries surmised. At the same time Setzer took precautions to evade responsibility. Neither the place nor his name appeared on the book. Servetus later testified that it was printed at Hagenau. Setzer was immediately suspect. The modern bibliophiles have confirmed the surmise because the initial letter on the first page of the *De Trinitatis Erroribus* is identical with one used in a number of works issued under the mark of Setzer.[1]

Servetus was not altogether naive in supposing that the book might receive serious attention. In as much as Erasmus had decried dissension over such thorny questions, Servetus endeavored to press a copy upon him; but he was rebuffed. The attitude of Erasmus had been made plain when he was asked by the Town Council of Basel for an opinion of Oecolampadius's attack on the Catholic food laws. Erasmus replied that the tract was "learned and pious, if anything can be which dissents from the judgment of the Church."[2] In other words the argument was cogent, yet not to be entertained. For to reject the authority of the Church is to disrupt the bond of society and the unity of Christian Europe. Erasmus would defer discussion of the Trinity to the Judgment Day.

As for Luther, he had once said, "If my soul loathes this word *homoousios* and I am unwilling to use it, I shall not on that account be a heretic, for who will compel me to use it provided I hold to the substance which was defended in the councils from Scripture?"[3] Melanchthon had been in receipt of a letter from Zell of Strassburg proposing to eschew all such terms as *substantialiter, essentialiter, realiter, naturaliter, localiter, corporaliter, transubstantialiter, quantitative, qualitative, ubiqualiter,* and *carnaliter.* The reference was to the Lord's Supper, but some of the same terms were used also with reference to the person of Christ and the Trinity. Melanchthon agreed.[4] Observe, however, that Luther's objection was only to the term *homoousios.* He disliked it because it was not in the Scripture; yet the doctrine he retained. Soon both he and Melanchthon discovered, as the fathers at Nicaea had done long before, that scriptural terminology does not suffice to exclude the interpretations of those who are adroit at placing their own sense upon language not devised to refute them. In order to safeguard biblical meanings, the Council of Nicaea had been driven to employ extra-biblical terms. The Protestant reformers found themselves driven to the same expedient.

Yet Servetus did have a hearing. The Strassburgers, though abundantly warned against him, were friendly and receptive. Bucer called him *Michael dilecte* and Capito was thought to favor his views.[5] When the book appeared some "lauded it to the stars."[6] Oecolampadius wrote to Bucer that "the book is particularly pleasing to those who hate our Church."[7] He did not say to him what he said to Zwingli: that partisans of the book were to be found in Strassburg.[8] That was true. Sebastian Franck from Strassburg wrote to a friend, "The Spaniard, Servetus, contends in his tract that there is but one person in God. The Roman Church holds that there are three persons in one essence. I agree rather with the Spaniard."[9] Bucer complained of those who supported Servetus out of impious curiosity, to whom Capito indiscreetly gave a handle;[10] Capito was exhorted from Berne to write and clear his escutcheon.[11]

Oecolampadius, of course, was convinced from the outset that the book was "thrice and four times blasphemous and impious." He feared for the reputation of the Swiss churches lest in France they be deemed "the authors of such blasphemy." Let Bucer write a refutation "howsoever this beast may have broken in."[12]

Bucer moved slowly with refutations. To Servetus he wrote:

> I am ready, as soon as I am free from my public responsibilities, to give you my reasons point by point and at length as to why I do not agree with you. You may expect from me not the least danger. But as to your intention of staying here, I have warned you before not to do so. In my opinion the magistrate will scarcely suffer you, if discovered, to remain. But as for me, you will not be molested while you are here, so long as you disturb and seduce no one, and I should like to see you given permission long enough for me to examine your work with care.[13]

At length Bucer satisfied himself and refuted the work in a public lecture.[14] Thereafter the disapprobation was general. The magistrates forbade the sale of the work in Strassburg.[15]

Servetus then turned back to Basel, where a similar action had already been taken.[16] The Town Council had consulted Oecolampadius, who advised them that "Servetus's book contained some good things which were rendered dangerous by the context. The work should be either completely suppressed or read only by those who would not abuse it."[17] The Council accepted both alternatives; the sale was prohibited, yet sufficient copies were retained for Oecolampadius to supply one for Zwingli.[18]

Servetus entered no remonstrance to the Council, but addressed Oecolampadius in the hope that the copies destined for France and collected in Basel might not be confiscated. He also requested permission to stay in the city. His petition concluded with a plea for religious liberty.

> If you find me in error on one point you should not on that account condemn me in all, for according to this there is no mortal who would not be burned a thousand times, for we know in part. The greatest of the apostles were sometimes in error. Even though you see Luther erring egregiously at some points you do not condemn him in the rest ... Such is human frailty that we condemn the spirits of others as impostors and impious and except our own, for no one recognizes his own errors ... I beg you, for God's sake, spare my name and fame ... You say that I want all to be robbers and that I will not suffer any to be punished and killed. I call Almighty God to witness that this is not my opinion and I detest it, but if ever I said anything it is that I consider it a serious matter to kill men because they are in error on some questions of scriptural interpretation, when we know that the very elect may be led astray.[19]

Whether Oecolampadius replied we do not know. We find Servetus again in Basel,[20] though for just how long there is no means of telling. The following year, 1532, he published – again with Setzer – *Two Dialogues on the Trinity*, in an effort to allay criticism. The work opened pretentiously with retraction of everything in the former book, not however as false but only as immature.[21] The accommodations were largely verbal. Whereas before Servetus had made Christ the Son of God, not by nature, but by grace, now to grace he would add nature, because to the Son *naturally* belongs the glory of the Father. He would admit two natures in Christ provided nature be understood to mean a *natural* property.[22] Previously he had been unwilling to call the Holy Spirit a person. He would do so now in the sense that the Spirit after the departure of Christ became *personalized* by dwelling in us, though properly speaking there is no person in the Spirit.[23] In the former work he had distinguished the incarnate Son from the pre-existent Word. Now he was prepared to say that the Word is Christ. Nevertheless the Word had no substance properly speaking until Christ was revealed and his substance became palpable.[24]

The point at which the new work went beyond the preceding was in expanding the Erasmian program of mediation among the contending parties by agreeing in part with them all. But in consequence, since they were at odds, to agree in part with one meant by the same token to disagree with the others. At the moment the most agitated doctrine among the reformers was that of the Lord's Supper. The Strassburgers were endeavoring to mediate between the Lutherans and the Swiss. Servetus may have been consciously rallying to their program in the hope that they would then lend him a readier ear on the doctrine of the Trinity. At any rate he agreed with Oecolampadius and Bucer that there is a real though not a physical presence in the Lord's Supper. "The body of Christ," wrote Servetus, "is mystically eaten."[25] "It is through the Spirit that we eat and drink the flesh of Christ."[26] "Only figuratively do we speak of the bread as the body of Christ."[27] From such a view Bucer could find no ground for dissent.[28]

At the same time Servetus adopted from Luther his device for safeguarding the physical presence from crassness. Luther held that the body of Christ is divine, spiritual flesh; it is not localized but universally diffused.[29] Servetus likewise held to the ubiquity and the deification of Christ's body. It is not localized.[30] "Christ walketh upon the wings of the wind ... and sitteth upon the circle of the earth. He measureth the heavens with a span, and the waters of the sea in his hand."[31] Yet he is

DE TRINI‑
TATIS ERRORIBVS
LIBRI SEPTEM.

Per Michaelem Serueto, aliàs
Reues ab Aragonia
Hispanum.

Anno M. D. XXXI

DIALOGO‑
RVM DE TRINITATE
LIBRI DVO.

DE IVSTICIA REGNI CHRI‑
sti, Capitula Quatuor.

PER MICHAELEM SERVETO,
aliàs Reues, ab Aragonia
Hispanum.

Anno M. D. XXXII.

*Title Pages of the Genuine Editions of the De Trinitatis Erroribus
and the Dialogorum de Trinitate Libri Duo*

not, as Luther said, in sewers and other unsavory places,[32] but "in spiritual things and that which is capable of his habitation."[33] His flesh is divine and consubstantial with God.[34]

Even more was Servetus essaying the role of mediator between the sectaries and the established Church. His views in many respects resemble those of Caspar Schwenckfeld and Melchior Hoffman. Both were concerned as to the nature of the flesh of Christ. Schwenckfeld inquired as to the kind of flesh eaten in the Sacrament and answered that the body of Christ was a glorified body.[35] The view of Servetus of the deified flesh was very similar. Hoffman could not see how the sinlessness of Jesus could be conserved if his flesh were like our flesh and subject to infirmity and sin. Even the virgin birth was not a sufficient safeguard unless it were posited that Christ in the process of birth was not contaminated. He was born not of Mary but simply through Mary, said Hoffman. Without knowing it, he was reproducing the view of the ancient Gnostics. Here too Servetus's theory of the deified body sounded similar. But Servetus also differed from both men. Schwenckfeld dated the glorification of the body of Christ from the resurrection. Servetus said that the body fell like manna from heaven[36] and – disagreeing with Hoffman – that Christ's flesh was like our flesh because our flesh also is capable of deification.[37]

To these men themselves the differences loomed larger than the similarities. Schwenckfeld, when likened to Servetus, was at pains to exculpate himself. "I had many conversations with Servetus," he said, "and I have read his books, and since some have supposed that I derived my doctrine of the glorified body from him, I have refuted the charge in my tract *On the Origin of Christ's Flesh*. There is some good in his books but, on the fundamentals of the Christian faith, he errs egregiously, and his book *On the Errors of the Trinity* is damnable."[38] Despite all such disclaimers, the Town Council of Ulm, in 1538, united the two men in a common condemnation.[39]

The historian must continually remind himself that a bout is possible only between boxers who stand in the same ring and observe the same rules. However much each might repudiate the other, Servetus had left an impress upon the sectarian movement. And Servetus's own attitudes were profoundly affected by his intercourse with the apocalyptic dreamers who sought to restore the primitive Church by admitting only heartfelt believers baptized in mature years, in token of an experience of the new birth.

The conclusion of the whole matter was that Servetus could not agree altogether with anybody.

> All seem to me to have a part of truth and a part of error and each espies the error of others and fails to see his own. May God in His mercy enable us without obstinacy to perceive our errors. It would be easy to judge if it were permitted to all to speak in peace in the Church that all might vie in prophesying and that those who are first inspired, as Paul says, might listen in silence to those who next speak, when anything is revealed to them. But today all strive for honor. May the Lord destroy all the tyrants of the Church. Amen.[40]

For the time being, however, the challenge of Servetus tended only to infuriate the tyrants. Protestants and Catholics coalesced in one common repudiation. In Luther's *Table Talk* we find this note: "When a most virulent book against the Trinity was edited in 1532 he said, 'These people do not think that others have had their temptations over this article, but I do not think one should oppose the Word of God and the Holy Scripture.'"[41] "When Melanchthon complained that the views of Servetus were spreading in Italy, Luther said that 'Italy was full of dangerous opinions from which dreadful abominations would arise.'"[42] Luther evidently had not seen the book — or he would have been still more incensed over the attack on his doctrine of justification and on his determinism.

Melanchthon had read the book *On the Errors of the Trinity*, and wrote to a friend: "I find Servetus acute and subtle enough in disputation, but not very solid. He seems to me to have confused imaginings ... On justification he is plainly demented. As for the Trinity you know I have always feared this would break out some day. Good God, what tragedies this question will excite among those who come after us!" Again: "I am reading Servetus a great deal. He entirely distorts Tertullian ... Irenaeus himself is confused. I hope to talk with you personally about these questions soon." To another correspondent he wrote:

> In Servetus there are many marks of a fanatical spirit. On justification you see that he derides the doctrine of faith ... He is completely astray on the difference between the Old and the New Testament, since he takes the Holy Spirit away from the prophets ... He misinterprets Tertullian and as it seems to me even Irenaeus. This does not please me that Servetus does not make Christ truly a natural Son of God. That is the gist of the controversy ... I am getting out a new edition of the *Loci*.[43]

The successive editions of that work were increasingly abusive of Servetus. In the edition of 1535 we read that "Servetus, a Spaniard, renewed the heresy of Paul of Samosata, but in most confused fashion."[44] In the editions after 1543 Servetus became "astute and impious … blowing smoke perfidiously before his hearers in his treatment of Irenaeus and Tertullian … We have sufficiently and clearly refuted the fury of Paul of Samosata, Photinus and Servetus."[45]

The judgment in the Catholic camp was no more favorable. At the Diet of Ratisbon, in 1532, the German Cochlaeus (who also nosed out and stopped the first printing of Tyndale's New Testament) discovered on sale a copy of the book *On the Errors of the Trinity*. He hastened to tell Quintana, probably not without a measure of glee, that Spain also had a heretic. The good man was thoroughly outraged that a Spaniard of his personal acquaintance should be guilty of a work containing the most impious and unheard-of heresies, and he took care that the pestilent book should be suppressed. Cochlaeus also came across the *Two Dialogues on the Trinity*. "The author," said he, "is a man of pungent and vehement temper, well versed in Greek and Hebrew, but that is the common disease of almost all the recent theologians."[46]

Girolamo Aleandro (Jerome Aleander), Luther's adversary at the Diet of Worms, wrote in April, 1532:

> I well believe that we are near the end of the world. There has been sent to the Diet a work in seven books, composed by an Aragonese Spaniard called Mihel Serveto, alias Dereves, entitled *On the Errors of the Trinity*. I should have sent the book by this post except that I have to return it. I will try to get you another. There will be plenty about … I never saw or read anything more nauseating, though the man is very keen. The confessor of the Emperor[a] says that he knows him, a man of twenty-six years,[b] and of brilliant parts, but a great sophist. Since the work shows a wide reading in Scripture and a polish of style of which he is not capable, the confessor thinks that he may well have conceived the plan, but that for the style and wealth of material he must have received help in Germany, in which parts he has been now for over a year, in Strassburg and Basel, where he helped Oecolampadius for some months. Erasmus wrote the other day in a letter that this Spaniard tried to send the work to him, but he would not lend an ear. Now he has sent a copy to the Bishop of Zaragoza. I will see what the princes will do about such a book, of which they all complain. And if nothing else, I will get together a committee of theologians, especially Spaniards – there are about six – that, when the book has been censored and condemned by the authority of the Holy See, they may write to Spain to make proclamation to burn the book

---

[a] Quintana
[b] He was actually twenty-one.

and the effigy of the heretic *al modo di Spagna,* because they say he may have left behind some impression of his heresy and he has already sent the book. The Most Reverend Legate will write to his vicar at Huesca in Spain to make such an execution, since the heretic is of his diocese. That is all that can be done for the present. These heretics of Germany, Lutheran or Zwinglian, wherever the Spaniard may be, ought to punish him if they are so very Christian and evangelical and defenders of the faith, as they boast, because he is as much opposed to their profession as to the Catholic. In some passages of his work he contradicts Luther by name, and yet he is in Lutheran territory.[47]

One observes with interest that it was Servetus himself who sent a copy of his book to the Bishop of Zaragoza. In other ways, too, information crossed the Pyrenees. Two of the officers of the court, [Comendador Mayor don García de Padilla and Hugo de Uriés, señor de Ayerbe], discovered both of the works of Servetus and denounced him to the Supreme Council of the Inquisition in Spain. The Council, on May 24, 1532, sent instructions to the inquisitors at Zaragoza to find out immediately where the said Miguel Revés came from in Aragon, "his family, age, where he studied, how long ago he left the country, what relatives he has and their condition and quality. Find out from his relatives whether he has written to them, and how long ago, by what route and from what place, and if he has written obtain the letters." A summons to answer the accusation of the Holy Office was then to be posted in due form in the Cathedral of Zaragoza on a holy day as well as in his native place [Alcolea or Cariñena, according to the documents]; further investigation was to be made in all secrecy at the court.

The inquisitors realized that this solemn summons would be but a futile gesture so long as Servetus remained in Germany. They therefore added this postscript:

After writing the above and thinking further on this question, which is of such great import for our Christian religion, we deem it expedient to try every possible means to lure the said Miguel Revés back to Spain, enticing him by promises of favors or other offers, and if this fail then exert pressure. A few suggestions to that end are appended. Use them or such of them as commend themselves, but in such a way that those with whom you deal may not suppose that the Holy Office would use any pressure other than to bring him back to the Church, which is indeed the case, so that others of our nation who are abroad may be recalled to the faith, seeing the good treatment accorded to him. For this purpose it is not wise to publish the edict so ceremoniously as we said. Rather it should be read with dissimulation so that no one may suppose or understand that the said Revés is summoned by the Inquisition, for that would be to notify his relatives and friends and they would alert him to accept no offer that might be made. And never mind about affixing the edict to the church doors, or if you do, let it be done at an hour when no one can read, and take it down at once before anyone has read it. This precaution is necessary in order that you may use the proposed suggestions. If they fail the case is closed. As for the inquiry which we mentioned with regard to his person, lineage and other qualities, it would seem well to entrust this to some person who would secure the information with secrecy and dissimulation so that no one would suppose that he was sent by the Inquisition. Let this be done with secrecy and despatch as the importance of the case requires, etc.

Along with these instructions, practically identical letters were sent to the Archbishop of Zaragoza and to the magistrates of the city, calling their attention to a "certain case of large importance for the service of God and of your Majesties and for the honor of our Spanish nation." Spaniards were sensitive to the gibe of being Marranos, and orthodoxy, as we have seen, had come to be a matter of national reputation.

From the next letter of the Supreme Council, we learn that the person entrusted with the delicate mission of ensnaring Servetus was his own brother, who had been sent to Germany for the purpose. The Council approved of the measures to forbid the sale of the works of "Luther, Oecolampadius, Revés and other reprobates."

Not until after five and a half years do we find any report from the fraternal mission. On the 13th of March, 1538, the Supreme Court sent this word to the Inquisition of Aragon: "Some time ago we wrote you to let us know how stands the case of Miguel Revés alias Servetus. We are informed that there is in the house of his father a brother, who was a chaplain of the Archbishop of Santiago, and that he went to Germany to bring him back, but without success. Find out where is the said Miguel Serbeto [sic] and let us know, as well as the state of the case." On the 3rd of May, the Supreme Council wrote again saying: "We have received the deposition of Juan Serveto and we are surprised that you did not examine the friar, and the other persons named as witnesses. If they are not there, you should find out where they are in order to examine them … You ought to find out where Miguel Servecto [sic] is, who maintains him, what are his plans, and if there is any hope of his coming here, and advise this Council." With this notice the case drops from the record.[48]

Unfortunately the deposition of Juan Serveto is not preserved. One would like to know whether he met his brother and where and when and what snares he employed to entice him, and still more to know whether he accepted his mission in good faith. He may well have done so. Religion constituted a deeper bond than blood, and the honor of Spain transcended the claims of a brother. One recalls the well-known case of Alfonso Díaz, who in similar fashion went to Germany to recall his brother, Juan. At first he attempted to terrify him by prospects of hardship if he stayed and to allure him by promises of benefices if he returned. At last Alfonso feigned conversion to Protestantism and proposed that they set out together to win Italy for the Gospel. When this ruse failed, through the warnings of Bucer and others, Alfonso caused Juan to be assassinated. The murderer was caught, but was saved by the intervention of Charles V, Holy Roman Emperor and King of Spain.[49]

Not only in Spain but also in Toulouse the Inquisition was on the watch for Servetus. On June 17, 1532, a decree was passed for the apprehension of some forty fugitives, students, monks, and even an apostolic protonotary – and among the first, "Michel de Serveto alias Revés."[50]

Where should he go? Humanist, Reformer, and Catholic joined in a common condemnation. His books were suppressed and his presence would not be acceptable in Basel or Strassburg. The Inquisition was on the watch in Spain and in Toulouse. Servetus even thought briefly of America as a possible asylum. About a decade later, in an unpublished first draft of the preface to a new theological work, he wrote these words:

> When I was a young man, scarcely twenty, I was moved by a certain divine impulse to treat of this cause, having been taught of no man. When I began, such was the blindness of the world that I was sought up and down to be snatched to my death. Terrified on this account and fleeing into exile, for many years I lurked among strangers in sore grief of mind. Knowing that I was young, powerless and without polish of style, I almost gave up the whole cause, for I was not yet sufficiently trained ... O most clement Jesus, I invoke thee again as divine witness that on this account I delayed and also because of the imminent persecution, so that with Jonah I longed rather to flee to the sea or to one of the New Isles.[51]

By this, of course, he meant America, probably South America. Perhaps he thought of joining the Welser expedition in Venezuela.[52]

The reference to Jonah was not altogether apt, for Jonah was fleeing to Tarshish to evade his commission to Nineveh. Servetus had already delivered his word to the people of Nineveh and they had not prostrated themselves in sackcloth and ashes. Better then, he concluded, to depart from Nineveh unrepentant and, since the New Isles were incredibly remote, to seek a Tarshish nearer at hand.

MICHAEL VILLANOVANVS

LECTORI S.

NON ABRE fuerit, Lector amice, de Claudio nostro pauculis hic praescribere, ac demum quid noua hac editione praestiterimus cognouisse. Fuit Ptolemaeus Alexandriae Aegypti urbe regia oriundus, Graecus, aliter, quibus tunc Aegyptus imbuebatur, abundè doctus: tametsi & Rhodi egerit aliquando: Philosophus, Astrologus, iuxta ac Mathematicus strenuus, quod & eius monumenta testantur. Floruit sub Traiano, Hadriano, & Antonio Pio Caesaribus. Tanta in orbe perlustrando eius sui solertiae plus quàm Herculea gloria, at terrarum orbem sine bello inuadens, sub regulam quandam censeri coëgerit, & nobis fructum descriptum tradiderit. Nec id soli praestitit, sed caelestia terrestribus coniunxit, eorum mensuras in una collegit. Fuit Strabone, Plinio & Pomponio Mela posterior, sed qui illos & priores omnes in Geographico artificio facilè superarit. Interpretes eius fuerunt Nicolaus Angelus Florentinus, Ioannes Bercherus et Bilibaldus Pirckheymerus. In priori etiã libri annotatiões scripsit Bercherus, sed ita, ut tã in eo quã in aliis multa desyderentur. Nos uerò meliore quaeq; sequuti uires omnes ac neruos intẽdimus, in corruptis emendandis, & reclusis explicãdis. Periculosus utraq; parte labor, nec alicui hactenus attentatus: sed pius, & quenã nobis impetret, si uabi locorũ lectiori nõ fecerimus satis. Illud ne tacuerim, ex aliis codicibus cũ graecis tũ latinis, aliorũq; autorũ assidua lectiõe, locos ad multa nullis nos restituisse: quorũ cãturias aliquot referre operæprecium foret, at specimen aliquod gustatori praeberetur, sed unius Narbonensis Galliae exempla sat erunt. Libro ij. capi. 10. tabula 3. Europae, Chetire ciuitas priùs legebatur, quam ex graeco codice Betire fuerit legendum, quae est Biterrensis ciuitas, uulgò dicta Besiers: Stephanus etiam Betarrã nominat: Mela, Plinius & Strabo Biturram. Fossae marinæ ibidem legebatur, cum Fossas Marianas à Mario Ro. consule dictas scriptores omnes testentur, quas nunc Aquas mortuas uocamus. Item flumen Sicarus in altero exẽplari legebatur in altero Tisera, si nutro modo fuerit legẽdũ, sed Hisera siue grecam exemplar, siue aliorum scripta, & maximè Caesaris commentarios quis inspiciat. adstipulatur etiam hodiernum nomen quod idem Isarus uulgo retinet. Nec illos taceam qui pro Arari fluxio ibidẽ scriperent Anar, & pro Dubi Baden, Cepero pro Cessero, Loxenuiorum pro Auenniorum colonia, Sempos populos pro Sentijs, quas hodie Dignenses. Omisse quoq; Cabellicorũ colonis duas Massiliae facere, alter an alter an nos graecam. Orobios insuper scribitur ab statuit, qui Obris ceteris dicitur. Emendasseutue etiam si heuisset Tolossitani, qui ad Garunnæ, non Iberis fluuij ripam consistit. Sed ut nobis non licuit inueterans illas horographicat tabulas renouare, ita eorum errata nobis adscribi non debent. Longitudinum & latitudinum numeros, quos contẽdunt, ne cui sim morosus, hic subticebo, cum si satis legenti & conferenti paturint. Nec in ea re à Ptolemaei mente descedimus, sed tãtum iuxta priores types librariorum restituimus errata. Libro octauo qui suprà alios, si Bilibaldo & Erasmo credimus, castigatione desyderabat, aduertat simul mediocriter in Mathematicis peritus, non solum in urbibus à Ptolemaeo ibi descriptis, sed in aliis quibusq; cunq;, maiorum dierum quantitates, & ab Alexandriae distantiae metiri queat. Illud item liceat, siue ordinem aliquando praeposterum, nec eundem esse in Ptolemaei traditione & nostra interpretatione, parumper ab ipso commissa transpositione locorũ. Vt inter Nemetes & Vangiones Germanos hodie populos in tabula Belgicae Galliae commemorantur: & inter Liburniae portum & Populoniã praemontoris siue Populeniã urbẽ in Tyrrheno Italiae pelago. Not enim uera nomina in margine reddidimus, sed ipsi priores posui, qui eo quo ipse pẽdebat ordine posteriores esse debuere. Eodem latiore inter Telamonem Hossen & Cossas transpositio est. idem conuicisus in Alpium montium nonnullis, quod Andreas Alciatus in Taciti annotauit. In Liguria maritimos Iacobus Breccilias ordinem à Vtolemeo alium ita docuit. Sed hactenus de ijs quae corruptè legebãtur. Scholia deinceps adiecimus, quò lectio esset dilucidior suauior & planior: quae quantum adiumenti lectori sint allatura, eorum esto iudiciũ, qui lectionis usu experimentũ fecerunt. in euoluendis sanè cum Graecorum tum Latinorum poëmatibus, historijs, & alijs scriptis cũ de regionibus, ciuitatibus, montibus, & fluminibus, quod persaepe sit, sermo inciderit; si sic ad nostri Ptolemaei lectionem quã describat: urbis uetusta cum priscis & poëtarum nominibus cõiunda, & ad nostri temporis sermonem coaptata, iucundē at̃ nouum & pro cãdubio lectori sunt allatura: cum nuda Ptolemaei lectio parũ uenusta hactenus uisa sit. Et quò magis tyronum animos ad hanc lectionem intenderemus, materiã lingua tanquam faciliore pluribus urbiũ uocabula explicauimus: ut cum Gallis gallicè, cum Germanis germanicè, cũ Italis Italicè, & cũ Hispanis hispanicè loqui uideremur: quorũ omniũ regiones aidimus, & linguas at̃q; nouimus. In reddendis sermoni uernaculo urbiũ nominibus, scriptorũ autoritate, propria experiẽtia, certissiues coniecturis, quoad eius fieri potuit summo conexi sumus in hac praesertim secunda editione, in qua nulla prioris errata castigauimus. Ceterum plurima eorum quae à Ptolemeo sunt descripta, cum sint excisae, nos silẽtio praeteriuimus. At si ubi desolatarũ eodem aut proxime loco urbes aliae successere, nos in structura loco scripte describere subrogauimus, in mergine quidem, nerũ ipsam Ptolemaei scriptam inuioletum esse uoluimus. Quam nostrã operam ad prouinciarum orbis notitiem & praesentium cum praeteritis collationem, quae suius est exercitatio, maxime facere, nemo, ni fallor, inficiaturus erit: nisi zoilus quispiam sit frontis pusilla, qui aliorũ sudores nequeat sine liuore dimetiri. Tu uerò quisquis sis candidus lector, nostras spero uigilias acceptas probataq; feres. Vale.

Ad eundem.

Si terras & regna hominum, si ingenia quaeq;
Flumina, caeruleum si mare nosse iuuat,
Si montes, si urbes populosq; opibusq; superbas,
Huc ades, haec oculis prospice cuncta tuis.

Michael Villanovanus to the Reader
From the 1541 Edition of Ptolemy's Geography

Chapter 5

Michel de Villeneuve, Editor

When the whale disgorged this Jonah, he appeared somewhere in France as Michel de Villeneuve, from Villanueva, the village of his upbringing in Spain. His movements in France are not altogether clear, but apparently he went first to Paris.[1]

In France, as in every other country in Europe at that juncture, liberty was on the wane. No longer could Bishop Briçonnet harbor in his parish a bellicose reformer like Guillaume Farel; no longer could Marguerite, the king's sister, secure immunity for Evangelicals of questionable orthodoxy. The king himself, François I, was a prince of the Renaissance whose religion sat lightly. His attitude toward heresy fluctuated in accordance with his desire to form an alliance with the pope, the Turks, or the Lutherans. He might intervene on occasions to save a distinguished Humanist from the toils of the Inquisition, while leaving the lesser breed to fry. François was not the man to withstand the prevailing temper at a moment when throughout Europe the rival religious camps were girding for war.

The great question which confronted every land was whether a house divided against itself can stand. Experience has subsequently demonstrated that it can. Religious diversity is not incompatible with social stability. But few at that time believed it possible and their very belief made them right. Two religions can exist side by side amicably only if they think they can. France was to be rent for half a century before making the great experiment of the Edict of Nantes, whereby the Huguenots received recognition along with the Catholics.

Michel de Villeneuve arrived in Paris just at the time when the ruling powers were beginning to discern that diversity in religion was a menace to public tranquility. The disposition to suppress innovators was growing and the machinery for suppression lay to hand. France employed three agencies: the civil courts, the local clergy, and the Inquisition. That the civil courts should have jurisdiction over heresy was greatly to the distaste of the Church. The arrangement preferred was that the ecclesiastics should determine guilt and the so-called secular arm should merely execute the penalty. But in France the local *parlements* – the term, by the way, means a court and not a parliament – were empowered to arrest, examine, and condemn those deficient in the faith. The Parlement de Paris was to be particularly active.[2] The local clergy might also occupy themselves with cases of heresy. To this procedure the Church, of course, had no objection, but it feared that judges personally acquainted with the accused might be too lenient. That had been the reason in the first place for the organization of the Inquisition. And in France, alongside the civil courts and the clergy, the Inquisition also was allowed to operate with the full collaboration of the royal power. Each of these agencies, when Michel de Villeneuve was resident in France, was epitomized in an individual. The president of the Parlement de Paris was Pierre Lizet. The most outstanding of the French ecclesiastics was the Cardinal, François de Tournon; and the indefatigable Inquisitor was Matthieu Ory.

Lizet, whose red nose the Huguenots jeeringly compared to a Cardinal's hat,[3] had already entered upon his office in 1529.[4] He was to attain notoriety for his implacable prosecution of heretics during the reign of Henri II, when the Paris Parlement sent so many to the flames as to earn for itself the sobriquet *La Chambre Ardente*. In his latter days, Lizet penned a defense of the burning of heretics which blended all of the traditional themes with strains of French nationalism. Spain was not the only land which made the maintenance of the faith a point of national honor.

The president of the Parlement gathered up the time-worn arguments for the constraint of heretics. The nub of it all was this: that heresy is the supreme crime because it is *lèse majesté* against the divine sovereign, because it destroys souls for eternity rather than merely shortening life in the body. It is worse than matricide because it rends Holy Mother Church, the Immaculate Bride of Christ. It is worse than treason because it breaks the bond of civil society and disintegrates Christendom; it is worse than counterfeiting because it devalues the truth of God. If thieves be impaled, homicides beheaded, counterfeiters burned in oil, and parricides consumed in acid, shall we then spare these pseudo-Evangelical Lutherans whose crime exceeds parricide? In the Old Testament, idolaters were stoned and the earth opened to swallow schismatics. Under the new dispensation these penalties are not in abeyance, for the gospel says "Compel them to come in." If it be objected that the tares are to be left until the harvest, recall that the concern of the Master was not for the tares but only for the wheat and, if the tares can be clearly distinguished, there is no reason why they should not be cast into the fire. Severity is an ultimate kindness; just as the amputation of a putrid member may save a body, so the stake may turn tares into wheat or may protect the wheat from the insidious scab. Have not the great Christian emperors, Theodosius, Justinian, and Charlemagne, placed their swords at the service of the Church?

And now especially to France, continued Lizet, was the charge committed to defend the Immaculate Spouse of Christ. In Exodus 25, the Lord ordered that the lily be placed upon the candlestick. Now the lily is the symbol of France and her rulers must see to it that the lily remains upon the candlestick.

> Wherefore, O judges of France, gird on your armor that with fire and sword the heretics may be exterminated from the land. In no better way can our country be defended than by maintaining the unity of the Christian faith which is the very foundation of the Christian monarchy. Let us with fury avenge the insult to the divine Majesty lest the penalties meet for adulterators of Catholic doctrine be turned against the whole people of France.[5]

The most eminent among the French clergy was Cardinal François de Tournon,[6] who occupied a position similar to that of Wolsey in his prime. In the affair of Henry VIII, Tournon was charged with safeguarding the interests of France, and it was Tournon who arranged the marriage of Henri II and Catherine de Médicis. In 1536 the cardinal was made the Lieutenant General of the king for all the provinces of the southeast. A panegyrist describes the cardinal as a grand prince, firm, incorruptible, vigilant, indefatigable, endowed with all the talents requisite in one responsible for religion, justice, finance, and war. And when the heretics raised their heads he was the tutelary angel of France to protect her from the plague. In council he addressed King François, saying:

If, by a fatal complaisance to your subjects Your Majesty persists in condoning heresy, grant that mine eyes be not required to witness the triumph of error, mine ears to hear the pang of blasphemy. Let me retire to solitude that by my supplications I may avert the storm from the Kingdom and bring a blessing upon your sacred person.[7]

At the Colloquy of Poissy, Tournon was the Catholic spokesman. There he recalled the glorious defense of the faith by Clovis, Charlemagne, Philip Augustus, and St. Louis,

who was more eager to adorn his diadem with virtues than to embellish our annals with victory. Do we now repent of the piety which made our Kingdom so flourishing? Does heresy expect to find an asylum at the foot of the throne? The great Henri II would not tolerate a heretic at his court and now a legion of ministers do not scruple to approach the throne uttering blasphemies in the presence of the most Christian king.[8]

Matthieu Ory, Inquisitor of Heretical Pravity for the Realm of France, spared no effort in tracking down men subversive of the faith.[9] In a tract dedicated to the Very Reverend François de Tournon, the Inquisitor made a defense of his métier. He pointed out that the New Testament, in the Acts of the Apostles 19:19, commended the burning of occult books. "If, then," he asked,

dead books may be committed to the flames, how much more live books, that is to say, men? Scripture says that a witch should not be allowed to live and heretics are spiritual witches. The law of nature enjoins that a corrupted member be amputated. The tares, of course, were not to be rooted out in Christ's day when the rulers were not yet Christian. The case is altered now.[10]

If all of this rhetoric savors to the modern reader of hypocrisy, one does well to recall that these zealots — the best of them at any rate — were genuinely concerned to save souls from the eternal fires. Here is a report from Huguenot annals of an examination conducted by Ory at Lyons on September 11, 1553, of a Protestant named Denis Peloquin. Ory besought him not to expose himself so lightly to the flames and reminded Peloquin that his life was in his own hands. The latter replied that he would be in grave peril if his life were not in the hands of One greater than himself. The next day Ory sent an assistant to say that the Cardinal de Tournon was well disposed and desired to save Peloquin and to restore him to his former condition. Tournon would give him a new robe and send him to one of his houses. The Huguenot replied that he was well enough content with his black robe unless he might exchange it for the white robe of the Apocalypse.[11] Such a response seemed to the Inquisitor to be an obstinate repudiation of proffered mercy.

These three men, then – Lizet, Tournon, and Ory – constituted a triumvirate for the prosecution of heresy through the lay courts, the local clergy, and the Inquisition. Servetus was to encounter all three. Despite the protection afforded by his pseudonym, he did not refrain from provocative activities. However clandestine his operations, they did not elude detection.

His initial concern, of course, was to find some way of making a living. Apparently he betook himself first to Paris, although this is not quite certain. He may have gone first to Lyons, though in that case he would have left very shortly for Paris, where in 1533 he was studying at the college of Calvi. The choice of Paris was not too wise for a religious refugee because Paris was the center where the hounds against heresy were beginning to display their fangs.

In the year 1533, Nicolas Cop, in his inaugural address as the Rector of the University of Paris, blended the teachings of Erasmus and Luther in a manifesto of reform. In the turmoil which ensued, Cop took to flight. So also did a young man who has long [been] supposed to have been the author of Cop's address, since it survives only in a transcript in his hand. That young man was John Calvin. For two years he became a fugitive in France itself. On one occasion he ventured back to Paris in order to keep an appointment in the Rue St. Antoine with Michael Servetus, who, for some reason, did not appear.[12] One would like to know more about all this. Evidently Servetus had disclosed his identity in certain quarters. Perhaps his failure to meet the appointment indicates repentance of his indiscretion. At any rate Calvin and Servetus alike were speedily to leave Paris. Late in 1534, the posting of the placards against the Mass incensed the authorities. Calvin withdrew to Basel under the assumed name of Martinus Lucianus. Servetus, still as Michel de Villeneuve, went to Lyons. The two antagonists were not to meet for almost another twenty years.

The choice of Lyons by Servetus was as wise as any. Basel would not have done, for he had been expelled already. Toulouse would not have done, for there he was on the list of the proscribed. The north of France was no better. Calvin himself had been for a time imprisoned on suspicion of heresy in his native Noyon, and one wonders how he

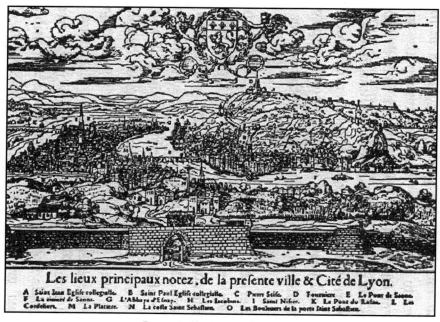

Lyons in the Sixteenth Century

ever escaped. Even Lyons, however, was by no means free from rigorism. The jurisdiction of the Parlement de Paris extended this far and, in 1536, the Cardinal de Tournon was to become the governor of the region. Still Lyons was a trade center intimately allied with Geneva higher on the Rhone, and with Germany beyond. Here were many openly or covertly hospitable to the Reform. Here Rabelais emitted his Gargantuan guffaws. And here the great printing houses rivaled Basel in output and boldness.

The most outstanding ecclesiastic of the region was the Archbishop, Pierre Palmier,[13] who had his residence at Vienne, sixteen miles from Lyons. An ardent Reformer when inducted into his see in 1528, he had at once commenced the renovation of the diocese, scrutinizing closely the education, attire, and demeanor of his clergy. Palmier was a man of cultivated tastes and extensive interests, and a patron of letters; but he could not be expected to condone heresy if flagrant instances were brought to his attention. In 1535, for example, a Lutheran preacher in his diocese was sent to the galleys. The Archbishop also was a close friend of Cardinal de Tournon, and shared with him repose as his guest at the Chateau de Roussillon. Yet, all in all, a more liberal prelate than Palmier one would scarcely find; and Lyons, with its suburbs, offered as promising an opportunity as any for carrying on without utter stultification.

Michel de Villeneuve undertook to support himself as a corrector and editor for the eminent publishing firm of Trechsel, consisting of the brothers Melchior and Gaspard. For them, he was to edit a number of works — two editions of Ptolemy's Geography, one in 1535 and a second in 1541, and an edition of Sante Pagnini's Bible in 1542. Various other labors and journeys were interspersed between these enterprises and will be discussed later. A topical rather than a strictly chronological arrangement commends itself for the period up to the publication of Servetus's great work in 1553. In the interim Villeneuve was to take up medicine and to publish a number of tracts dealing with this field. His activity in this regard will be discussed in the next chapter.

The two geographies and the Bible were issued from the same press. The Bible and one of the Ptolemys were made possible by the munificence of the same patron, Hugues de la Porte. They bore likewise the same printer's device, Samson carrying off the gates, with the legend *libertatem meam mecum porto*, "my freedom I carry with me." One cannot take this emblem as a key to the mind of Servetus, for presumably he had nothing to do with the choice. It is, however, a very interesting combination of medieval and Renaissance ideas. Samson carrying off the gates of the city was for the Middle Ages a stereotype symbol of Christ despoiling the gates of Hades. But the slogan used here, "my freedom I carry with me," suggests, rather, the Neo-Stoicism of the Renaissance — the philosopher, though he be a slave, might yet inwardly be free. Or perhaps this device is redolent of the more exuberant mood of the Renaissance with its swaggering confidence that man's energy can deflect the shafts of Fortune. Quite conceivably, all these interpretations would appeal to Servetus; covertly he was seething over the prevalent corruption and nurturing his spirit on the grandiose drama of the Apocalypse. He liked to think of himself as an emissary of Michael the Archangel, and it would not be too much of a leap to conceive of himself as Samson carrying off the gates.

The tasks which he undertook entailed, however, much of the pedestrian. They were directed not to the exhilaration of the spirit, but to the filling of the belly. He was earning his living as an editor, and he

C L A V D I I

PTOLEMAEI
ALEXAN:
DRINI
Geographicæ Enarrationis,
Libri Octo.

EX BILIBALDI PIRCKE-
ymheri tralatione, sed ad Græca & prisca exemplaria à Michaële Villanouano
secundò recogniti, & locis innumeris denuò castigati. Adiecta insuper ab eodem Scho
lia, quibus & difficilis ille Primus Liber nunc primum explicatur, & exoleta Vrbium
nomina ad nostri seculi morem exponuntur. Quinquaginta illæ quoque cum ueterum tum
recentium Tabulæ adnectuntur, varijsq; incolentium ritus & mores explicantur.

Accedit Index locupletiss. non hactenus uenaisca.

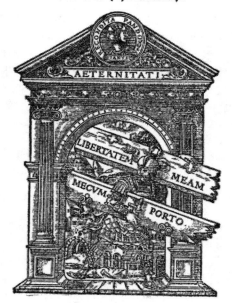

Prostant Lugduni apud Hugonem à Porta.

M. D. XLI.

Title Page of the 1541 Edition of Ptolemy's Geography

took on the books assigned. The collation of texts and the emendation of readings was plain donkey work. Yet every book assigned fed his gluttony for knowledge and editors in those days enjoyed uncommon liberties by way of prefaces, annotations, and even revisions in the text.

Villeneuve was called upon first to edit a geography.[14] The subject evoked intense interest in his century, though strictly speaking what passed for geography was more exactly ethnography. Nowhere was the term *humanism* more appropriate to describe the attitude of the Renaissance to the world about. The human was more intriguing than the environmental. Interest centered not on maps but on men. Not peaks, plains, deserts, oceans, nor fauna and flora, but manners, costumes, superstitions, religions, constitutions, laws, and learning – these were the topics elaborated in successive geographies. All of this, of course, is not to say that no advance was made in cartography and that no interest was displayed in latitude, longitude, nomenclature, and contours. Such names as Regiomontanus and Waldseemüller would alone suffice to prove the contrary. Yet, to a large degree, the maps and the descriptions were not correlated. The picture would show the locality, while the text talked about the inhabitants.

The great explorers of the age did not alter the attitude.[15] They too were not scientific observers of terrain so much as seekers of the lost paradise or the fountain of eternal youth. They saw what they went out to see. Columbus himself reported the singing of a nightingale in a land where no nightingale has otherwise been known to sing.

The preoccupation with men presumably accounts for the comparatively slight concern for the new discoveries. After all, were cannibal chieftains to be compared with the sheiks of Arabia or the princes of Cathay? For more than a century after Columbus Europeans still looked more to the east than to the west. A census of books on travel and discovery, published in France from 1480 to 1609, divides them into four classes in the order of popularity. The first class consists of books on Turkey, the second of works on India, the third covers the remainder of Asia, including Palestine, and the fourth has to do with America. Then, in addition, a few books were devoted to Africa and Scandinavia. The impressions of voyages to Jerusalem well nigh equaled the treatments of the New World. Not until after colonization began in earnest in the seventeenth century did the interest shift.[16]

With Servetus the case may well have been different. Though he still regarded Jerusalem as the center of the earth,[17] yet the New Isles had occurred to him as a possible haven for a religious refugee. But he could not allow himself free rein while editing; his task was simply to bring out a new edition of a work often issued already – the geography of Claudius Ptolemy, an Alexandrian of the second century A.D. This work was as much the starting point for geography as was that of Aristotle for logic, Galen for medicine, or Euclid for geometry. In the fifteenth and sixteenth centuries, Ptolemy's geography had been published in Greek and in Latin translations. Then began continuous revisions in the light of expanding knowledge, until the term Ptolemy came to apply to any work consisting of maps and descriptions of highly variable content.

Villeneuve was commissioned to begin, not with the original Ptolemy, but with the revision already made in 1525 by Willibald Pirckheimer of Nuremberg. And back of his work lay still other revisions, notably that of Leonard Fries of Strassburg in 1522. Fries in turn drew from that of Waldseemüller in 1513. This was the man who fastened upon the New World the name *America,* and he it was who designed the maps which Fries redrew with some embellishments and which then passed unchanged through the editions of Pirckheimer and those of Villeneuve in 1535 and again in 1541. The accompanying descriptions consist of deposits and successive accretions.

Villeneuve discharged his task with diligence. In the edition of 1535 he enumerated some eighty works which he had consulted by way of preparation, and this list was augmented in the edition of 1541. The introduction of modern place names was not an innovation, for Fries in 1522 had an alphabetical table of equivalents in the back. There he noted, for example, the *Augusta Raurica* was now called *Basel* and *Basilea.* Villeneuve added merely that the French called it *Basle.*

The structure of the work was predetermined. There were fifty maps, of which only two dealt with the Western Hemisphere. The first was a map of the globe on which, in the midst of the present Brazil, stood in bold characters the word *America,* precisely where Waldseemüller had first placed it. The word does not appear on the more detailed map of the New World. The focus there is Cuba, called Isabella's Island and flying the flag of Spain. The legend beneath explains that this land was discovered in 1492 by the Genovese Columbus, Captain of the King of Castile. To the description of his exploits, Villeneuve added a protest against calling the land America. "Columbus was the discoverer of a continent and of many islands which the Spaniards now happily rule. Wherefore they are utterly wrong who call this continent America, since Americus went to this place long after Columbus."

The bulk of the work deals with Asia, Africa, and Europe in proportions dictated by the taste of the age. Servetus took occasion in his addenda covertly to rebuke the west by the example of the east. "Remarkable it is," he comments, "that the Arabs, though contiguous to the mighty empires of the Medes, Persians, Greeks and Romans, have conserved their freedom and have been conquered by none. And, indeed, they adopted the religion of Muhammad entirely of their own accord, in which they persist."

When Servetus came to deal with Europe, his insertions had about them something of the mordant. A religious enthusiast, doomed to ruminate in the cloister of his own heart, surveyed the panorama of this Europe where none dared proclaim the truth of God from the sacred Word save at peril of his life. Servetus injected into the description of Germany this proverb: "Hungary produces cattle, Bavaria hogs, Franconia onions, turnips and licorice, Swabia harlots, Bohemia heretics, Bavaria again thieves, Helvetia hangmen and herdsmen, Westphalia liars, and all Germany gluttons and drunkards."

Of course Servetus did not make this up. He was drawing from that genre which the Germans call *ortsneckerei*. We might call it "locality ribbing," the flinging of jibes at places, of which in the United States the special butts are Missouri, Texas, California, and Boston. Europeans relish these thrusts of nation against nation and town against town. The story was told, for example, that if the Devil were to fall to earth dismembered, his head would land in Spain by reason of pride, his heart in Italy because of treachery, his belly in Germany for gluttony, his hands among the Turks and the Tartars for pilfering, and his legs in France for dancing.[18]

Servetus did not invent this sort of thing but plainly he relished it. The strictures of his own composition on the various lands are more candid than kindly. "The Scots," he said, "are prone to vengeance, ferocious, well built but negligent of their persons, envious and contemptuous. They revel in lies and do not seek peace like the English." This was toned down in the second edition. "The Irish are inhospitable, uncouth, cruel and more addicted to hunting and games than to agriculture." This was retained in the second edition. "The English have a language difficult, because of diverse origin, to pronounce. They have recently fallen away from the Church of Rome."

"The Germans are very devoted to the service of God except that they do not readily abandon positions which they have once adopted." Servetus had had experience on that score.

> The condition of the German peasants is dreadful. They live sparsely in the country, squatting in huts of mud, wood and straw. For food they have oatmeal and cooked vegetables and for drink they take water and whey. Officials in each section harry and exploit them. That is why there was recently a revolt of the peasants in a conspiracy against the nobles. But the poor always fail.

The comments on the Italians were even more caustic. "The Venetians pretend to forgive injuries but, if an opportunity presents itself, no one takes a more cruel revenge. They continually emit the most horrible oaths and blasphemies against God." The Spaniard is here retaliating for the Italian jibes at the Marranos. "Proud Rome, widowed of her rule over the peoples, has become the seat of the supreme pontiff who is assisted by the purpled cardinals ... The Neapolitans dress sumptuously and are redolent of perfume."

In the section on France, Servetus recorded, "The King's touch cures scrofula. I myself saw the King touching many victims of the malady but I did not see that any were cured." In the second edition this was altered to read, "I have heard that many were cured."

No people in the whole work fared worse than the Spaniards. Villeneuve introduced a comparison between the French and the Spaniards, much to the prejudice of the latter.[19] "The French," he said, "are talkative, the Spaniards taciturn and better at dissimulation." Was he thinking of his own brother as an emissary of the Inquisition?

> The French are buoyant, volatile and convivial and entirely free from the hypocrisy and gravity of the morose Spaniards ... In France guests are received most civilly in the inns ... in Spain harshly and boorishly, so that the tired traveler is forced to ask for food from village to village ... In Spain the Inquisitors assume great authority against the heretical Marranos and Moors and act with the utmost severity, and there is another remarkable sort of justice, called the *Hermandad* (Brotherhood), for it is a sworn fraternity of citizens, who at the sound of a bell come together in thousands to pursue the delinquent throughout the whole province. Runners are sent to all the other states so that it is almost impossible to escape. The captive is bound to a stake and shot with arrows ... The Spaniard is

restless in mind, vast in endeavor, highly gifted and impatient of instruction; half taught he thinks himself learned.

The second edition adds, "So that you will scarcely find a learned Spaniard save abroad." This covered Servetus's own case.

This passage comparing Spain and France drew fire from a quite unpredictable quarter. The German cosmographer, Sebastian Münster, published an edition of Ptolemy at Basel in 1540. In the preface, he paid tribute "To the most learned Michael Villanovanus, who had not spared himself any emendations, explications and illustrations." Then Münster paid him the compliment of incorporating in his own work the comparison of France and Spain, but with no indication of the source. The sense of literary property was not acute in that period. The passage in this form came to the attention of a Portuguese scholar, named Damião de Góis, who arraigned Münster for railing so atrociously against the Spaniards when he had never visited their country and did not know what he was talking about. Münster replied by disclosing that the author was Michael Villanovanus.[20]

But nothing in the whole book produced the same reaction as the description of Palestine, which concluded with the words:

> Nevertheless be assured, reader, that it is sheer misrepresentation to attribute such excellence to this land which the experience of merchants and travelers proves to be barren, sterile and without charm, so that you may call it in the vernacular the "promised land" only in the sense that it was promised, not that it had any promise.

This passage was deemed infinitely worse than any strictures on the Spaniards. Did it not give the lie to Moses, the very mouthpiece of God, who had referred to Palestine as the land of promise flowing with milk and honey? Servetus, to obviate this criticism, in the 1541 edition of the Ptolemy, retained the map of Palestine but left the page for the description completely blank.

The irony of it all was that this passage was not of his own composition. He had taken it bodily from the edition of Pirckheimer who, in turn, had borrowed it from Leonard Fries. There was only one inadvertent change: through the successive printings the form *laudatam,* applied to the Holy Land, had been turned into *laudantem.*[21] The passage actually is a part of the literature of revulsion against the crusades. As a matter of fact, the crusades, rather than the Old Testament, caused Palestine to be called the Holy Land. This characterization is not discoverable prior to the year 1100. Then, when the whole crusading enterprise fell through successive disasters into disrepute, there were those who boldly depreciated Palestine as a barren waste unworthy of so much blood.[22] Of all this Servetus was presumably unaware and carried over the passage as it was because he had nothing better to substitute.

Instead of omitting it in his second edition, he might have been on more defensible ground if he had followed the example of Sebastian Münster who, in his Ptolemy of the year 1540, had amplified the passage in the interests of precision:

> Jerusalem is located in an excellent land, which at one time flowed with milk and honey and now has become a source of salvation and a nutriment of life. This land at first God blessed above all others. So long as the people were upright their country was opulent, fertile, well-watered and abundant. But when they turned from the Lord to idols no pest were they spared. Then the curses pronounced by God in Deuteronomy 27 fell upon them so that now the land is not excellent but most miserable, scabby, sterile, without charm, devouring its inhabitants, as travelers to this day testify.

Such a clear demarcation between the Mosaic period and the present might have obviated criticism. Servetus merely omitted the passage. He was to hear from it again.

To the Bible he was to devote much more arduous and assiduous labor than to the Ptolemy. The edition of the Sante Pagnini Bible is alone well known. Two other and earlier editions, having been issued anonymously, were not accredited to Servetus prior to the recent discovery in the archives of Lyons of the following contract:

> Monsieur Michel de Villeneuve, called also Villanovanus, Doctor of Medicine, residing now at Lyons, appeared in person and contracted with the Honorable Hugues de la Porte (and others named), in consideration of presents received, to edit the Bible in six volumes, checking glosses, orthography, accents, punctuation and diphthongs, restoring Greek and Hebrew letters for Latin transcriptions, inserting in the Old Testament the notes of Jerome or Gabinius and, in the New Testament, those of Erasmus and Robert Etienne, in accord with directions to be given by M. Claude Guilliaud, Doctor of Theology at Paris and Canon at Autun. Villeneuve shall feed the manuscript to two or three presses which shall commence at the Easter Fair and shall continue until the work is done, for which he shall receive four hundred pounds ... Done at Lyons in the house called

Luxembourg on Monday the 14th day of February of the year 1540.[a] Gaspard Trechsel, publisher (and others named), residents of the said city of Lyons, witnesses.[23]

The completion of this work consumed four years and was discharged on the 20th of August, 1545, not in six but in seven volumes. An unsigned preface by the editor is undoubtedly from the pen of Servetus, who defended the incorporation of medieval glosses against those who condemned whatever was not couched in Ciceronian Latin. A one-volume octavo edition appeared in 1542 and also long remained unrecognized.[24]

The edition of the Pagnini Bible bore the name Villeneuve and served only to augment his doctrinal derelictions. The offense lay in the theory of Scripture. The medieval interpreters assumed a fourfold sense. The first is the plain historical meaning, though if the passage be inconsistent or devoid of sense this might be eliminated. Then came the allegorical for doctrine, the moral for ethics, and the anagogical for hope and comfort. The Protestant reformers rejected all save the historical. Nevertheless, they saw in the prophecies of the Old Testament predictions fulfilled in the New Testament and in the events of the Old Testament foreshadowings or types of the New. God, as Lord of history, they assumed, in unfolding the great drama of redemption, vouchsafed anticipatory intimations of his ultimate purpose for the salvation of mankind. The serpent which Moses set up in the wilderness for the healing of people was, according to John's Gospel, a type of the lifting up of the Son of man upon the Cross. The three days of Jonah in the belly of the whale prefigured the time that the Son of man should be in the heart of the earth, according to Matthew. And the apostle Paul saw in Isaac the type of the Son according to the Spirit, and in Ishmael, of the Son according to the flesh. The Middle Ages, as already noted, regarded Samson carrying off the gates as a type of Christ breaking the gates of Hell. The sacrifice of Isaac was similarly a type of the Crucifixion; and the three days' journey of Abraham and Isaac to Mount Moriah was another anticipation of the time that Christ lay in the tomb.

Servetus rejected all save the first of the four traditional senses of Scripture. The historical alone is valid, he claimed. Thus far he was on common ground with the Protestants. But he also rejected prophecy.

---

[a] By our reckoning, 1541.

He retained typology, although the type, said he, can be discovered only in that which actually happened in history. We have, then, first to establish the *fact* and that is why we must learn Hebrew and recover the plain, literal sense of the words. Then and then only shall we be in a position to seek for deeper meanings:

> Scripture has a double face ... and contains beneath the oldness of the letter that killeth the newness of the Spirit that giveth life, so that when one sense is elucidated it would be wrong to omit the other, the more so because the historical discloses the mystical. We have tried, therefore, in our notes to restore the literal old historical sense everywhere neglected, so that through it as a type the true mystical sense might be known, and we all, with unveiled face, might clearly see Jesus Christ, our God, the end of all, veiled in shadows and figures, on which account the blind Jews saw him not.

The task assigned to Servetus in editing the Pagnini Bible appeared to give little scope for the elaboration of these ideas expressed in the preface. The work had first been issued in 1528. The distinctive feature was the separate numbering of the verses, which Villeneuve did not retain. An unauthorized edition had appeared at Cologne in 1541 at the hands of Melchior Novesianus.[25] Villeneuve had this edition also before him. His additions to Pagnini and Novesianus consisted only of new chapter headings and marginal annotations in so infinitesimal a type that one would scarcely have thought to detect in them any portent of his trial and execution.

But one of the most signal prophecies of the Old Testament was flatly rejected. It was the famous reference, in Isaiah 7:14, rendered in the Vulgate: "Behold, the Lord himself shall give you a sign and a virgin shall conceive." This was taken in the early Church to be a prediction of the virgin birth. But unfortunately the word *virgin* was derived from a mistaken translation in the Septuagint, the Greek version of the Old Testament. The Hebrew word means simply "young woman," as the Jewish exegetes were never slow to point out. Villeneuve entirely agreed with them and his marginal annotation indicated that the one who should conceive was the wife of Hezekiah.[26]

As for typology, Villeneuve was insistent that the historical reference must first be recognized. Therefore, frequently in the book of Isaiah, when the edition of Pagnini or Novesianus referred the passage to Christ, Villeneuve would add, "under the guise of Hezekiah or Isaiah or Cyrus." The Song of Songs in the Middle Ages had commonly been interpreted as an allegory of the love of Christ for the Church. In the edition of Villeneuve the chapter headings which usually conveyed this interpretation were entirely omitted.

The cardinal passage, and the one which was to occasion reproach, was the great fifty-third chapter of Isaiah which, throughout the Christian centuries, had always been regarded as depicting the actual sufferings of Christ: "He was despised and rejected of men, a Man of sorrows and acquainted with grief … He was wounded for our transgressions, He was bruised for our iniquities and by His stripes we are healed." The gloss of Villeneuve was this: "The incredible and stupendous mystery refers to Cyrus because the sublime sacrifice of Christ lies hid beneath the humble types of history."

The String Quartet of Plato, Aristotle, Galen, and Hippocrates

Chapter 6

Doctor of Medicine

The contract which in 1541 engaged Michel de Villeneuve to edit the Bible in six volumes referred to him as *Docteur en Médecine*. Such indeed he had become. The enlargement of his skills and activities was due in no small measure to a new friendship formed in connection with his editorial work. During the period when he was engaged by the firm of Gaspard and Melchior Trechsel, their presses published several works from the pen of a distinguished medical humanist of Lyons, Symphorien Champier.[1] He was one of the more ebullient figures of the Renaissance; he did not scruple to don nobility by constructing a genealogy. He was deterred by no inhibitions from essaying war and theology, patristics and the poetry of passion, chivalric biography and the pursuit of medicine. He was one of the disseminators in France of the Florentine Neoplatonism and an ardent reconciler of discrepancies in the classical tradition. A woodcut in one of his works displays the rival Greeks, Plato and Aristotle, Galen and Hippocrates, constituting a string quartet. One notes the absence of any of the Arabs, against whom Champier sided in matters medical with Galen, the Greek. Champier was a man of public spirit who patronized the University of the Trinity and, in particular, the medical school.[2] His public influence is evident in that when the Town Council proposed a tax on wheat he dissuaded them by citations from "authors Hebrew, Greek, Egyptian and Latin" and induced them instead to put the tax on wine. In consequence there was a riot in which his house was sacked. The city made appropriate restitution and he continued his honorable and somewhat belligerent career.[3]

Champier had become embroiled in a controversy which for sheer triviality may give comfort to theologians when reproached with a contentious spirit by men of science. Champier was battling with a fellow Galenist, Leonhart Fuchs of Heidelberg, the eminent botanist whose herbal is a landmark and whose name is perpetuated in that of the flower called, after him, *fuchsia*. A woodcut portrait of him from his famous book displays him holding a flower.[4] Fuchs was, by profession, a doctor. He had attacked certain theories of Champier; he, in turn, had denounced the work of Fuchs to the Inquisitor of Paris, by whom it was burned. In defense of his friend and patron, Michel de Villeneuve entered the lists, in a pamphlet significant chiefly because it evidences his first interests in matters medical. [5]

The tract, *In Leonardum Fuchsium Apologia*, curiously begins with a point of theology, and the men of science may if they wish ascribe the contentiousness of Fuchs, Champier, and Servetus to the fact that they were also theologians. Fuchs was an ardent Lutheran, while Champier did not scruple to invoke the Inquisition – and incidentally he was a warm friend of the Cardinal, François de Tournon, to whom several of his works were dedicated. The theological interests of Servetus we well know. He begins his *Apologia* by proclaiming himself a disciple of Symphorien Champier and a loyal son of Mother Church who cannot restrain himself when he contemplates the heresies of Leonhart Fuchs.

Leonhart Fuchs

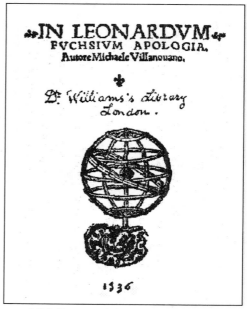

Title Page of the Tract Against Fuchs

Thus the heretic decries the heretic. If one finds this amazing, one should reflect that he who cares enough about religion to be a heretic not infrequently considers the religion of another to be erroneous and pernicious. The particular point here was one on which Servetus did agree with the Catholic Church — namely, that salvation is not exclusively by faith apart from works. He had already attacked Luther on that score. And one should not too promptly brand as a hypocrite a man who regarded the pope as the beast of the Apocalypse and yet considered himself a loyal son of Mother Church. Such attitudes were not necessarily incompatible. Yet the suspicion will not down that this fugitive for faith who, if his views were known, would have been banished or burned in any land of Europe, was endeavoring to create a diversion by raising the cry of heresy against another.

Then came the medical matters. Fuchs and Champier differed as to the meaning and use of a drug called scammony, a resin extracted from roots. It is a very powerful cathartic which, unless modified, occasions gripes. Champier strongly discountenanced its use as more dangerous than Cerberus and Beelzebub.[6] The quarrel with Fuchs was as to whether the scammony prescribed by the Greeks in larger doses was actually the same as that prescribed by the Arabs only in smaller quantities. Fuchs argued for identity and Champier for diversity. The latter appears to have been correct — for the United States Dispensatory for 1947 reports differences in the strength and even the composition of scammony according to locality.

The next point had to do with the origin of syphilis. Even to this day the problem has never been altogether solved whether this disease was newly imported into Europe by the returning sailors of Columbus or whether it was an unparalleled flare-up of some earlier malady.[7] The difficulty lies in the inexactitude of medieval descriptions of venereal diseases. But the difference between Fuchs and Champier did not lie here. They were both agreed that it was a new disease. The question was whether to regard it as of natural or of supernatural origin. Champier claimed that it was both new and an evidence of the wrath of God.

This point particularly appealed to Servetus. One is not to suppose, however, that by this he was thinking of a specific punishment for sexual irregularities. The disease in that unsanitary age, totally inexperienced in preventive measures, could be quite innocently acquired. The point was rather that mankind in general deserved the wrath of God. What should one say of a generation which refused to listen to the plain teaching of the Word of God and which sent Moors and Jews to the stake for rejecting a doctrine which Scripture did not require? Servetus was a smoldering Savonarola – or better might one say an Anabaptist prophet in disguise, covertly pronouncing doom upon a stiff-necked and adulterous generation.

Probably on the advice of Champier, Servetus went to Paris and studied medicine. There he became associated with a very distinguished circle. His teachers were Jacques Dubois, Jean Fernel, and Johann Guenther von Andernach. His colleague in dissection was the great Vesalius.[8] Guenther paid this tribute to his assistants in dissection:

> My first helper was Andreas Vesalius, a young man marvelously diligent in anatomy, a practitioner of pure medicine unalloyed. And after him, Michael Villanovanus was closely associated with me in dissection. He is well versed in every branch of literature, and in Galen is second to none. To these two I both lectured on Galen and showed them what I had discovered through the examination of muscles, veins, arteries and nerves.[9]

Dissection in those days presented difficulties for the medical student at the point of obtaining an adequate supply of cadavers – not through any interdiction by the Church, but because the law allowed for this purpose only the bodies of those executed for crime. The bodies of malefactors were granted only to doctors of reputation, but they could conduct dissections in public without hindrance. Rabelais, for example, in 1534 dissected at Lyons in the presence of his students. Servetus may quite possibly have been among the audience. Étienne Dolet celebrated the occasion by composing a poem in which the corpse expresses gratification at being thus enabled to exhibit the wonderful artifice of the Creator.[10] When such official grants were not adequate, students like Vesalius sometimes had recourse to stealthy despoiling of the gallows. Felix Platter at Montpellier even appropriated the newly interred from a monastic cemetery until sternly reprimanded by his father.[11] So far as we know, Servetus never had recourse to any such expedients.

He supported himself while pursuing anatomy partly by publication. A treatise *On Syrups* may have produced a tidy income since it went through six editions. The syrups in question were sweetened decoctions which served as a base for astringents, cathartics, tonics, and the like. In other words, Servetus was continuing those pharmaceutical studies to which he had been introduced by Champier and of which his little excursus on scammony had been a foretaste. The Greeks and the Arabs were divided as to the use of syrups. Servetus here, as in theology, took an eclectic position. "In this controversy," he said in the preface to his tract, "if I may judge, neither side is right, but I do not wish to enter as censor and, by condemning both sides, incur the enmity of all. Nevertheless, lest out of fear I withhold anything which may be useful to humanity I here set forth what I think to be more nearly the truth." If he thus at certain points disagreed with one, it was only because he was agreeing with the other. Now Galen was followed, now Hippocrates, and now the Arabs. Fundamentally, however, the medical philosophy of Servetus was that of the Greeks.

And for that reason the tract *On Syrups* devoted the major portion of the space not to the specific subject at all but to the theory of digestion. According to the Arabs, the process is one in the sick and another in the well, and cures are frequently to be effected by the employment of contraries. Servetus, following the Greeks, contended instead that digestion is the same process whether in health or in sickness. Its purpose is first of all segregation, and then assimilation of the appropriate and elimination of the inappropriate. There is, according to Hippocrates, a nature of man which conducts these processes, and the art of the physician is simply to assist nature. Assimilation is best aided by natural means such as repose, sleep, massage, baths, warm food and drink; citrus fruits are especially commended. Here was an unwitting anticipation of vitamins. For elimination and the arresting of maladies, the syrups have their utility. At this point the Arabs received their due.[12]

Another way to earn a living was by lecturing. On one subject Servetus was already well prepared by reason of his editing of the Ptolemy in 1535. He now undertook to give instruction in geography before distinguished audiences. Among his hearers was Pierre Palmier, the Archbishop of Vienne.[13] Now, the science of earth is close to that of heaven; friends therefore suggested to Servetus that he should rise from the terrestrial to the celestial and combine geography with astronomy. In the sixteenth century that was bound to involve astrology.

And few in that day would take umbrage. Astrology had become almost the stepdaughter of the Church, even though astrological determinism was incompatible with divine Providence, let alone with the intervention of God. Yet, did not the Bible say that the stars in their courses fought against Sisera? And God did not disdain to employ a star to inform the Wise Men of the birth of Christ – albeit a very special star from which no warrant can be inferred for casting horoscopes. The Bible might thus yield certain favorable inclinations toward astrology. The cult of the stars, however, is not properly Jewish or Christian but rather classical. Particularly in the age of the twilight of the gods, the ancients in search of religious assurance looked with wonder and comfort upon the chaste beauty and the starlit majesty of the southern night. Was there not here some faint intimation that neither blind chance nor the sheer caprice of noxious spirits governs the lives of men, but rather the beneficent purpose of a rational power which has woven into the tapestry of heaven the evidence of law-abiding energy? The world soul animates the universe alike in the bodies above and in those below. And what is discoverable on high may, then, be taken as a guide for that which is beneath. The moon affects the tides, the weather, the menstruation of women, and the temperaments of men. The conjunctions of planets and constellations give clues to forthcoming events.

These views received an enormous reinforcement with the revival of Aristotle among the scholastics of the thirteenth century. An examination of the compatibility of astrology with the Christian position was thereby necessitated. An accommodation was found through the word of Augustine that the stars affect the bodies, though not the wills, of men. On this basis astrology could be employed as an aid to medicine.[14] Such was the view of Aquinas. A distinction was drawn also between plain astrology, which today would be called astronomy, and judicial astrology, or the art of forecasting. Even this foretelling was allowed by Aquinas, provided the predictions were general rather than specific.

Such discriminating safeguards did not prevent a lush development of the worst features even in high ecclesiastical quarters. Pope Julius II allowed an astrologer to determine the date for his coronation. Leo X established a professorship for astrology in the College of Sapienza; and Paul III was particularly addicted to the cult. Kings and emperors engaged court astrologers. In medical circles the body was marked off according to the signs of the zodiac, that bloodlettings or operations might be conducted under a favorable configuration. Diseases were attributed to stellar influence – hence the name *influenza*. The Humanist movement brought no diminution – in fact, the contrary, because of the enthusiasm for classical sources. And, if Pico della Mirandola protested, it was largely because of the influence of Savonarola.

Astro;ogical Medicine
The body demarked according to the signs of the zodiac
for blood-letting from the propitious part at the appropriate time

Nor did the Reformation bring a decisive break. Luther, to be sure, scoffed at the diviners: "I am the son of a peasant. My father wanted to make me into a burgomaster. I became a master of arts, then I became a monk. My father didn't like it. And then I got into the Pope's hair and married an apostate nun. Who could have read that in the stars?"[15] Yet Melanchthon was so steeped in astrology that he actually changed the "date" of Luther's birth in order to provide him with a more propitious horoscope.

At the same time church councils and medical faculties took measures to curb the hordes of quacks and charlatans while kings favored only felicitous predictions. The flood of forecasts which presaged and did much to set off the Peasants' War in Germany was not the sort of prophecy that a stable government would relish. In consequence, astrologers were now curried and now harried. Yet a modern author has estimated that there were in Paris in the sixteenth century some 30,000 mountebanks battening on the credulity of the populace.[16]

The charge was now brought before the Faculty of Medicine of the University of Paris that Michel de Villeneuve was one of these charlatans. Thereupon the aggrieved Villeneuve promptly wrote and committed to the printer a defense of astrology in which he pointed out, with perfect propriety, that Plato, Aristotle, Pythagoras, Galen, Hippocrates, and many others were all partisans of the art. Not only that, but they recognized the validity of astrological medicine. In this regard Servetus was distinctly moderate. He did not allocate portions of the body to the constellations. His point was rather that the weather affects the body and the stars affect the weather. The phases of the moon have a bearing on temperature. Prognostications of the weather can be made with some degree of confidence, though one must bear in mind that the observable signs may be invalidated by some supervening force. "Thus when the almanacs have predicted rain," said Servetus, "I have predicted from the constellations that winds would supervene and dispel the clouds and, when they have predicted cold, from other signs I have shown that the winter would be mild." The point was that the doctor should be versed in weather forecasting, just as, likewise, he should study geography to learn how climate varies with locality (a point which Servetus in his geographies had not deemed worthy of mention). Those who decline to avail themselves of all aids are ignoramuses. "So blind are they that they never lift their eyes to the heavens to behold that this most beautiful mechanism was not established by God in vain.

And why have signs been established by the Creator, as Scripture testifies, if not that they may signify something?"

Servetus went beyond astrological medicine simply in the form of weather forecasts, however, and verged on the more dubious aspects of the art. He reproached "a certain ape" for leaving astrology out of account in his investigation of the causes of syphilis. And then the very Servetus who rejected the predictions of the prophets of the Old Testament proceeded, himself, to foretell the future. He had made the perfectly valid observation that on the night of the 13th of February, 1538 (actually at 13h 9m 21s),[17] Mars, while in the neighborhood of the star called *Cor Leonis* or Lion's Heart, had been eclipsed by the moon. "Hence I predicted that in this year the hearts of the lions would be more avidly excited, that is, the minds of princes would be induced to martial enterprises, much land would be devastated by fire and sword, the Church would suffer, certain princes would be killed, pests would ensue, which may God avert."

Servetus really did not need astrology for this. Brooding with intense fervor over the mystery of iniquity that rejected the light and slew the prophets, he foresaw the impending vengeance of the Lord. He had considered syphilis a foretaste of the woes to come, and now the eclipse of Mars was a portent.

Dean Thagault of the Medical Faculty, hearing of the forthcoming *Apology for Astrology*, resolved to intervene.[18] "Because I was Dean of the faculty," he recorded, "I went to remonstrate with Villeneuve. I came upon him in the act of dissecting a cadaver with the help of another doctor. I told him not to bring out his Apology. He was abusive in the presence of several scholars and two or three doctors."

The Faculty of Medicine requested the Parlement de Paris to issue an injunction against the printing of the *Apology*. But Servetus, having been tipped off, gave the printer a fee to hasten the work and distributed many copies without charge. He even boasted that he had outdone the Dean.

The next step was to bring Villeneuve to trial before the Parlement convened under the presidency of Pierre Lizet, who was so desirous that the land of the lily should be pure in the faith. The record has this entry:

> Monday, March 18, 1538, behind closed doors, President Lizet presiding – The case of the Rector of the University of Paris and the Dean of the Faculty of Medicine against Michel de Villeneuve.

The speaker for the Rector of the University complained that Villeneuve practiced judicial astrology which is forbidden by many constitutions both canon and civil, since knowledge of the future is reserved for God. The accused, who is an intelligent man, cannot be ignorant of all this. Yet he has cast divinations based on nativities which the Theological Faculty finds most reprehensible. He takes fees for this and has captured the minds of students by his mellifluous poison. Pico says that astrology "is a pestilent beast of mercenariness which corrupts philosophy, adulterates medicine, weakens religion, fosters superstition, pollutes morals, defiles the Church and makes men miserable, anxious and distraught." Yet this Villeneuve has written an apology in which he declares on the basis of an eclipse of Mars that "The hearts of the lions will be avidly excited, that is, the minds of princes will be induced to martial enterprises, much land will be devastated by fire and sword, the Church will suffer, certain princes will be killed and pests will ensue." And a little further on he says, "There will be languor, misery and death." We demand that he be inhibited from the practice of judicial astrology and that all copies of his Apology be confiscated.

The representative of the Faculty of Medicine complained that when the doctors remonstrated graciously Villeneuve had replied insolently. He had published not so much an apology as an invective against those who candidly admonished him. He, a student, accuses his teachers of imperiousness. He owes them respect as masters and instead he calls them monsters. He has enlisted the aid of Jean Thibault.

That was a sore point. Thibault was the court astrologer. First he had served with the Emperor, Charles V, and now was attached to François I of France. The Medical Faculty regarded him as a colossal charlatan and had sought to suppress him, but in vain, presumably because of the royal favor. If this man now rallied to the side of Villeneuve, the latter would perhaps enjoy immunity because of the king's influence in the background. On the other hand, since Villeneuve was not in the king's employ, he might be suppressed – and this would be to score both against Thibault and against the king.

Then the defense spoke and conceded that the faculty had displayed admirable moderation toward Villeneuve – a foreigner. Enmity had arisen because he had said that doctors ought to understand the science of astrology. But as for judicial astrology he had said nothing. He was accused of it, indeed, but there were students who attended his lectures who would testify that he spoke only of the effect of the stars upon material things and declared this knowledge necessary for doctors. His assailants retaliated by dubbing him a charlatan and he, being aggrieved, came out with an apology. He did say that the eclipse pointed to disaster, but he added: "which may God avert." And as for the reference to "languor, misery and death," those were not his words but a citation from Hippocrates. Villeneuve had declared himself ready to submit to the judgment of the theologians. As for his calling the doctors a pest, the reference was only to the ignorant among them. Nevertheless they cited him before the inquisitor for the faith as if he were suspect of heresy. And, although such a citation (when the case was already in the hands of the Parlement) could be considered an abuse, nevertheless to show that he had nothing to fear for his reputation he appeared and proved that he was as good a Christian as those who pursued him.

What nerve! This man, who knew that the inquisitor could burn him if his identity were disclosed, had the temerity to appear of his own accord. He must have been very dexterous in keeping the examination strictly to the question of astrology. And on that point he could demonstrate his rectitude. His indiscretions could be more than matched by the examples of the popes and emperors. One wonders, incidentally, who this inquisitor was. In all likelihood it was not Matthieu Ory – who otherwise would at once have recognized Servetus when later he fell into his clutches.

The Dean of the Medical Faculty in his account interjects: "The President of the Parlement[a] harangued the offender at length and the members of the court gnashed their teeth at Villeneuve."

The court record gives the sentence: "All the issues of his *Apology* should be called in and confiscated. Villeneuve should show respect to the faculty, and they in turn should treat him as parents do their children. He should not practice judicial astrology, whether in public or in private, on pain of being deprived of those privileges which the King confers on the students of the University of Paris."

Whether or not this squabble prevented Servetus from taking his degree is not clear. He asserted later at Geneva that he was a Doctor of Medicine of the University of Paris.[19] Nevertheless his name does not appear among the *diplomés* at Paris. This does not necessarily prove that he lied, because the complete records may not have been preserved. It is plain, at any rate, that the contract to edit the Bible at Lyons referred to him as *Docteur en Médecine,* and this among those who were familiar with his record at Paris.

---

[a] Pierre Lizet.

In any case, the greatest fruit of the Parisian period was not a degree but a discovery which has given to the name of Servetus an imperishable place in the annals of science. He was the first in the West to grasp the pulmonary circulation of the blood – or more accurately, the transit or circuit of the blood in the lungs, since no return occurs to the point of departure.[20]

To understand precisely what Servetus discovered one needs to have in mind the views of Galen from which he diverged. This ancient master taught that the blood is continuously generated in the liver to which it never returns, having been consumed in the nutriment of the body. The blood is communicated from the arteries to the veins in part by anastomosis at the extremities, and in part through the wall of the heart by means of interstices which do not appear in an autopsy because of the cooling and contraction ensuing at death. In the lungs, as well as at the extremities, according to Galen, there is an anastomosis, but not a continuous flow; if any blood returns from the lungs to the heart, it is only by reason of a leakage of the valves. Galen failed to discern the course of the blood in the lungs because he misconceived the function of the lungs, the aeration of the blood being assigned not to them but to the left ventricle of the heart. He suggested with genuine divination that air is needed by the body for the same reason as by a flame; in both instances, he supposed that the function of the air is to expel the waste products of combustion, which process in the body takes place in the left ventricle. The lungs, to use a modern figure, served in Galen's system as a carburetor to provide the proper mixture of air and spirit which then passes into the heart and expels the fumes.[21]

Servetus retained the Galenic view of the origin of the blood in the liver and, for that reason, did not attain an understanding of the circulation of the blood throughout the body.[22] His advance lay rather in an accurate delineation of the course of the blood in the heart and the lungs. His first correction of Galen was the direct result of dissection. The transmission of the blood from the right to the left ventricle, he observed, is not by way of the septum, "for this middle wall, since it lacks orifices, is not suitable for this communication, even though something might seep through." Without a microscope Servetus was not in a position to make an absolute assertion of impermeability, but he was prepared to say that the primary course could not be through the septum.

Secondly he observed that the pulmonary artery is too large for the function assigned to it in the Galenic system, where it is needed only to transmit a very small portion of the blood to the lungs for their nutriment. This Servetus denied. "The great size of the arterial vein[b] ... has not been made so great, nor is the purified blood expelled with such force from the heart into the lungs simply for their nutriment." This passage deserves a special emphasis because recently several modern writers have assumed that since Servetus was not emancipated from the Galenic theory of the continuous manufacture of the blood in the liver for the feeding of the body, he must, therefore, have supposed that only a little blood went to the lungs for that purpose and no more. Hence, they assume, he cannot have believed that the whole blood stream passes through the lungs.[23]

This assertion, to be sure, is not made by Servetus in so many words, but it is a legitimate inference from the statements that the blood goes through the lungs for some other reason than for their nutriment and that the artery is too large for this function alone. Why, then, does the blood pass through the lungs? Servetus had the correct answer. It is for the sake of aeration, whereby the fuliginous vapors of Galen are expelled and the blood changes color. This process takes place in the lungs, not in the heart. To quote Servetus more fully:

> The vital spirit is generated from a mixture made in the lungs of the inspired air with the elaborated refined blood, which is communicated from the right ventricle to the left. This communication does not, however, take place, as commonly supposed, through the middle wall of the heart, but by an elaborate device the refined blood is driven from the right ventricle of the heart over a long course through the lungs. By the lungs it is prepared and made bright. From the pulmonary artery it is transferred to the pulmonary vein. Then in the pulmonary vein it is mixed with the inspired air and is purged of fumes by expiration ... Moreover it is not simply air, but air mixed with blood which is sent from the lungs to the heart through the pulmonary vein, so that the mixture takes place in the lungs and the bright hue is given to the spiritous (arterial) blood by the lungs, not by the heart. In the left ventricle of the heart there is not a place large enough for so copious a mixture, nor is that elaboration sufficient for the bright tint. Moreover the middle wall, since it lacks orifices, is not suitable for this communication and elaboration, even granted that something might seep through.[24]

A question of some interest has arisen, in connection with his discovery, as to whether Servetus enjoys a complete priority. Here, as so often in the history of science, independent investigators came upon

---

[b] i.e. the pulmonary artery.

the same truth almost coincidently. Frequently unseemly quarrels have ensued as to who should receive the palm. For the advance of knowledge the discovery alone matters and not the discoverer, but man is driven to the noblest endeavors not without a touch of vanity. In this instance, however, there was no rivalry between Servetus and Realdo Colombo, the other contestant, for, to the best of our knowledge, neither knew of the discovery of the other. So far as the priority of the announcement is concerned, there is no problem at all. Colombo's *De Re Anatomica* came out in 1559. The discovery of Servetus was announced in the *Christianismi Restitutio* in 1553; the circumstances of the publication will be related in a subsequent chapter. The priority of publication, then, is not in question but only the time of the actual observation.

The point may appear too trivial to be worthy of pursuit. Yet there may be a certain interest in recording what can be known. A pupil of Colombo said that his work had been commenced *abhinc multos annos,* "for many years." Such a statement obviously admits of no precision. In the case of Servetus it is possible to be more exact. There is today in the Bibliothèque Nationale at Paris a manuscript of Servetus's work containing the passage on the pulmonary transit of the blood. This manuscript differs in a number of respects from the printed edition, and it is not in the author's hand. Is it a transcript deliberately modified from the printed work or is it a faithful copy of an earlier draft which we know to have existed in 1546?

The priority of the Paris manuscript is well nigh settled by a comparison of the citations from the editions of printed works. Servetus in his very first publication, *On the Errors of the Trinity,* had regretted his inability to obtain a copy of the works of Clement of Alexandria. They were not printed in Greek until 1550, and in Latin the following year. Now the printed edition of the *Restitutio* of 1553 has three citations from Clement of Alexandria and these do not appear in the manuscript.[25] Again the works of Philo of Alexandria appeared for the first time in Greek in the year 1552, though Latin translations had come out in 1527 and 1538. The Paris manuscript of Servetus cites Philo five times in Latin but lacks the two citations in Greek which appear in the corresponding portions of the printed edition.[26] One can scarcely question, therefore, that the Paris manuscript is earlier than the printed book. Since earlier, then presumably it is derived from the manuscript of 1546.

The dating of the manuscript, however, has ceased to be pertinent to the priority of discovery because the laurel has passed alike from

Servetus and Colombo to an Arab, Ibn An-Nafis, of the thirteenth century, who recorded the impermeability of the septum and the aeration of the blood in the lungs. He was not so explicit as Servetus, however, in denying the Galenic theory that the blood serves to nourish the lungs nor did he call attention to the size of the pulmonary artery. Yet his observations were extremely significant. There remains then but the question of whether his findings may conceivably have influenced either Servetus or Colombo. The likelihood is that they did not. For although a portion of his work was translated into Latin and appeared at Venice in 1547, it is not the part which contains the allusions to the pulmonary transit of the blood. The question can only be whether the translator, Andrea Alpago, who had access to the full Arabic text, may have grasped the significance of what lay before him and may have communicated his observations to others.[27] In any case, the differences in detail render dependence dubious.[28]

A question vastly more interesting than the priority of discovery is the philosophy of man without which even dissection might never have led Servetus to his significant observations. One recalls that his findings are announced in a work on theology. One must understand that for him theology, philosophy, physiology, and psychology were not compartmentalized. He was a son of the Renaissance with its exuberant appropriation and development from antiquity of the concept of the cohesiveness of the universe. All reality holds together in rational integration because the whole, as the Stoics held, is pervaded by that reason which enables man to understand and the world to be understood. Because of this immanent rationalism, the same fundamental principles are exhibited in every area of existence and varied disciplines are interrelated, such as mathematics, music, and astronomy. In this spirit Albrecht Dürer studied proportion alike in architecture, in the structure of the human body, and in the designing of the letters of the alphabet. The eclectic period of late antiquity, and similarly the Renaissance, believed in the ultimate unity of all systems of philosophy and religion. Renaissance men sought to encompass all disciplines and harmonize all systems. In this spirit Symphorien Champier had placed the rival leaders of Greek philosophy and medicine in a string quartet. Servetus was in this tradition in his belief that physiology, psychology, and theology are intimately bound and the place of their conjunction is man.

A second principle, likewise prevalent in that generation, was the belief that the immanent animating force in the universe is something more than the placid reason of the Stoics. Rather it is a dynamic and creative energy, the very being of God the Creator, who suffuses all with his spirit, obliterating all cleavages, drawing all things unto Himself, and infusing nature with such superabundant and harmonious excellencies that man should lose himself in rapturous adoration. Such was the view of Giordano Bruno. This reverence and delight stimulated the endeavors of the first astronomers, such as Kepler, and by the same beliefs Servetus was impelled to study the motion of the blood.[29]

For Servetus, however, there was a third reason and this too was characteristic of his age – the problem of personal salvation. His question differed chiefly only in vocabulary from that of Luther as to how to discover a gracious God, how to feel oneself attuned to the universe. Not by faith alone, was the answer of Servetus, but by a union of man with God. His earliest work, as we have seen, appropriated from the Church fathers the belief that man by communication with the God-man, Christ Jesus, may himself become a son of God and, in some sense, divine.

Yet man is not so born. How, then, does this transformation come to pass? The answer is that there must be already in man some area of divinity which may serve as a point of expansion. The mystics used a varying terminology – such as the spark, the seed, or the light in man. Servetus was able to avail himself of all three of these terms, but the locus of God in man which he preferred was another traditional concept, namely that of the soul. "For," declared Servetus, "our soul is a certain light of God, a spark of the spirit of God, having an innate light of divinity." He distinguished in current fashion the three kinds of spirit in man – the natural, the animal, and the vital – but then in accord with the temper of his age reduced them all into one. "In all these there is the energy of one spirit and of the light of God."[30] This again means that he would make no sharp distinction between soul and spirit.

The soul according to the Biblical account was breathed by God into man. The divine principle was thus injected by respiration. But respiration is directed to the purification of the blood. At once Servetus then grasped the meaning of the Hebrew doctrine that the soul is in the blood.[31] And how appropriate that it should be located in something that moves! It is not, said he, in the heart, the liver, or the brain, for these are static; being in the blood, it is able to course through the body.[32] As Symphorien Champier had said, *Sanguis est peregrinus,* "the blood is a traveler."[33] How easily this idea might have led to the discovery of the full circulation! So far Servetus was not in a position to go. He did, however, follow the blood to the brain; there the soul in the blood, he assumed, vivifies all the faculties of the body, since the soul animates the body, as in turn it is animated by God.

Thus far, however, he had discovered no solution for his religious problem of personal salvation, because the blood and the soul and the respiratory system are in every human being, whether saved or lost: those who are endowed with all of these physical functions may yet be alienated from the universe and estranged from God. There must then be something beyond respiration. The answer is that respiration must become again inspiration, as generation must lead to regeneration. For Servetus these were not so much two processes as aspects of one divine operation. He was never quite sure whether he was talking the language of physiology or religion and, for that reason, he has become difficult to comprehend in an age of the secularization of science. For Servetus there was only an enhancement of natural processes in ascending from respiration to inspiration, generation to regeneration, from sight to insight, from birth to new birth in the spirit. For him the vital spirit of Galen was identified with the Holy Spirit of Christ. "By the breath of God through the mouth and the ears, within the heart and brain of Adam and his children, the celestial aura of the Spirit, the spark of the idea, was in essence conjoined with the matter of spiritualized blood and the soul was made." "Just as by air God makes ruddy the blood, so does Christ cause the Holy Spirit to glow."[34]

Here is the Renaissance faith in the unity of all reality. Servetus drew no compartmental lines. With the Victorian poet he would have said that he who understands the flower in the crannied wall is able to understand what God and man are. To grasp the meaning of the movement of the blood might well unlock the meaning of the movement of the stars. He who really understands all that is involved in the breathing of man has already sensed the breath of God.

The Archangel Michael Vanquishing the Devil

Chapter 7

The Restoration of Christianity

Servetus left Paris to practice medicine in the provinces. He was for brief periods at Lyons and Avignon and then two or three years at Charlieu. Only two incidents of this period are known – a fight and nearly a wedding. The first was occasioned by the jealousy of a rival physician whose partisans fell upon Servetus while he was on his way by night to attend a sick patient. He was wounded and, in turn, injured one of his assailants. In consequence he was for two or three days under arrest.[1] As for the wedding, he confessed under later cross-examination that he had been on the point of uniting himself with a girl of Charlieu but had desisted, believing himself to be impotent by reason of castration at the age of five on one side and rupture on the other.[2] As a medical man he should have known that by neither would he have been impaired. In any case this testimony ill comports with a statement on another occasion that he had dedicated himself to celibacy by preference.[3]

One may surmise the real reason to have been that he could never have found a wife who could be trusted with his secrets. Only if he could have first gradually inducted a girl into his ideas would it have been possible, and that he could scarcely have done without giving her a very extensive preliminary education. On the other hand, to have lived with a wife while concealing from her his inmost ruminations and clandestine publications would have been galling and precarious. If an unsympathetic wife, were she Catholic or Protestant, had come to suspect his heresies, she would have been bound to report him and would not have placed the marriage bond or personal attachment above loyalty to the faith.

Sometime after 1540 Servetus transferred his residence to Vienne, a suburb of Lyons.[4] One inducement was the gracious patronage of Pierre Palmier, the Archbishop of Vienne, who had been an auditor of his lectures on geography in Paris. Another reason was that the firm of Trechsel had established a branch printing office at Vienne. For the next dozen years approximately, Servetus engaged both in editing and in the practice of medicine. The second edition of the geography came out in 1541, the edition of the Pagnini Bible in 1542; the contract to edit the Bible in six volumes was signed February 14, 1540/41, and the work as previously noted continued over four years. In addition, Servetus formed a liaison with another publisher, of Huguenot leanings, Jean Frellon, for whom he translated some grammatical works into Spanish and edited a Spanish translation of Thomas Aquinas.[5]

The dozen or so years at Vienne were the most tranquil in the career of Servetus. He went quietly about his labors, enjoying the esteem of the gentry. Among his clients, for example, was Guy de Maugiron, lieutenant governor of Dauphiny, a veteran of the Battle of Pavia, a commander high in the councils of the king.

[For a considerable portion of the time, he was living in the archiepiscopal palace as the almoner of the Archbishop Pierre Palmier. To be sure, His Reverence was seldom in residence, and his friendship with Servetus went back to their earlier days together in Paris. Yet it is a piquant spectacle to observe this heretic composing his explosive *Restitution of Christianity* in the very palace of a prince of the Church.

At the same time, Servetus was active as a public citizen. He served on a commission to direct the building of a bridge across the Rhone, and when a dispute arose as to whether it should have one arch or two, he voted for two and won. He also advised diverting the waters of the river in order to facilitate the driving of the pile. His fellow physicians elected him the prior of the Confraternity of St. Luke with special responsibility to oversee the apothecaries and to minister to the indigent at the hospital. Into this office he was solemnly inducted.[6]]

Yet all the while Servetus well knew that if his innermost convictions were disclosed, few among his friends would treat him better than if he were a carrier of the cholera. Guy de Maugiron, for example, at the behest of the king, had posted with fifty horse to Lyons because of a rumor that certain Lutherans were plotting a scandal on Corpus Christi Day in 1546.[7]

Nevertheless, Servetus could not bring himself indefinitely to bear no witness. He would not heedlessly expose his life. The pseudonym was not to be abandoned. He would not invite prompt extinction by a refusal to attend Mass. His testimony should be anonymous and clandestine, but for that reason, perhaps, all the more copious and pungent. Throughout the unruffled decade, by the bedsides of the sick, he was engaged in eschatological reveries; while editing Thomas Aquinas in Spanish he was seething with revulsion against the usurper of the keys of the Kingdom.

A new book was under way. Its actual publication will concern the next chapter. The title was to be *Christianismi Restitutio,* that is, the restitution or restoration of Christianity, a theme dear to Erasmus and all the Christian Humanists. The new work was very largely to incorporate the earlier; but in several respects it showed the impact of new influences. The first was the Neoplatonism popularized in France by Symphorien Champier; the second was Anabaptism, with which Servetus had made his contacts at Strassburg. The term Neoplatonism in this context must be broadly construed. The movement was in the main Platonic stream, but highly eclectic. The priests of the cult drew from Plato himself, from Posidonius and Philo, Plotinus, Proclus, Iamblichus, Clement of Alexandria, Dionysius the Areopagite, Hermes Trismegistus[8] and even from the Zoroastrian Oracles and the Jewish Cabala. Neo-Gnostic would be as appropriate a designation as Neoplatonist. Strains of Stoic pantheism were not excluded.

The primary view of God, however, was the Neoplatonic picture of the ultimate One, the fount of dynamic being engaged in perpetual self-elaboration through emanations, and in constant self-expression through intermediaries such as reason, wisdom, and word, comparable to rays of light. The emanations descended from the primal One and reality in consequence was graded in terms of distance from the source. Man stands at the center of the chain of being. According to Pico della Mirandola, the great proponent of the new school, man, by his own endeavor, is able to sink or rise in this scale even to the point of union with the One. Thus he will be made god with God.

In all this the name of Christ has not been mentioned, but one perceives how readily he could be identified with the reason, wisdom, word, and the light rays proceeding from the One, and how the process of unification with the One might be facilitated by a prior union with the Supreme Intermediary.

From the Hellenistic tradition Servetus took the picture of God as the primal abyss of being, with reference to whom no name can be named:

> For what can man conceive with regard to God unless He has rendered Himself visible? ... Much rather is He hidden. The mind fails in thinking of God for He is incomprehensible. The eye does not see Him because He is invisible. The ear hears Him not, nor ever has heard unless He spoke with a human voice. The hand does not touch Him because He is incorporeal, the tongue cannot declare Him for He is ineffable. No place can hold Him since He is not to be circumscribed. Time cannot measure Him because He is immeasurable. God transcends all things and exceeds all intellect and mind. There are those who think that only by negatives are we able to define God. If one reflects upon light or anything else known to us, one plainly observes that God is not light but above light, He is not essence but above essence, He is not spirit but above spirit, He is above anything that can be conceived. The true knowledge of God is that which teaches not what He is but that which He is not. No one knows God unless one knows the way in which God has made Himself manifest.[9]

And God has rendered himself manifest through intermediaries such as Logos, wisdom, and idea, all of which are identified.[10] God becomes immanent since in him are the archetypal ideas after which particular existences are fashioned.[11] He is the very principle of form within the forms which give individuation.[12] Since every existence consists of matter and form, and the form is a part of God, then everything must have a portion of God. "If you exclude the divine idea nothing can be called stone, gold, flesh, soul of man nor man, since it is the divine idea which gives specific and individual existence."[13] "God 'essentiates' the essences. He confers essence upon the celestial spirits. From Him emanate the race of divine essences which in turn infuse His essence into other beings. God himself is in them and the light itself of His word radiates in them."[14] "He sustains all things in their essence so that any creature devoid of that sustenance is reduced to nothing."[15]

God as "essentiating" may be said, therefore, to be in every existence, having without mutation in himself the form proper of that particular entity.

> Since He contains in Himself the essences of all things, He exhibits Himself to us as fire, stone, electrum, a rod, a flower or what not. He is not altered but a stone is seen in God. Is it a true stone? Yes, God in wood is wood, in a stone He is stone, having in Himself the being of

stone, the form of stone, the substance of stone. I consider, therefore, that this is true stone having the essence of the form, although lacking the matter of stone.[16]

These passages naturally have given rise to the characterization of Servetus as a pantheist. He is rather an emanationist. God confers being, essence, particularity upon all that is and God sustains all things. Without him nothing can be: "God fills all things, even Hell itself."[17]

Since the eternal Word, identified with Christ, is but a mode of God's self-expression, then what is said of God may be said also of Christ. That very passage in which God is said to "essentiate" all things is extended to Christ. The Father himself conferred the power of essentiating on Christ and He confers essence upon all other beings. All things are through Him and in Him. He bears, carries, and sustains all by the word of His power. In Him all things consist whether terrestrial or celestial. He is the dispenser of light, sending it forth from His substance.[18]

The reference to light introduces a concept drawn from the Neoplatonic tradition and particularly congenial to Servetus, who was fond of describing the self-disclosure of God and the working of Christ in terms of light. There was a warrant for this, of course, in Biblical tradition. God is light, and the Father of Lights, who clothes himself with light as with a garment. He it was who at the Creation said, "Let there be light," and who now shines in our hearts. His glory appeared in the face of Moses, and in the face of Christ, who is the light of the world. "This is the light that lighteth every man that cometh into the world." We give thanks to God "who hath made us meet to be partakers of the inheritance of the saints in light." These and other passages Servetus used freely in his earlier work.[19]

These biblical passages have the ring only of metaphor. In the Platonic tradition, however, light was to be infused with the quality of a metaphysical principle. The point of departure was the passage in Plato's *Republic* where the sun is said to be "the offspring of the good which the good begat like to itself that he might be in the visible world to sight and the objects of sight what the good is in the intellectual world to thought and the objects of thought."[20] The Neoplatonists lifted such language out of the region of metaphor when Plotinus abstracted light from material things and identified it with Logos and form.[21] Proclus made light the bond between the upper and the lower world. For Philo and Hermes Trismegistus, light became a mediator in the way of ascent. Said Hermes, "God is life and light and the Father from whom man is born. If then you learn that you are yourself from life and light, to life you will return."[22] The fathers of the Church blended these traditions. Augustine accommodated the Neoplatonic doctrine to the biblical account by distinguishing uncreated from created light. Subsequent scholastic speculation made much of light as a form.[23]

Servetus was acquainted with this literature and appropriated from it the picture of light as both created and uncreated, as the bond between the corporeal and the spiritual, the substantial form of all things or the origin of the forms.[24] Inasmuch as light gives being to all things and God is light, the drift toward immanentism is apparent. The following passage well illustrates the combination of physical, metaphysical, and religious conceptions:

> The earthly material (in the Creation) is called *tohou* and *bohu,* without form and void, because it had not as yet been made a participant of light. Whence again you conclude that form is from light. Not only are the forms and existences of things from light, but also souls and spirits; since light is the life of men and the life of spirits. Light is of all things in this and the other world the most beautiful. In the idea itself of light everything consists in that it shines. Light alone, both celestial and terrestrial, both spiritual and corporeal, informs and transforms, and from her is the whole form and adornment of the world. The Creator placed light forms in things that they should be no longer in dark and formless chaos. Nothing could of itself produce the form of light nor a natural image in a mirror or in the eye unless it contained light in itself as a form. Light is the visible form of all things. Light itself variously transforms clay into resplendent stones and water into lustrous pearls. In regeneration it is light which informs and transforms our spirits, as also light will substantially transform our bodies in the final resurrection.[25]

The application of some of these ideas to the person of Christ illustrates the peculiar elements in the Christology of Servetus. The denial of the pre-existence of the Son must be understood in accord with the doctrine of forms. The Word is the form. This pre-existed with the Father. The flesh is matter. The Son is the combination of the two and necessarily could not antedate the union, although as to the form one may speak of the pre-existence of the Son.[26] Then the whole light metaphysic is applied to Christ as in the following passage:

> There is one brightness of the sun and another of the moon, another of fire and still another splendor of water. All these were disposed in light by Christ, the architect of the world, who is the first principle in whom

ΘΕΟC

Hermes Trismegistus

all things consist, celestial and terrestrial, corporeal and spiritual. He created the material elements and substantially endowed them with light forms, bringing forth light itself from his treasures.[27]

One further passage may be cited because it exhibits the manner in which these varied themes were drawn together in lyrical rhapsodies of Christological mysticism:

Christ fills all things. On account of him God made the world and by him the world is filled. He descends to the lowest depths and ascends to the loftiest heights and fills all things. He walks upon the wings of the wind, rides upon the air and inhabits the place of angels. He sits upon the circle of the earth and measures the heavens with his span and the waters in the hollow of his hand ... It is fitting that now Christ should walk among us as once he walked amid the camp of Israel. Now Christ walks among the candlesticks, that is, in the midst of the churches, as the Apocalypse plainly teaches. Behold now the tabernacle of God is with men and He will dwell with them. Our inner hearth is the place where Christ dwells among the sons of Israel. His place is not in any particular part of heaven as some think ... He dwells above all heavens and within us. They have a carnal sense who separate Christ from us by placing him at the right hand of the Father. But we say that he is in that heaven to which the angels do not attain. He is in the third heaven where and whence he fills all things, beyond every place and beyond every tangible body. He is a spiritual body in the new heaven which is within us. In Christ alone is God and in him is all the origin of deity. Nowhere does God breathe save by the spirit of Christ. Nowhere does He speak save by the voice of Christ. No one does he illumine save by the light of Christ. The body of Christ is communicable to many in the Lord's Supper, by a marvelous bond uniting us in one so that we are the members of his body from his flesh and from his bones. The body of Christ and the body of the Church are one flesh as the flesh of man and wife are one flesh ... They are mistaken who say that Christ cannot be eaten and would place him in some locality in heaven. They do not know where God is who do not know Christ. We never have anything of God in the world unless it be Christ, nor shall we ever have anything to the day of judgment when Christ shall present us in the presence of the Father.[28]

The second new factor in Servetus's thinking apparent in *Christianismi Restitutio* is that of Anabaptism. The very title of his book is reminiscent of these circles. If Erasmus and the Christian Humanists aspired to restore the primitive Church, their efforts were largely confined to the recovery of documents. The Anabaptists went further and reconstituted actual congregations in accord with what they believed to be the ancient pattern. If the church of Luther and Calvin be called that of the Reformation, the church of the Anabaptists might be called that of the Restitution. The very expression itself served as a title for a number of Anabaptist tracts. Anabaptist influence affected the doctrine of Servetus particularly on the subjects of man, the Church, and the future.

Strictly speaking, however, his doctrine of man was not exclusively Anabaptist but rather a blend of Catholic, Renaissance, and Anabaptist ingredients. With the Catholic Church he held that the natural man is capable of fulfilling the natural law. Were not Zacharias and Elizabeth, the parents of John the Baptist, accounted just, although unacquainted with Christ? And the redeemed man is able to co-operate with God in the work of salvation. Faith alone does not suffice, for faith will pass away, whereas love alone abides. Faith lights the lamp which is kept burning only by the oil of love.[29]

Servetus agreed likewise with the Renaissance picture of man, situated at the middle of the great chain of being and able of his own power and motion to descend or ascend until united with God. For Servetus, of course, this view was Christianized, as it had already been among the Eastern theologians. Man, said Servetus, is free. From the stars he receives only inclinations and temperaments.[30] As for fore-ordination, predestination, election and reprobation, these were the inventions of Simon Magus.[31] Man is capable of union with Christ and, through Christ, with God. "The divine has descended to the human in order that the human might ascend to the divine."[32]

> Our inward man is nothing but Christ himself. This is not to say that we are equal to Christ; for that matter we are not equal to each other. But Christ communicates to us His glory, "The glory which thou gavest me I have given them that I may be in them as thou Father in me." Christ is called our inward man because he communicates to us His spirit whereby we are renewed from day to day. The more Christ renews our spirit by the fire in His spirit, the more he insinuates Himself into our body, the more is our inward man said to grow in Christ. He is formed in us and the outward man declines. Our inward man consists of the divine element from Christ and the human from our nature so that truly we are said to be participants of the divine nature and our life is said to be hid in Christ. Oh, incomparable glory! Will not the Kingdom of God be in us if Christ who is in Heaven be in us, making us that which He is? Our inward man is truly heavenly, has come down from Heaven of the substance of God, of the divine substance of Christ, not of the blood, not of the will of the flesh but of God. Our inward man is God as Christ is God and the Holy

Spirit is God. As the psalmist said, foreshadowing this truth, "I have said, ye are gods." As the one God in many makes them Gods, so the one Christ in many makes them both Christs and Gods.[33]

The specifically Anabaptist element comes to the fore in the picture of the redeemed man who is begotten in baptism. "Our inward man is born in baptism having the incorruptible armament of the spirit."[34] The miracle which God aforetime wrought in the Red Sea and Jordan is wrought for us again in the sacred laver. In baptism the heavens are opened.[35] Baptism, according to the apostle Paul, entails dying with Christ to sin and rising with him to newness of life. Commenting on this passage, Servetus inquired:

> What shall render you equal to a friend who for you has suffered death? Will it not be that you shall be ready to die for Him? There is nothing more acceptable that we can render to Christ, nothing more fit to discharge our debt, although there is an infinite difference between His death and ours on account of the excellence of Him who suffered without desert for those deserving of death. When, then, for Christ you suffer the cross and death remember first that you owe this to Christ who suffered such for you. Remember secondly that for you this means not death but life itself and the destruction of death. Fear not, then, to suffer death for Christ which is his due and so precious in His sight. All the more because it is not death but the breaking of Satan's chain and the coming into the freedom of glory and the life abiding ever in Christ. The eternal life we know and taste and have truly present even now, from which we are not separated by death because always the inward man lives in us. This we know and the resurrected Christ within we experience. And by experience we know that like Him we are to rise, because like him we are revived in the inward man.[36]

One can understand why, if baptism involves so much, it should be denied to children. "What heavens have they seen opened?" asked Servetus.[37] This is not to say that they are lost.[38] They are born innocent and, like Adam, do not become capable of either their best or their worst until after eating the fruit of the tree of the knowledge of good and evil, which commonly happens about the twentieth year.[39] Then the Devil numbs the heart, defrauds the brain, and inebriates the senses.[40] Baptism should preferably be deferred, after the example of Christ, until the thirtieth year.[41]

Such a view plainly brought Servetus into collision not only with the Catholics but with all of the leading reformers who retained infant baptism. They did so because of their theory of the Church; for they compared the church to ancient Israel, the chosen people of the Lord, into whose membership babies were initiated by circumcision. Servetus denied the analogy[42] and the reason was that the Church for him was not a community, self-perpetuating through propagation, but rather a fellowship in the spirit. Whether in his mind it would have any outward form at all is not too plain, for said he, "The celestial Jerusalem, the heavenly paradise, the Kingdom of Christ is within us with a glory far greater than the glory of Eden."[43] At this point he may have diverged from the Anabaptists. Nor did he claim that perfection is actually attained. Though our inward man cannot sin, the inward man is not the whole man and we do repeatedly fall short.[44]

He may have gone beyond the Anabaptists in his spiritualization of the Church, but all the more was he at one with them in decrying the baptism of babies. Christ explained to Nicodemus the meaning of the new birth. That which is born of the spirit is spirit; he who is born of the spirit hears the voice of the spirit and sees the Kingdom of God and understands its mystery — all of which cannot apply to children.[45] They should not be baptized but dedicated with such a prayer as this:

> O God who of old declared Thyself to be the God of Abraham and of his sons, protect now and preserve for Thy Kingdom these children. O most clement Jesus, son of God, who with such love took the children upon Thy knees and blessed them, bless now and direct these children that by heavenly faith they may share in Thy celestial Kingdom. O most tender Jesus, Son of God, who from the womb was most innocent, grant that we may walk without guile, with the simplicity of these children, that the Kingdom of Heaven may ever be reserved for us.[46]

To give baptism then to these children who have not experienced the mystery of regeneration is an abomination, a desolation of the Kingdom of Christ. The baptizers of infants do not wish Christ to reign in his saints. They will not suffer us to reign with Christ because they do not permit us to rise with Him. "Woe, woe to you baptizers of babies who have shut the Kingdom of Heaven to men, into which you do not enter nor suffer us to enter! Woe! woe!"[47]

Servetus could not bring himself simply to thunder his woes into the void. He did have a concern at least for a fellowship of the spirit on earth and wished to gain living converts. Rome would not listen. Basel, Strassburg, and Wittenberg were deaf. But in the meantime a new center of Protestantism had arisen; its center was at Geneva. The reform had been facilitated by a political revolution in which the citizens threw off the authority of the Duke of Savoy and of the bishop. This was accomplished only by means of a military alliance with the Swiss city of Berne, and Berne was Protestant.

The Genevans had their first taste of the new gospel when the men from Berne stabled their horses in the cathedral and put the images of the saints down the wells. After the withdrawal of these iconoclasts came Guillaume Farel, the red bearded, bellowing against the priests of Baal. Civil war was barely averted. The Reform was introduced. Farel felt himself unequal to directing the very movement which he had inaugurated. When, then, that young scholar, John Calvin, passed through the city of Geneva, Farel laid hold of him with the demand that he stay and take over leadership. All Calvin's qualms, remonstrances, and excuses were crushed with threats of eternal fire, and he became the reformer of Geneva. He already had a name by reason of his *Institutes of the Christian Religion*. This was issued at Basel in the year 1536, and began with that magnificent preface addressed to the king of France, where, said Calvin, no place is found for the proclamation of the true gospel:

> Therefore it seemed to me fitting that I should declare to you the confession, making plain the nature of that doctrine against which the furious so rage and with fire and sword trouble thy Kingdom. I do not fear to confess that I have myself embraced that doctrine which they clamor to exterminate by prison, exile, proscription and fire on land and sea.

Surely one who, with such courage, undertook to instruct the king of France would himself be amenable to instruction as to the true gospel.

Servetus resolved by correspondence to establish that interchange which in the flesh he had missed some years ago in Paris. Of all the reformers, Calvin appeared to be the one who might be disposed to listen. Geneva in some respects resembled an Anabaptist colony in the rigor of its discipline. These Huguenots boasted even of their pale faces in contrast with the ruby nose of Pierre Lizet, their persecutor.

Servetus scarcely understood how deep were his differences with Calvin. For Calvin, God was so high and lifted up, so unspeakably holy, and man so utterly unworthy, that no union between God and man could be thinkable. Man's only hope of redemption is through Christ Jesus who was from all eternity the Son of God; and the only hope of society is through the company of the elect who, from before the foundation of the world, have been chosen to achieve God's purpose. The doctrine of election was thus the very core of Calvin's system.

Tentatively at least he was prepared to regard the children of the elect as themselves among the chosen and for that reason to baptize babies.

Through the mediation of Jean Frellon – the Huguenot publisher at Lyons for whom Servetus had already edited several works – the correspondence with Calvin was commenced.[48] Undoubtedly the pseudonym Michel de Villeneuve was employed, just as Calvin signed himself Charles Despeville. But neither was deceived as to the identity of the other. Servetus adopted a condescending tone and undertook to instruct John Calvin on Christology and on infant baptism.[49] Calvin replied courteously and at length but not to the satisfaction of Servetus, who told Calvin that he cut his throat with his own sword and urged him to read carefully the fourth book, on baptism, of a manuscript which appears to have been sent with a previous letter.[50] This is our first notice of the new theological work in progress, the *Christianismi Restitutio.* Calvin, somewhat nettled, replied again at length but added that he was too busy to write whole books when all he had to say was already contained in the *Institutes,* of which he sent a copy. Servetus annotated it with insulting comments and returned the *Institutio.*[51] Calvin never sent back the *Restitutio.*

Servetus persisted and sent in all some thirty epistolary discourses[52] until Calvin informed Frellon that he regarded their mutual friend as a satan to waste his time.[53] On the very same day Calvin wrote to Farel, "Servetus has just sent me, together with his letters, a long volume of his ravings. If I consent he will come here, but I will not give my word, for should he come, if my authority is of any avail I will not suffer him to get out alive."[54] One observes from this letter that Calvin was aware of the identity of Servetus and one notes that he did not betray him to the Catholic authorities. He would give no assurance of what would happen, however, were Servetus to come to Geneva. Servetus sent one more letter requesting the return of his manuscript.[55] There was no answer.

The last illusion had been destroyed. Rome, Zaragoza, Toulouse, Basel, Strassburg, Wittenberg and now Geneva had repelled his word. Where, then, was there any hope? Only in the Lord God of Hosts who will give "beauty for ashes, the oil of joy for mourning, the garment of praise for the spirit of heaviness."[56]

The time is fulfilled, meditated Servetus; the three ages near their accomplishment. Here one catches the strains of medieval Apocalypticism with its periodization of history into three phases. Servetus developed the theme. Three princes, said he, have arisen against Christ: the first in the foreshadowing was Absalom, the second in the flesh was Caiaphas, and the third in the spirit was the papacy. Three voices have cried in the wilderness: the first was Cyrus, the second was John the Baptist, and the third is the voice of the liberators. Three times has the spirit of Christ come: first at the Creation, secondly at Pentecost, and for the third time in the Paraclete.

The four horsemen of the Apocalypse have already appeared: "And I saw and behold a white horse and he that sat on him had a bow, and a crown was given to him and he went forth conquering and to conquer." This is the papacy, using the temporal sword to fight with the kings of the earth. "And there went another horse that was red and power was given to him that sat thereon to take peace from the earth." This signifies the cardinals. "And when he had opened the third seal behold and lo a black horse." This means the Dominicans in their black robes. "And when he had opened the fourth seal I looked and behold a pale horse." This points to the mendicant orders.[57] Now nothing should impede but that the papal mountains and the Babylonian hills should be brought low.[58] The archangel Michael girds himself for Armageddon.[59] Michael Servetus should be his armor bearer. "You take offense," wrote Servetus to Calvin, "that I mingle in this fight of Michael and desire that all godly men should do so. But read this passage carefully and you will see that it is men who will fight there, exposing their souls to death in blood and for a testimony to Jesus Christ."[60]

Nowhere is one more inclined to recognize Anabaptist influence than here. One is reminded of Michael Stifel who predicted the last day on Saint Michael's,[61] and apart from any play on names, these eschatological and Messianic reveries recall all the new Enochs and Elijahs of the chiliastic phase of Anabaptism.

When, then, should the end come, according to Servetus? In all such calculations the key figure was 1260 – the number of days spent by the woman, in Revelation, in the wilderness.[62] These days were taken to be years and the device for determining the end was to select some date which, when added to 1260, would slightly exceed the present. Servetus took the time of Sylvester and Constantine as the point of departure because this was the period of the fall of the Church. If the computation was reckoned from the beginning of the reign of Constantine in 305, the date would be 1565, but, if from the Council of Nicaea – which for Servetus constituted more particularly the fall – the year would be 1585.[63] Servetus was discreet enough not to name the precise date, yet he was sure that the time was at hand when, "Singing hallelujahs we shall come to the fountains of living water and the supper of the Lamb."[64]

Spurned by Calvin, Servetus addressed a letter to one of the ministers in Geneva, Abel Poupin:

> Your gospel is without God, without true faith, without good works. Instead of a God you have a three-headed Cerberus.[65] For faith you have a deterministic dream, and good works you say are inane pictures. With you the faith of Christ is mere deceit effecting nothing. Man is with you an inert trunk, and God is a chimera of the enslaved will. You do not know the celestial regeneration by water and you have as it were a fable. You close the Kingdom of Heaven before men ... Woe! Woe! Woe! This is the third letter that I have written to warn you that you may know better. I will not warn you again. Perhaps it will offend you that I meddle in this fight of Michael and wish to involve you. Study that passage carefully and you will see that they are men who will fight there, giving their souls to death in blood and for a testimony to Jesus Christ. Before the fight there will be a seduction of the world. The fight then follows, and the time is at hand ... I know that I shall certainly die on this account, but I do not falter that I may be a disciple like the Master. This I regret, that I am not able to amend for you some passages in my works which are with Calvin. Goodbye, and do not expect to hear from me again. I will stand above my watch. I will consider. I will see what He is about to say, for He will come. He will certainly come. He will not tarry.[65]

---

[a] Referring of course to the Trinity.

CHRISTIANI-.
SMI RESTITV,
TIO. ✓

Totius ecclesiæ apostolicæ est ad sua limina vo-
catio, in integrum restituta cognitione Dei , fidei
Christi , iustificationis nostræ , regenerationis bapti
smi, & cœnæ domini manducationis. Restituto de-
nique nobis regno cælesti, Babylonis impiæ captiui-
tate soluta , & Antichristo cum suis penitus de-
structo.

בעת ההיא יעמוד מיכאל השר
καὶ ἐγένετο πόλεμος ἐν τῷ ὀυρανῷ,

M· D· LIII·

[handwritten:] Danielis Márkos Szent-
Ivani Transylvanæ-
Hungari.

Londini 1665 die
13 Maii

Nunc Michaelis Almasi
Futuro Episcopo dandus.

Title Page of the Vienna Copy of Christianismi Restitutio, 1553

Chapter 8

Brush with the Inquisition

Servetus did not recover his manuscript but he had kept either copious notes or another draft. The work was rounded out and to it were added the thirty letters to Calvin and an *Apology to Melanchthon*. The next problem was to get a publisher, who would have to be bold or else unaware of what was involved. Servetus sounded out Martin Borrhaus at Basel. The reply was: *"Michael carissime,* why your book cannot be published at Basel at this time I think you will sufficiently understand ... Basel, the nones of April, 1552, *Martinus tuus."*[1]

Closer at hand and perhaps more favorably disposed was the printing firm of the brothers-in-law Balthazar Arnoullet and Guillaume Guéroult of Lyons, with a branch at Vienne. Arnoullet was the businessman and Guéroult the literary partner. He had rendered some of the psalms into verse, which of itself betrayed Huguenot leanings. Arnoullet had connections with Calvin; Guéroult's relations with Geneva were of another sort.

A clue is given in a little work which the firm published with the title of *Emblems*. It consisted of woodcuts and rhymes by Guéroult, much after the manner of the later fables of La Fontaine. One tells of a bankrupt who took a rope to a secret place to hang himself but, finding there a pot of gold, made off with the treasure and left the rope. The secreter of the cache, finding it gone, employed the rope.

This yarn is dedicated to "A.P." These initials stood for Ami Perrin, the head of the party of the political Libertines, the chief enemies of Calvin at Geneva. They had thrown off the yoke of the duke and the bishop and did not relish the reign of the saints. Once the malcontents had banished Calvin. The Libertines were restive under his recall.

LE PREMIER
LIVRE DES
EMBLEMES.

Composé par Guillaume Gueroult.

A LYON,
Chez Balthazar Arnoullet.
M. D. XXXXX.

Title Page of Guéroult's Emblèmes

Guéroult himself had been at Geneva and, taxed with sexual irregularity, had been brought to trial. He was let off with only a trivial fine and banishment, through the intervention of Pierre Vandel, another chief of the party. Smarting with resentment, Guéroult came to Lyons. He was not loath to publish a book galling to Calvin, provided responsibility could be disclaimed.

Arnoullet was different; he appears to have been deceived. He need not have known the degree of obnoxiousness of the book in order to feel the need for grave precaution if it were Protestant at all. He did consent to publish, but only on condition that the work be undertaken with the utmost secrecy and all the cost be borne by the author, with a bonus in addition.[2] The work was commenced on St. Michael's day, the twenty-ninth of September, 1552, and was completed on January the third, 1553. The manuscript was burned leaf by leaf as the printed pages were set in type.[3]

A thousand copies were struck off and a number sent to the Frankfort fair; others went to a bookseller at Geneva, through whom probably a copy came into the hands of a friend of John Calvin, a certain Guillaume Trie. This man had a Roman Catholic cousin, named Antoine Arneys, living at Lyons. The Catholic had reproached the Protestant for living in a city devoid of ecclesiastical order and discipline. Feeling was high at that particular moment because five Protestant students from Berne had been arrested while passing through Lyons, and had languished in prison since the first of May, 1552. The ecclesiastical tribunal had condemned them on May 13, but they appealed to the Parlement de Paris; the Swiss cities interested themselves on their behalf, enlisting the good offices of Cardinal Tournon. But this treacherous zealot so delayed the appeal that it was rejected on February 18, 1553.[4] Shortly afterwards Trie learned that the arch-heretic Servetus had printed a most blasphemous book under the very eyes of the cardinal but was unmolested. The news was too good to keep. On February 26, 1553, the Protestant of Geneva wrote this letter to the Catholic of Lyons:

My dear cousin,

Thank you very much for your fine remonstrance. I have no doubt that your attempt to recall me is actuated by friendship. Although I am not a learned man like you, I will do my best to answer your points. With the knowledge that God has given me I shall have something to say, for thanks be to God, I am not so poorly grounded as not to know that Jesus Christ is the head of the Church [from whom she cannot be separated, and without whom she has neither life nor health] and that she consists only in the truth of God contained in Scripture. So whatever you may tell me about the Church I will hold it for a phantom unless Jesus Christ presides there with all authority and the Word of God reigns as foundation and substance. Without that your formalities are nothing. Forgive the liberty I take, which is not merely to maintain my cause, but to give you occasion to look better to yourself. To be brief I am astounded that you reproach me with our lack of ecclesiastical discipline and order [and that those who teach us have introduced a license to set confusion everywhere;] whereas, thank God, I see vice better conquered here than in all your territories. And although we allow greater liberty in religion and doctrine, we do not suffer the name of God to be blasphemed [nor do we allow false doctrines and opinions to be disseminated without reprimand.] I can give you an example which is greatly to your confusion [since it is necessary to mention it.] You suffer a heretic, who well deserves to be burned wherever he may be. I have in mind a man who will be condemned by the Papists as much as by us or ought to be. For though we differ in many things, yet we have this in common that in the one essence of God there are three persons and that the Father begat his Son, who is eternal Wisdom before all time, and that he has had his eternal power, which is the Holy Spirit. So then, when a man says that the Trinity, which we hold, is a Cerberus and a monster of hell, and when he disgorges all possible villainies against the teaching of Scripture concerning the eternal generation of the Son of God [and that the Holy Spirit is the expression of the Father and the Son] when this man blatantly mocks all that the ancient doctors have said, I ask in what place and esteem will you hold him? This I say to obviate any reply which you may make that we are not agreed as to what is error. You will admit that what I have told you is not merely error, but such detestable heresy as to abolish the whole Christian religion. I must speak frankly. What a shame it is to put to death those who say that we should invoke but one God in the name of Jesus Christ, that there is no other satisfaction than that which is made in the passion and death of Jesus Christ, that there is no other purgatory than his blood, that there is no other service agreeable to God than that which He commands and approves in His Word, that all pictures and images counterfeited by men are so many idols which profane His majesty, that one should observe the sacraments according to the mode ordained by Jesus Christ. Yes, and one is not content simply to put these men to death, but they must be most cruelly burned. And now here is one who will call Jesus Christ an idol, who will destroy all the fundamentals of the faith, who will amass all the phantasies of the ancient heretics, who will even condemn infant baptism, calling it an invention of the devil. And this man is in good repute among you, and is suffered as if he were not wrong. Where I'd like to know is the zeal which you pretend? Where is the police of this fine hierarchy of which you so boast? The man of whom I speak has been condemned by all the churches which you reprove, yet you suffer him and even let him print his books which are so full of blasphemies that I need say no more. He is a Portuguese

Spaniard, named Michael Servetus. That is his real name, but he goes at present under the name of Villeneufve and practices medicine. He has resided for some time at Lyons. Now he is at Vienne where his book has been printed by a certain Balthazar Arnoullet, and lest you think that I am talking without warrant I send you the first folio. You say that books which keep solely to the pure simplicity of Scripture poison the world, and if they get out, you cannot suffer them. Yet you hatch poisons that would destroy Scripture and even all that you hold of Christianity.

I forgot myself in giving you this example, for I have been four times as long as I intended ... Geneva, Feb. 26.[5]

The first four leaves of the *Restitutio* were attached.

One wonders how so much information had reached Geneva. The identity of Servetus was no problem. Calvin would at once recognize the thirty letters addressed to himself. The initials *MSV* could easily be deciphered. Even more incriminating was the introduction of a dialogue in which one interlocutor says to the other, "I perceive that you are Servetus."[6] Curiously, this reference is lacking in the Paris manuscript; if other evidence were lacking, one might infer that the manuscript was later and the copyist feared to record the telltale name, rather than that Servetus had inserted it in the printed book. Yet the plain fact is that it is in the printed book. He may have felt, as he did at Paris, that boldness was the best defense. The problem, then, is not to know how Servetus was recognized but how the news of the secret press of Arnoullet and Guéroult leaked to Geneva. There is, however, no question but that it did.

Arneys, the cousin at Lyons, lost no time in placing these documents before the inquisitor Matthieu Ory, who called in the vicar of Lyons; together the two examined the evidence from Geneva. It was decided to send word at once to Cardinal Tournon, who was then at the Chateau de Roussillon below Vienne. Ory wrote on March 12, instructing a subordinate of the cardinal to act so secretly that his left hand should not know what the right was doing. "Ask his Lordship verbally," ran the instructions, "and let us know whether he is acquainted with Villanovanus, a doctor, and Arnoullet, a publisher."[7] The cardinal promptly gave order to Maugiron, the lieutenant governor at Vienne, to act with great diligence and secrecy. "I know," wrote Tournon, "that you would not spare your son for the honor of God and His Church. I need say no more ... March 15, 1553."[8]

On the 16th of March, the judges assembled at the house of Maugiron and word was sent to "Michel de Villeneufve" that they had something to tell him. When he took two hours in coming they began to fear that he sensed danger, but he appeared at last and with a very confident air. The judges told him that they had information against him, which warranted their searching his premises. Servetus answered that he had lived in Vienne for a long time, and had associated with preachers and doctors of theology, who had not suspected him of heresy. He was quite ready to open his premises to remove all suspicion. Search was then made, but the officers found merely two copies of the tract on astrology. Servetus had evidently made good use of his two hours.

On the following day, March 17, the judges, knowing that Arnoullet was out of town, called in his partner, Guéroult, and subjected him to a long grilling without receiving the least enlightenment. An examination of his house, press, and papers revealed nothing. The printers were then examined individually and shown the leaves of the *Restitutio*. Did they recognize the characters, and how many and what sort of books had they printed in the last eighteen months? They answered that the leaves had not come from their press and that in the last two years they had printed nothing in octavo, as the catalogue would show. After the individual examinations, the judges summoned all the printers, compositors, and servants of Arnoullet, together with their wives and domestics, and warned them to disclose nothing about the examination lest they be accused of heresy. Arnoullet returned on the next day (the 18th), and his replies tallied with those of his brother-in-law.

The baffled judges took counsel with the Archbishop of Vienne, Pierre Palmier, to whom Servetus had dedicated the second edition of his geography. The archbishop, once the pupil and patron of Servetus, pointed out the insufficiency of the evidence and sent word to Ory to come himself to Vienne. Ory came and suggested that Arneys be requested to write back to Geneva for the full text of the *Restitutio*. Ory then posted back to Lyons and dictated the letter himself.

Here is the reply which came from Guillaume Trie:

My dear cousin,

When I wrote the letter which you have communicated to those whom I charged with indifference, I did not suppose that the matter would go so far. I simply meant to call your attention to the fine zeal and devotion of those who call themselves the pillars of the Church, although they suffer such disorder in their midst, and persecute so severely the poor Christians, who wish to follow God in simplicity. Inasmuch as this glaring instance had been brought to my notice, the occasion and subject seemed to me to warrant mentioning the matter in my letters. But since you have disclosed what I meant for you alone, God grant that this may the better serve to purge Christianity of such filth, such deadly pestilence. If they really wish to do anything, as you say, it does not seem to me that the matter is so very difficult, though I cannot for the moment give you what you want, namely the printed book. But I can give you something better to convict him, namely two dozen manuscript pieces of the man in question, in which his heresies are in part contained. If you show him the printed book he can deny it, which he cannot do in respect of his handwriting. The case then being absolutely proved, the men of whom you speak will have no excuse for further dissimulation or delay. All the rest is here right enough, the big book and the other writings of the same author, but I can tell you I had no little trouble to get from Calvin what I am sending. Not that he does not wish to repress such execrable blasphemies, but he thinks his duty is rather to convince heretics with doctrine than with other means, because he does not exercise the sword of justice. But I remonstrated with him and pointed out the embarrassing position in which I should be placed if he did not help me, so that in the end he gave me what you see. For the rest I hope by and by, when the case is further advanced, to get from him a whole ream of paper, which the scamp has had printed, but I think that for the present you have enough, so that there is no need for more to seize his person and bring him to trial ... Geneva, March 26. [9]

Thus we see that John Calvin supplied the evidence to the Roman Catholic Inquisition! He had long preserved the secret of Servetus. At length under the importunity of a friend he succumbed.[10] Not the least of the counts on which he must answer is that he denied his share in the affair. Servetus later not infrequently reproached him for his treachery,[11] and even after the execution the charge would not down. Calvin entered a categorical denial:

They say that I did nothing else than throw Servetus to the professed enemies of Christ as to ravening beasts, that I was responsible for his arrest at Vienne in the province of Lyons. But how should I come to have such sudden familiarity with the satellites of the pope? to be on such good terms? It would be highly incredible indeed that letters should pass back and forth between those who have no less difference than Christ and Belial. So there is no need for many words to refute so futile a calumny, which falls with a mere negation.[12]

Calvin's words have been construed as strictly true in the sense that he had exchanged no letters of his own with the inquisitors, but this is only to save him from a lie by making him guilty of a subterfuge.

The material supplied did not yet satisfy the inquisitor, because there was no proof that Villanovanus was Servetus, nor that he was the author of the *Restitutio*. Further queries were sent to Geneva. Guillaume Trie answered in the following letter:

My dear cousin,

I hope that I shall have satisfied your requests in part at least by sending you the handwriting of the author. In the last letter which you have received you will find what he says about his name, which he disguised, for he excuses himself for having assumed the name Villeneufve, when he is really Servetus alias Revés, on the ground that he took the name from that of his native town.[13] For the rest I will keep my promise, God willing, that if there is need I will furnish you with the manuscripts which he has printed, which are in his handwriting like the letters. I should have endeavored already to secure them if they had been in this city, but they have been at Lausanne for two years.[14] If Calvin had had them I think, for all they are worth, he would have sent them back to the author, but since he (Servetus) had addressed them to others as well, they have kept them… [Understand that it is not only recently that this wretch has striven to trouble the Church, trying to lead the ignorant into the same state of confusion as himself. Twenty-four years ago the leading churches of Germany rejected him and cast him out. If he had been found there, he never would have been permitted to leave. The first and second letters of Oecolampadius addressed him by the title that properly belongs to him: Servetus the Spaniard, denying that Christ is the Son of God, of one substance with the Father.]…

As for the printer I am not sending you the proofs by which we know that it is Balthazar Arnoullet and his brother-in-law, Guillaume Guéroult, but we are well assured nevertheless and he cannot deny it. It is quite possible that the work was done at the expense of the author and that he has taken the copies, in which case they will have left the shop. I have been brief because the messenger insists on leaving at once, having delivered your letter late … When you have finished with the letters let me have them back … From Geneva on the last day of March.[15]

On the 4th of April there was a great assembly at the Chateau de Roussillon. Tournon, Ory, Palmier, and the vicars gathered with the ecclesiastics and doctors of theology. Ory placed before them the documents from Geneva, namely the letters of Guillaume Trie, seventeen manuscript letters of Servetus to Calvin, and a printed book.[16] The proof was complete and it was decided that Servetus and Arnoullet should be arrested. After dinner Palmier and his vicar [Louis Arzellier] returned to Vienne and made plans with the sheriff [Antoine de la

Court] to arrest both at the same time. At six o'clock the grand vicar went to the neighborhood of Arnoullet's house and sent him word to bring a copy of the New Testament, which he had lately printed. When Arnoullet met the request, he was carried off to the prisons of the archbishop. The sheriff discovered Servetus attending to the sickness of Maugiron, the lieutenant general. The doctor was informed that there were many sick and wounded prisoners at the palace, as in truth there were. Would he come and visit them? "M. de Villeneufve" replied that apart from his professional obligation he would be delighted to come of his own accord. While he was making the rounds in the royal prisons the sheriff sent word to the vicar to join him and the two informed the doctor that he was himself a prisoner. He was committed to the jailor with instructions to guard him securely and treat him according to his station. He might retain his valet, a lad of fifteen years, and his friends might visit him that day.

On the next day, April 5, Palmier sent word to Tournon of what had happened and invited Ory to come to Vienne for the examination. The inquisitor so pressed his horse that before ten o'clock he was with the archbishop. After dinner they commenced to examine Michael Servetus. The record begins:

> On the fifth day of the month of April of the year 1553, we, Brother Matthieu Ory, Doctor of Theology, Penitentiary of the Holy Apostolic See, Inquisitor General of the Faith in the kingdom of France and for all Gaul, and Louis Arzellier, Doctor of Laws, Vicar General of the Most Reverend Monsignor Pierre Palmier, the Archbishop of Vienne, and Antoine de las Court, Lord of Tour de Buys, Doctor of Laws, Sheriff and Lieutenant General for the district of Vienne, we went to the prisons of the palace at Vienne, and in the criminal chamber caused Michel de Villeneufve to be brought before us ... and examined him as follows.[17]

In reply to their questions, Servetus, after swearing on the Gospels to tell the truth, gave a brief autobiography in which he passed over all references to his dealings with the Protestants. Of his publications he mentioned only the medical works and the geography. He had corrected a few others. Then they showed him from a printed book pages 421-424, on baptism, and inquired as to the marginal annotations. For long it was supposed that the book in question was the *Restitutio,* but the pages do not correspond. They fit precisely the Latin edition, printed in Strassburg in 1543, of Calvin's *Institutio.* This was the copy sent to Servetus and returned by him with contemptuous annotations.[18] The inquisitors asked not whether he had written this, but how he interpreted it. He replied in a sense satisfactory to the Church, and then examined the handwriting carefully. It had been done so long before that he was not sure whether it was his, but after a more careful examination he thought it was. If anything was contrary to the faith he would submit himself to the judgment of the Church.[19]

On the next day, April 6, he was again sworn on the Gospels and examined as to the letters. The first he managed well enough [although he asserted that he was named de Villeneufve, that he was born in Tudela and that he had not written any books besides those mentioned before]; but at the second [on being interrogated on letter 16, which deals with free will] he broke into tears and said,

> My Lords, I tell you the truth. When these letters were written at the time that I was in Germany about twenty-five years ago,[a] a book was printed in Germany by a certain Spaniard called Servetus. I do not know where he came from in Spain, nor where he lived in Germany, except that I have heard it was at Hagenau, where it is said his book was printed. This town is near Strassburg. Having read the book in Germany, when I was very young, about 15 to 17, it seemed to me that he spoke as well or better than the others. However, leaving all that behind in Germany, I went to France without taking any books, merely with the intention of studying mathematics and medicine as I have done since. But having heard that Calvin was a learned man, I wanted to write to him out of curiosity without knowing him otherwise, and in fact I did write, requesting that the correspondence should be confidential, and for brotherly correction, to see whether he could not convince me, or I him, for I could not accept his say so . . . When he saw that my questions were those of Servetus he replied that I was Servetus. I answered that although I was not, for the purposes of discussion, I was willing to assume the role of Servetus, for I did not care what he thought of me, but only that we should discuss our opinions. On those terms we wrote until the correspondence became heated, and I dropped it. For the last ten years there has been nothing between us and I affirm before God and you, sirs, that I never wished to dogmatize or assert anything contrary to the Church and the Christian religion.

A third examination elicited nothing new.[20]

After the second examination Servetus sent his valet to the monastery of St. Peter to recall a debt outstanding to the sum of 300 écus.[21] Had he waited an hour it would have been too late, for the inquisitor notified the jailor that "M. de Villeneufve" should speak to no one

---

[a] They were written from Vienne.

without permission and should be carefully guarded. The precautions of the inquisitor were not without warrant. In the back of the prison garden there was a flat roof from which one could reach a corner of the wall and from there leap into the courtyard. Although the garden was always carefully locked, prisoners of rank were allowed to walk there and attend to their necessities. Servetus went out in the evening and carefully surveyed the terrain. On the morning of the 7th he was up at four and asked the key from the jailor, who was going out to cultivate his vines. The good man, seeing the bathrobe and nightcap, never surmised that the prisoner was fully dressed and had his hat under the robe; he gave him the key and left shortly afterwards with his workmen. When Servetus thought them sufficiently distant, he dropped his velvet nightcap and fur bathrobe under a tree and leapt from the terrace to the roof into the court without hurt. He quickly gained the Rhone gate and passed into the suburbs, according to the testimony of a peasant woman, who was examined three hours afterwards.[22]

Not until after two hours was his escape discovered. The jailor's wife first found out and staged a mighty spectacle, tearing her hair, beating the servants and her children and all the prisoners encountered. Emboldened by anger, she scrambled over the roofs of the neighboring houses. The judges, too, did their duty. The sheriff ordered the gates to be closed and guarded that night and the ensuing. After a proclamation at the sound of a trumpet nearly all the houses were searched. Lyons and other cities were notified, nor was it forgotten to find out whether Servetus had anything in the bank. All of his money, papers, and effects went into the hands of justice. The sheriff was suspected of complicity in the escape because Servetus had cured his daughter of a dangerous illness. Curiously enough, in the records, the deposition of the jailor reached the admission that he gave the key to Servetus and the rest was blank.

The remainder of the month of April was spent in a further examination of the effects of "Villeneufve" and Arnoullet. The letters from Calvin were copied and the originals deposited with the clerk. On May 2, the inquisitor was informed that, in an out-of-the-way house, Arnoullet had two presses which he had not specified in the report. At once the inquisitor, vicar, and bailiff went out to see. They discovered three printers and confronted them with proof that they had worked on the book. Let them tell the truth and, if they had erred, ask for mercy. The workmen in terror fell on their knees. One confessed that they had printed a book in octavo called *Christianismi Restitutio,* but they had no idea that it contained heresy and heard of it only after the trial commenced. Then they were afraid to say anything lest they should be burned. "Villeneufve" had printed the work at his own expense and had corrected the proof. The work commenced on St. Michael's day of the last year and was finished on January 3. On the 13th, at the request of "de Villeneufve," five bales were sent to Pierre Merrin at Lyons.

Here was news for the cardinal and the archbishop. The next day the inquisitor and the vicar made off for Lyons to examine Merrin. He admitted without concealment that about four months ago the barge from Vienne had brought him five bales with the label: "From Michel de Villeneufve, Docteur en Médecine, to Pierre Merrin, caster of type, near the Church of Our Lady of Comfort." The same day Jacques Charmier, an ecclesiastic of Vienne, had come to request him, on behalf of "Villeneufve," to keep the bales until called for, and said they were blank paper. Merrin had heard nothing more from "Villeneufve," no one had come for the bales, and he had never opened them to see whether they were paper or books.

The vicar removed the bales to the archiepiscopal palace. Jacques Charmier was then examined and asserted persistently that he did not know what was in the bales. He had been so intimate with Servetus, however, that he was condemned to prison for three years.[23]

On the seventeenth of June, the civil tribunal passed sentence on Servetus. Their verdict was expressly based in part on the material supplied by John Calvin. Villeneuve was declared guilty of scandalous heresy, sedition, rebellion, and evasion of prison. The sentence was that he should pay a fine of a thousand pounds to the king, and that as soon as apprehended he should be conveyed together with his books in a cart from the palace through the streets and accustomed places to the market place, and thence to a place called Charnève. There he should be burned at a slow fire until his body was reduced to ashes. Under the circumstances the sentence should be executed in effigy.

Every detail was carried out. His picture was hanged for a moment to dull its sensibilities and was then burned, with the five bales of "blank paper."[24] The sentence of the ecclesiastical court was not passed until December 23.[25] Maugiron obtained permission from the king to have the confiscated goods awarded to his son, and this was the Maugiron whom Servetus was attending when arrested.[26]

Balthazar Arnoullet, in the meantime, remained in prison. Here, on July 14, he wrote to his friend Bertet to go to Frankfort and secretly destroy the copies of the *Restitutio,* so that not a leaf nor half a leaf should ever be found.[27] Arnoullet excused himself for not having signed the last three letters. He feared a longer detention of his person. The day before, he made his purgation before six of his neighbors and would be entirely clear in a week. Bertet was wrong that avarice led him to accept the *Restitutio*. Guéroult deceived him and, when asked whether the book was according to God, replied affirmatively and said he had a good mind to translate it into French. Guéroult is further blamed for having absconded without settling his accounts or saying good-bye. Bertet has heard that the inquisitor has his name. Arnoullet cannot say — "but I assure you that I was examined a dozen times and never mentioned a soul. I was asked about a good many whose names I will tell you when we are together." Arnoullet announces his intention to live away from the power of their enemies and the enemies of the truth. He is going to Geneva. He adds in a postscript: "I have given the carrier ten sous and would have given him more except that you will be surer of this letter if he expects something at your end."[28]

The destruction of the issue of the *Restitutio* was so thorough that today only three copies survive. One is at Edinburgh. The first sixteen pages are missing and have been supplied in manuscript from a form divergent from the printed text and presumably copied from the draft of 1546. It is in this manuscript that the reference occurs to the New Isles as a possible asylum. The second copy is at Paris and carries the name of Colladon — to be encountered in the trial at Geneva. The third is at Vienna; it had been the property of a Transylvanian nobleman, Markos Szent-Yványi, who was living in London in 1665. The work was reprinted in 1790.[29]

Geneva in 1550

Chapter 9

Why Geneva?

The next news of Servetus is an entry in the records of the Genevan Consistory: "On August the 13th of the present year Michael Servetus was recognized by certain brothers and it seemed good to make him a prisoner that he might no longer infect the world with his heresies and blasphemies, seeing that he was known to be incorrigible and hopeless."[1]

The 13th was a Sunday. Absence from church would have entailed an investigation. Attendance would attract less attention. Servetus went, therefore, to the service as a part of his plan "to keep himself hid as much as he could."[2] But "certain brothers from Lyons," espying him, carried the news to Calvin,[3] who caused him to be arrested by the magistrates.[4] In accord with the law, Calvin's secretary, Nicolas de la Fontaine, went to prison as surety that any penalties would be discharged if the accusations were not sustained.[5]

Why, one is compelled to ask, was Servetus so rash as to expose himself at Geneva? His own statement in the courtroom with regard to his coming was that

> he had lodged the night before his arrival at Louyset and entered alone on foot. His plan was not to stop but to go to Naples and there to practice medicine. With this intent he lodged at the Inn of the Rose and had already requested the host and the hostess to engage a boat to take him further up the lake where he could pick up the road for Zurich. He had concealed himself as much as he could that he might be able to go on without recognition.[6]

He was, then, on his way to Italy, but could he have found no other route than through Geneva? He must have been aware of the peril because he well knew that the incriminating evidence with which he had been confronted by the Catholic Inquisition in France had been supplied directly or indirectly by John Calvin. He probably did not know of Calvin's remark to Farel that if Servetus came to Geneva he would not get out alive if Calvin had his way but he certainly knew that Calvin had declined to give him any promise of immunity. Servetus had seen enough at Basel to realize that the reformers had not abandoned the attitude of the Catholic Church toward heretics and certainly not toward blasphemers.

As for Calvin's views about the treatment of heresy, Servetus obviously could not have known the refutation which Calvin had not yet published against him. Yet from Calvin's collaboration with the Inquisition, Servetus might have divined that his view did not differ vastly from that of Ory, Lizet, or Tournon. As a matter of fact, Calvin was not at all deterred by their example from the exercise of constraint in religion.

> Because the Papists persecute the truth, should we on that account refrain from repressing error? As Saint Augustine said, the cause, not the suffering, makes the martyr. To be sure in the early days the sword was not used on behalf of the Church because miracles were then available. Admittedly Christ did not use the sword, but Peter acted in the spirit of Christ when he destroyed Ananias. The proposal of Gamaliel to wait and see the outcome before using constraint was the counsel of a blind man. The advice to leave the tares till the harvest was motivated only by consideration for the wheat.

Thus far Calvin was simply repeating the familiar arguments and explanations employed by the Catholics and also by the early Protestants, except the Anabaptists. Calvin declined even to avail himself of the distinction—drawn by Luther—between heresy, which should be immune from coercion, and blasphemy, which might be punished. For Calvin, either one was an affront to God. And that was the point where his intolerance became more intense than that of any of his predecessors. The purpose of constraint was not to make converts, inasmuch as the saved and the lost are already predetermined. The purpose was to vindicate the honor of God by silencing those who sully His holy name.

The full impact of Calvin's theory comes to expression in his comment on the injunctions of Deuteronomy, in the thirteenth chapter, with regard to the treatment of seducers who lead the people after false gods. Not even the closest relatives are to be spared but are to be taken beyond the camp and stoned to death. Calvin comments:

Those who would spare heretics and blasphemers are themselves blasphemers. Here we follow not the authority of men but we hear God speaking as in no obscure terms He commands His church forever. Not in vain does He extinguish all those affections by which our hearts are softened: the love of parents, brothers, neighbors and friends. He calls the wedded from their marriage bed and practically denudes men of their nature lest any obstacle impede their holy zeal. Why is such implacable severity demanded unless that devotion to God's honor should be preferred to all human concerns and as often as His glory is at stake we should expunge from memory our mutual humanity.[7]

Servetus could not indeed have read these words, but he might have divined their import; he could not have failed to know that in Calvin's eyes he was himself thrice over a heretic and a blasphemer. Servetus's picture of God as a self-expansive being with whom man can be united was for Calvin blasphemy against God and a travesty of man. The Calvinistic God is not an abyss of being but the sovereign Lord whose essence consists in His will. In His presence man, puny and unclean, should only sink in ashes, adore and obey. The picture of Christ in terms of the eternal Logos, combined, not eternally, but only temporally with the human Jesus, undercut for Calvin the unshakable grounding of salvation in the everlasting. The estimate of man as born innocent conflicted with Calvin's doctrine of original sin, and the assertion of man's freedom to affect his status clashed with foreordination, the very core of Calvin's view of God and of his hope for history. The denial of infant baptism destroyed the picture of the Church as an ongoing community; Servetus's description of the Church as a fellowship of the fervent bade fair to render it small and impotent in a social context. If, then, the seducer of the people should be taken beyond the camp and stoned, what mercy should be extended to Servetus?

Even if Servetus had only an inkling of all this, why — one must ask again — did he come to Geneva? Calvin did not pretend to know. "Perhaps he meant to pass through," was his comment. "We do not yet know with what intent he came."[8] Some of Calvin's modern apologists believe themselves to be better informed; this is by no means preposterous, since more evidence is at our disposal today than was accessible to any single contemporary of Servetus.

The explanation of Servetus's motives offered by these modern apologists for Calvin has assumed the form of an argument designed in a measure to extenuate his severity. The contention is that Servetus conspired to overthrow Calvin and his whole regime. Through Guéroult, Servetus was in league with the Libertines, it is claimed; for a month prior to his discovery, he had been lurking in Geneva engaged in machinations, looking toward a *coup d'état*.[9] Calvin, then, struck not only for the honor of God but for the preservation of the republic. What modern state would hesitate to extinguish an individual who threatened its very existence? Calvin, they say, did no more than any statesman of our own time would find himself constrained to do.

One may well debate whether this course of reasoning serves so much to exculpate Calvin as to incriminate the modern state. In any case, it misrepresents Calvin because it makes him into essentially a political figure. He did, of course, have a concern for the stability of the Genevan Commonwealth, and he did believe that heresy was heinous partly because it would blight all human institutions by bringing down the wrath of God. But Calvin cared for commonwealths and institutions only insofar as they embodied the truth of God; he had previously gone into exile, and would go again, if the Commonwealth were recreant to the faith. If, then, Calvin brought against a heretic a capital charge, the reason was not primarily that the republic might be secure but that the honor of God might be maintained.

Nevertheless, the picture of the collusion of Servetus and the Libertines has so far commended itself to reputable and careful historians that a detailed examination of the thesis is in order. The contention is that Servetus was conspiring with the Libertines and to that end had been in Geneva a month prior to his arrest. The only evidence adduced is a statement made by the Genevan Council some years later, after the Libertines had been completely crushed – some of them executed and others, like Perrin and Vandel, in flight. When a plea was then made to permit certain of the refugees to return, the Council – whose statement is extant only in a German translation – sought to discredit the Libertines on the ground that they had given "*vffenthalt* and favor to Servetus."[10] This word *vffenthalt* commonly means lodging. But in that day it meant also protection and, in this sense, was clearly used elsewhere in the same document.[11] This evidence, therefore, may be used to substantiate the claim that the Libertines endeavored to save Servetus but not that they entertained him in their homes.

On the other side we have the express statement of Servetus, already cited, which went unrefuted in the courtroom: that he had arrived only the day before. In addition, there is the testimony of Théodore de Bèze,

Calvin's colleague at Lausanne and later his successor, that Servetus was recognized "very soon" – indeed, "immediately."[12] Moreover, Calvin, as already noted, thought that Servetus perhaps intended only to pass through. Again, Calvin estimated that Servetus had been wandering for four months in Italy.[13] As to the place, this is a mistaken inference from a letter received from Italy;[14] the reference to the time, however, is significant. From the escape of Servetus at Vienne to the arrest at Geneva, exactly four months and six days had elapsed, from April 7 to August 13. If one allows in Calvin's calculations for a journey to and from Italy in addition to the four months, scarcely half a day would remain for any previous residence in Geneva.

But the month in the city is not essential to the argument. Wholly apart from any particular length of time, Servetus may have been in collusion with the Libertines. The attempt is made to sustain this point by calling attention to the extremely evasive, deceptive, and inconsistent statements of Servetus as to his relations with Guillaume Guéroult. The latter charged that Servetus had avoided him. When this was repeated in the courtroom, Servetus promptly denied the accusation.[15] But the next day he admitted that he had concealed from Guéroult a copy of the book.[16] Successive evasions culminated in the assertion that he did not even know the man's last name. He had never heard him called anything but "Maistre Guillaume."[17] Why all of this concealment and evasion, we are asked, if there were not something sinister about the connection? The answer is simple. Servetus was not seeking to clear himself from the taint of Guéroult but, rather, to clear Guéroult from any connection with himself. As a matter of fact Guéroult had fled to Geneva and was himself on trial. He was not released until September 5.[18] The first statement of Servetus was made on August 28. Quite conceivably, after the first blurted denial of having shunned Guéroult, Servetus was made aware of Guéroult's plight – or, not knowing, he may have reflected that, wherever Guéroult might be, to confirm his complicity would be compromising. Similarly, a little later in the trial, Servetus declined to give any testimony which would incriminate friends at Vienne.[19]

Further evidence adduced in favor of the conspiracy is that during the course of the trial Servetus became more insolent and overbearing. Why did he bait his accusers and his judges if he were not confident of powerful support? Calvin himself said that Servetus might have been saved if he had shown "the least sign of modesty, wherefore the conjecture is probable that he had some vain confidence from I know not where which ruined and lost him."[20] Calvin, one observes, did not invoke the Libertines. He did not pretend to know the source of this insolent defiance. One recalls that Servetus had displayed a similar temper in his trial at Paris and had escaped. He may have concluded that brashness is the best defense. His release at Paris was aided by the court astrologer. Perhaps on this occasion he may have supposed that the Libertines could secure for him permission to continue his journey. But that, however, would be very different from collaborating with them for Calvin's overthrow.

In explaining the demeanor of a long-hunted spirit, one should not press with undue confidence any correlation between an inner mood and an external event. Servetus may have been so long pent up that when once the sluice was opened the torrent poured. Then, again, if he did look for intervention, can one be sure as to the source? He may have been awaiting help, not from Perrin and Vandel, but from the archangel Michael. "The three ages," said Servetus, "are complete; the four horsemen have appeared; the vials of the wrath of God are about to be opened." Moreover, possibly not escape but *death* was what he envisaged, for had he not said that he must die in this encounter? Foreseeing no deliverance, he may have been resolved this time to make his testimony unabridged and unabated.

A further consideration is adduced to show that Servetus counted on the co-operation of the Libertines – namely, that he arrived at precisely the moment when Calvin was in a most critical situation. The struggle over the spiritual independence of the Church was just coming to a head. Calvin asserted with all the conviction of a Hildebrand that the Church alone should control excommunication; the Church alone must prevent the Lord's table from profanation. This is a spiritual matter, Calvin claimed, in which the magistrate has no right to interfere.

Philip Berthelier, one of the leaders of the Libertines, had been excommunicated, but the Council proposed to restore him. Calvin appeared before an extraordinary session on Saturday, September 2, 1553, and asserted that he would die a hundred times rather than subject Christ to such shameful derision.

The Council weakened and secretly advised Berthelier not to appear at the communion on the morrow. Calvin did not know this, however, and defiantly proclaimed in his sermon, "If anyone comes to this table, who has been excluded by the Consistory, I will do my duty with my life." Calvin came down slowly from the pulpit and placed himself behind the communion table.

> There must have been in that vast cathedral a great silence followed by a singular astonishment. Behind the table stands this man, pale, thin, broken, worn, who seems nothing but a breath, but whose eye, burning with a blind fever, looks over the audience to find the excommunicated man. The crowd, moved, subdued as only a crowd can be, looks too. Nobody! Nothing! Berthelier does not present himself. Berthelier is not there![21]

Calvin had won.

But this victory, so runs the argument, could not have been foreseen three weeks before, when Servetus arrived. At that time the situation was highly critical. Servetus, we are told, knew and counted on this fact. The only evidence adduced is a letter from Musculus, the minister at Berne, to Bullinger, the successor of Zwingli at Zurich, saying that "Servetus had recently come to Geneva to take advantage of the rancor with which the government pursued Calvin. He hoped to obtain a foothold from which he would be able to carry on the affair with the other churches."[22] This statement, emanating from Berne, was as much a guess as the supposition of Bullinger that "the providence of God brought Servetus to Geneva that she might have an opportunity to purge herself of the charge of heresy and blasphemy by punishing him as he deserved."[23] There is, then, no proof that Servetus was in collusion with the Libertines and the accusation of sedition is without foundation.

Yet further corroboration of the thesis is discovered in the withdrawal of Calvin after the first phase of the trial, and the entry of the public prosecutor who attempted to prove that Servetus from the outset had been a turbulent character. This charge, it is true, was made but was not sustained, and the prosecutor soon made his exit. Calvin re-entered, accompanied by theology, which alone affected the ultimate decision. The sentence mentioned only points of theology. The trial thus wore a political aspect, only in the broader sense that heresy was always regarded as socially subversive.

More plausible is the contention that the Libertines attempted to secure the acquittal of Servetus, though the evidence even here is not unimpeachable. Calvin had *heard* that Berthelier intervened at the examination in favor of Servetus.[24] Bullinger had *heard* that the Libertines supported Servetus out of hatred for Calvin.[25] Roset, a Genevan chronicler, said that Berthelier had been *accused* of favoring Servetus.[26]

Calvin declared that Perrin "feigned sickness for three days" – how could Calvin know that he was not really sick? – "but at length went to the council in order to deliver the scoundrel and was not ashamed to petition that the case be carried to the Two Hundred."[27] Of all this the official records know absolutely nothing. An anonymous account said that Perrin absented himself from the final sitting.[28] But he did not. The record shows that he was present.[29] After the collapse of the Libertines, the Genevan senate, as already noted, attempted to discredit the exiles on the ground that they had favored Servetus.[30] Over against this may be placed the deposition of Trolliet (1558) – the confidant of Perrin – to the effect that Vandel, Berthelier, and Perrin had not supported Servetus to his knowledge.[31] Vandel discountenanced a tract which criticized the treatment of Servetus,[32] and Berthelier denied that he had expressed disapproval of the verdict.[33] Bonivard, the famed one-time prisoner of Chillon, said that after the replies from the Swiss cities, the Libertines did not dare to give Servetus open support.[34]

Nevertheless, it would be precarious to press skepticism in this direction. Calvin's statement of what he had heard about Berthelier appears in the official records without a hint of contradiction, and one can scarcely feel that he was mistaken about Perrin's appeal to the Two Hundred, in spite of the silence of the official report. It is altogether possible that some of the Libertines out of spite for Calvin sought to release one whom he accused. Yet the party as a whole did not. Rigot, who prosecuted Servetus, was himself a Perrinist, and acted in entire independence of Calvin.[35]

A further supposition is that the Libertines communicated with Servetus in prison. The evidence is circumstantial and conjectural. Farel said vaguely, "There were some who gave him to hope that there was no danger."[36] Théodore de Bèze recorded that one of the Libertines, an employee of the government, "was *believed* to have whispered in his ear."[37] Bonivard, however, thought that the information was supplied by Claude, the jailor.[38] This guess has the merit of leaving uncontradicted the assertion of Servetus, in the presence of his accusers, that he had communicated with no one save with those who gave him to eat.[39]

The apologists find support for these conjectures in circumstantial evidence. The windows of the prison were locked.[40] Why, we are asked, if not to prevent any further communication with the outside?[41] But the explanation is much simpler. Servetus testified on one of the occasions at Geneva that he had escaped at Vienne through a window.[42] The authorities took the hint.

A further point is that during the course of the trial Servetus gave more precise information about Calvin's dealings with the Inquisition at Vienne. This information is supposed to have been supplied by the Libertines.[43] One should observe in this connection, however, that Servetus also gave increasingly precise information about his escape from Vienne.[44] Did he learn this from the Libertines?

Particular stress is laid on the fact that Servetus was sufficiently acquainted with the laws of Geneva to know that he could appeal to the Two Hundred. How did he discover that, some inquire, unless he was informed during the course of the trial? As if the Two Hundred were an esoteric society of which one could not have learned at Vienne! And for that matter Servetus said that he had been in Geneva before.[45] Even greater importance is attached to the coincidence that Servetus made the appeal on the 15th of September, while the Berthelier case was still pending. The crisis of the Berthelier case, however, had already been passed on September 3. A date in August would have been more timely.

But grant that there was communication, and it is by no means improbable, what then has been proved? Nothing more than that the Libertines may have attempted secretly as well as publicly to save Servetus. If both be true, Servetus is not thereby convicted of sedition. This alone is established: that there was a connection between the cases of Servetus and Berthelier, both of whom received help from the same quarter. The apologists would contend that the connection was so intimate that, had Calvin failed in the one, he must have failed also in the other, with the consequent collapse of his entire work. The Genevan Reformation was at stake. That is why he was so adamant, they claim; that is what enables us to understand and excuse his intolerance.

Not one of these suppositions is even probable. Had Berthelier been restored to communion Calvin would have gone into exile, but it is not likely that Servetus would have been released after the verdict of the Swiss cities. The Genevan Council could be inexorable enough without Calvin. On the other hand, if Servetus had been released, Calvin need not have lost the victory already attained over Berthelier. Certainly it is far from the truth that a milder treatment of Servetus would have been the undoing of Calvin's work. On the contrary, this exercise of severity plunged him into a prolonged and embarrassing controversy. Neither is it necessary to call in the Libertines to explain Calvin's rigor. The honor of God was at stake. Calvin, like Servetus, gave less thought to the Libertines than to the Lord.

176 ΙΟΥΣΤ.

Page from the Spurious Justin Martyr with which Calvin Confronted Servetus

Chapter 10

The Geneva Trial

The trial itself involved five phases. 1) First came a series of examinations on the basis of charges supplied by Calvin. 2) Further oral examinations by the public prosecutor followed. The correspondence with Vienne formed an interlude. 3) The trial continued in the form of a running debate between Calvin and Servetus, who took advantage of his ink and paper to address several pleas to the Council, among others an appeal to the Two Hundred. 4) The Swiss cities were consulted and their replies submitted to the Council. 5) On the basis of this material, the court deliberated and passed judgment.

In the first phase there were five examinations. First the lieutenant general, Tissot, made an investigation to see whether there was ground for continuance of the case. After the replies of Servetus, Nicolas Fontaine, Calvin's secretary and surety, supplied copies of the Ptolemy of 1535, of the Pagnini Bible, of the printed *Restitutio* and of the manuscript – the one which Calvin had not returned for printing of the book, but now supplied as an aid to burning the author. The accused and the accuser were then committed to the jailor, who was instructed to relieve Servetus of his valuables, consisting of sixty gold écus, a gold chain worth as much, and six gold rings.[1]

Nicolas then petitioned the Council for release, since the charges were sufficiently substantiated inasmuch as "the replies of Servetus were but silly songs." Incidentally Nicolas remarked that he had felt bound to defend the honor of Calvin and of the church at Geneva. (Local instead of national honor!) The report of the lieutenant persuaded the Council to make the next examination itself; this took place on August 15. This was the first hearing before the Council, but the second examination. As a result Nicolas was released from prison but only because Calvin's brother, Antoine, became surety in his stead.[2]

On the following day (August 16), the Council subjected Servetus to his third questioning. There were two significant changes in the court. Colladon, the Calvinist, appeared as advocate for Nicolas. This Colladon is the one, as previously noted, whose name appears in the Edinburgh copy of the *Restitutio.* The place of the lieutenant was taken by Philip Berthelier, the Libertine. Calvin heard that he had espoused the cause of Servetus, which is not all improbable since the Council invited Calvin to come himself the next time to defend his accusations. We may assume that he was present for the fourth examination, as a result of which Nicolas was entirely freed.[3] On the 21st, Calvin refuted the use which Servetus made of the Church fathers.[4]

The charges thus far leveled against Servetus, and his replies, are available partly in the public records, partly in Calvin's account. There were thirty-nine accusations which reduce themselves to a few groups. These deal with the earlier life and publications of the accused; with his doctrine, especially of pantheism, of the Trinity, immortality, and baptism; and with his abusiveness against Melanchthon and the church at Geneva.

As for Servetus's life, the accusation was made that, about twenty-nine years before, he had begun to trouble the churches of Germany by his errors and heresies; that he was condemned and had to flee to escape punishment. He answered that he had written a book, but had not troubled the churches so far as he knew. The letters of Oecolampadius were produced and, for some unaccountable reason, thus came for the first time to the eyes of Servetus. The next count referred to the book which had "infected many people." Servetus admitted the book but denied the infection.

He was next charged with continuing to sow his poison in the annotations on Ptolemy and in the comments on the Bible. The records of the Council compare interestingly at this point with Calvin's version. According to the public document, Servetus replied that there was nothing wrong with the Ptolemy. It sold publicly throughout Christendom and he had lectured on it at Paris. When the book was produced, and he was shown the passage on Judaea, he said that he had not written it, but that nevertheless there was nothing wrong with it. He understood it as applying to the present century rather than to the time of Moses. The court objected that since he included all who had written on the country he included Moses. This is the *official* account.

Calvin amplified by saying that Servetus "at first growled that he had not written the passage, but this cold cavil was at once refuted, for in this he was shown to be a clear impostor. Thus being driven in a corner he said there was nothing the matter with it. He was asked who but Moses could be meant by 'that vain preacher of Judaea'? 'As if,' he answered, 'no others had written on Judaea.'" Calvin retorted that Moses was the first and must have deceived the others, "but the dirty dog wiped his snout and said in a word that there was nothing wrong with it. And when he could think of no subterfuge would not make a clear confession."[5] So Calvin. Yet Servetus was right that he had not composed the passage. He might have added that he had omitted it from the second edition, and had he looked again at the first he might have shown that the phrase, "that vain preacher of Judaea," did not appear.

As for the Bible, Calvin said that Servetus soiled every page with "futile trifles and impious ravings." The comment on Isaiah 53 might serve as an example. "The perfidious scamp wrenches the passage so as to apply it to Cyrus, though adding that Christ is foreshadowed for whom alone this language is suitable. But, in the meantime, we are left with no satisfaction for sins, no means of propitiating God, no purgation. Everyone will admit that I was right when I told him that no author had so boldly corrupted this signal prophecy." One notes that Calvin did not take exception to the treatment of the virgin-birth passage in Isaiah 7.

On the doctrinal questions, Calvin furnished the following account of the discussion of pantheism:

> When he asserted that all creatures are of the proper essence of God and so all things are full of gods (for he did not blush to speak and write his mind in this way) I, wounded with the indignity, objected: "What, wretch! If one stamps the floor would one say that one stamped on your God? Does not such an absurdity shame you?" But he answered, "I have no doubt that this bench or anything you point to is God's substance." And when again it was objected, "The devil then will be substantially God?", he broke out laughing and said, "Can you doubt it? This is my fundamental principle that all things are a part and portion of God and the nature of things is the substantial spirit of God."[6]

Servetus in commenting on the encounter said, "Stamping your foot you said that you did not move in God. You must, therefore, have moved in the devil. But we move and are in God in whom we live. Even if you are a blind demon you are sustained nevertheless by God."[7]

As for the Trinity, Servetus declared that he did believe in it, that is, in the Father, the Son, and the Holy Spirit, three persons in God. He said, however, that he interpreted the word *person* differently from the

Moderni. Only those who placed a real distinction in the divine essence would he call Trinitarians and atheists.[8]

The charge that he denied immortality was stoutly repudiated. Servetus had never thought nor said nor written that the soul is mortal, but only that it is clothed with corruptible elements.[9] But he admitted without reservation his severest strictures on infant baptism. "It is an invention of the devil, an infernal falsity for the destruction of all Christianity." This he would hold unless convinced to the contrary. He did not believe that children are without original sin, but that redemption must wait until they are mature. He believed that God would not regard as mortal those sins which are committed before the age of twenty.[10]

As for the abuse of Melanchthon and Calvin, and of Geneva in his letter to Poupin, Servetus averred that it did not exceed the scurrility previously heaped upon him by the Reformers in printed books. He had no intention of injuring Calvin and wished merely to show his errors.[11] Later in the trial Servetus asserted that "it is common today in a matter of disputation that each should maintain his cause considering that the adverse party is on the way to damnation."[12] In other words, abuse is simply the technique of controversy.

With regard to the use of the Church fathers, Calvin related that

Servetus was in the habit of brazenly citing authorities at which he had never looked. A laughable and ridiculous example is given in the case of Justin Martyr, for when he complacently asserted that the fables of the Trinity and persons were unknown in his golden age, I called for a codex and put my finger on certain passages in which the holy man set forth our opinion no less clearly than if he had written at our request. But this genius of a Servetus, who was so proud of his linguistic accomplishment, could no more read Greek than a boy who has just started the alphabet, and, seeing himself trapped, brazenly asked for a Latin translation. "What!" I said, "when there is no Latin translation, and you cannot read Greek, nevertheless you pretend to be so familiar with Justin!"[13]

This was utterly unfair. Servetus knew Greek and knew it well, but his knowledge of Justin was based entirely on a fragment in a Latin translation by Irenaeus, as well as on quotations in an early author whom Servetus supposed to be Justin.[14] He had not had an opportunity to avail himself of the Greek text of Justin which had appeared in print at Paris only two years previously and which included both genuine works and those now known to be spurious. When, then, Calvin produced this edition and in good faith pointed to a passage from the pseudo-Justin which read, "The One is perceived in the Triad and the Triad is known in the One," Servetus, who had never seen it before, was naturally nonplussed.[15]

The examinations ended; the Council voted to give Servetus books and paper to present a written request. Inquiry should be made at Vienne as to why he was detained, and how he escaped, and the Swiss cities should be informed. The letter to Vienne was sent the next day, August 22.[16] This ends the first phase of the trial.

The second phase was marked by the entry of Rigot, the public prosecutor – himself a Libertine – who undertook to answer the prisoner's plea to the Council for liberation. Servetus based his petition on the ground that in the early Church there had been no criminal prosecution for doctrine, and that in the days of Constantine the maximum penalty for heresy had been banishment. He was not seditious and had never troubled their country nor any other. He did not approve of the Anabaptist attitude toward the magistrate. Inasmuch as he was a stranger in their city and ignorant of their customs, let them give him representation by counsel.[17]

The prosecutor replied that Servetus was wrong about the early Church. It was the pagan judges who "cared for none of these things." The Christians executed heretics from Constantine to Justinian. The plea for toleration was itself a confession of guilt. Servetus knew that he deserved death, Rigot claimed, but to avoid it he raised an objection against capital punishment for criminals. As for an advocate, the prosecutor continued, Servetus could lie well enough without one.[18]

Rigot subjected Servetus to two examinations in which an attempt was made to prove that his doctrines were subversive of the social order and that his life in consequence must be dissolute. The very plea for religious liberty was interpreted as a political menace, on the ground that it would take the sword of justice from the magistrate.[19] The teaching of Servetus that those under twenty could not commit a mortal sin was regarded as a license to the young to commit adultery, theft, and murder with impunity.[20] Examined as to his relations with the Jews and the Turks, Servetus said that he had not communicated with the Jews on matters of religion, and that he was not of Jewish extraction.[21] He had read the Qur'an, which was allowed at Basel. It was a bad book, but he had used only the good. He would no more aid Muhammad than the devil.[22]

This attempt to connect Servetus with the Jews and the Turks is highly significant in view of the popular belief that tolerance of his views would cause Europe to succumb to the Turk; it was remembered that the regions in which Paul of Samosata and Arius had once assailed the Trinity were now in the hands of the infidel.[23]

A long series of questions were designed to give the impression that he had been a turbulent character and lived loosely for years. Had he not been arrested for wounding someone in a brawl? Servetus in reply related the incident at Charlieu. Had he ever been married and, if not, how could he refrain so long? Servetus replied that he was physically unfit because of an operation and a rupture. Seeing that he had lived a dissolute life and had not had the grace to live chastely as a true Christian, what had led him to write on the fundamentals of the Christian religion? Servetus answered that he had studied the Holy Scripture with a desire for the truth and that he had lived as a Christian. (The prosecutor reverted to these charges in the second hearing.) How old was he when he was operated on and ruptured? Servetus said that he could not remember, but he was probably about five. Had he contemplated marriage at Charlieu? Yes, but had refrained because of his incapacity. He had remarked, had he not, that there were enough women in the world without marrying? Servetus replied that he did not remember having said it, but he might have done so in jest and to conceal his impotence. Had he not lived wantonly at Charlieu and elsewhere? Servetus answered No.[24]

There were many questions about the work *On the Errors of the Trinity* and about the relations to Oecolampadius, Bucer, and Capito, as well as about the printing of the *Restitutio* and the dealings with Arnoullet and Guéroult. The prosecutor continued: Did he not know that his book would greatly disturb Christendom? No, he thought that Christendom would profit, and the truth would be worked out little by little. What truth did he think was not already worked out? Calvin's doctrine of predestination, he retorted, and of the descent into hell. Did he then think that his doctrine would be accepted and that it was true? He answered that he did not know whether it would be accepted, but he thought it true, for things are often at first reproved which are afterwards received. If, then, he thought he would offend God in concealing his opinions, why did he not proclaim them in France? Because, he answered, we should not cast pearls before swine, and there was great persecution among the papists.[25]

The courier now came from Vienne accompanied by the jailor and the captain and brought a copy of the sentence, but not of the acts of the trial. Vienne assured Geneva that if the fugitive were returned, he would be punished so that there would be no need of any further charges. The jailor asked for an attestation from Servetus that the former had not assisted the latter's escape.[26]

Servetus was called and gladly exonerated the jailor. When asked whether he wished to be sent back to Vienne, he fell on the ground in tears and begged that he might be judged in Geneva.[27]

Maugiron sent word that the king had awarded the goods of the heretic to his son. Would the Council at Geneva kindly obtain from Servetus a statement of debts to be discharged? The property confiscated amounted to 3,000 or 4,000 écus. Servetus declined to give this information on the ground that his creditors would be molested by the Inquisition.

This ends the second phase of the trial. The public prosecutor made his exit. In the next scene Calvin and theology returned.

The third phase consisted of a written discussion between Servetus and Calvin, in Latin. The specification that it must be in Latin indicates that the documents were intended for the Swiss cities. The Council had already decided to keep them informed, and now Servetus made a direct appeal to their arbitrament. This statement comes from Calvin, who said in print that he gladly accepted the condition.[28] A letter to Bullinger of Zurich would indicate, however, that Calvin was anything but glad. "Our magistrates," he wrote, "cause you this trouble against our will. They have reached such a point of madness that they question everything we say. So if I assert that it is light at noon they begin to have their doubts about it."[29]

The discussion was not conducted in the best of temper on either side. Calvin's statement was submitted to Servetus, who scribbled it over with exasperated comments. The doctrine of the Trinity, of course, came in for discussion with special reference to the views of Irenaeus and Tertullian. Calvin asserted that Tertullian recognized a real distinction between the persons of the Trinity. Servetus commented, "You lie. Nothing of the sort was ever heard of in Tertullian, but only a disposition."[30] Calvin wrote, "If there were a drop of veracity in Servetus would he have dared to abuse this passage to the denial of a real distinction?" Servetus commented, "Unless Simon Magus had closed your eyes you would see that nothing was ever said there about a real distinction, but rather of a formal disposition." Servetus constantly flung the epithet of Simon Magus at Calvin through the belief that Simon was the father of the doctrine of predestination.[31]

A memorandum was submitted to the judges by the ministers of Geneva who said, "Servetus thinks the judges will not know how eloquent he is and what an unabashed reviler unless at the outset he calls Calvin a homicide and afterwards vomits many insults upon him." Servetus retorted, "Deny that you are a homicide and by your acts I will prove it. But in so just a cause I am constant. I do not fear death." The ministers continued, "This prodigious blaspheming chaos deserves no mercy." To this, Servetus appended: "Let mercy, therefore, be shown to Simon Magus."[32] The ministers asserted that "the man's utter lack of the spirit of meekness and docility is nowhere more apparent than in his furious assault upon infant baptism as a detestable abomination." Servetus wrote over against the word "meekness": "You should show it toward me even though I were possessed of an evil spirit."[33]

But this discussion was not mere reviling. Calvin and Servetus came to grips, not so much over the doctrine of the Trinity, however, as with regard to the nature of God and man. Servetus believed that Calvin's doctrine of original sin, total depravity, and determinism reduced man to a log and a stone.[34] Calvin believed that Servetus's doctrine of the deification of humanity degraded God and made deity subject to the vices and infirmities of the flesh.[35] That was why Calvin could not admit any spark of divinity in children, and when Servetus declared that they could not commit a mortal sin, Calvin answered, "He is worthy that the little chickens, all sweet and innocent as he makes them, should dig out his eyes a hundred thousand times."[36]

There is an extensive passage in Calvin's refutation which goes to the core of the controversy. He objects that the doctrine of divine immanence as set forth by Servetus means not simply that God sustains his creation but that God is enmeshed in his creation. The deification of man was for Calvin no less intolerable. Servetus claims, he says, that

> the spirits of the faithful are participants of the divine nature. In them is the substance of the eternal Spirit and their seats have been prepared from eternity: This perverse delirium about the eternal substance has often been refuted. What could be more ridiculous than to claim eternity in the case of those for whom God freely prepared a kingdom before even they were born? Regenerate souls are said by Servetus to be consubstantial with God; therefore, whatever they possess of right and justice is not conferred upon them by grace but implanted in them by nature. In that case, eternal life would be no longer at once a gift and a reward. And what becomes of the eternal essence of God? That single word of God, "I am that I am," sufficiently shows how impious it is to

transfer his eternal essence and divine eternity to creatures. I bear in mind that in another place Servetus babbles that we are in substance generated by God; and in no other way is divinity conferred upon us than in the same manner as Christ is taken up into God so that in us there is a hypostatic union of the divine and the human. But what does this conflation of God and man mean if not that God is made corruptible and is thereby condemned to extinction?[37]

For Calvin, then, the deification of humanity meant not the exaltation of humanity but the degradation of divinity and, with this, the extinction of everything that matters, whether in life, death, or eternity.

The Council voted to send the documents to the Swiss cities and, pending their reply, to let the case rest. This was on September 5.[38]

Calvin busied himself, in the meantime, with writing to the Frankfort pastors to destroy the copies of the *Restitutio,* which contained "a rhapsody composed of the impious ravings of all the ages."[39]

Servetus, after ten days, addressed this petition to the Council:

I humbly beg that you cut short these long delays and deliver me from prosecution. You see that Calvin is at the end of his rope, not knowing what to say and for his pleasure wishes to make me rot here in prison. The lice eat me alive. My clothes are torn and I have nothing for a change, neither jacket nor shirt, but a bad one. I have addressed to you another petition which was according to God and to impede it Calvin cites Justinian. He is in a bad way to quote against me what he does not himself credit, for he does not believe what Justinian has said about the Holy Church of bishops and priests and other matters of religion and knows well that the Church was already degenerated. It is a great shame, the more so that I have been caged here for five weeks and he has not urged against me a single passage.

My lords, I have also asked you to give me a procurator or advocate as you did to my opponent, who was not in the same straits as I, who am a stranger and ignorant of the customs of the country. You permitted it to him, but not to me and you have liberated him from prison before knowing. I petition you that my case be referred to the Council of Two Hundred with my requests, and if I may appeal there I do so ready to assume all the cost, loss and interest of the law of an eye for an eye, both against the first accuser and against Calvin, who has taken up the case himself. Done in your prisons of Geneva. September 15, 1553.

Michael Servetus in his own cause. [40]

In reply to the petition, the Council voted merely to give Servetus clothes at his own expense.

The prisoner now submitted his notes on Calvin's last reply, with a complaint that he had not been refuted from Scripture. He concluded, "Michael Servetus signs alone, but Christ is his sure protector." Another note explained why he had marked up Calvin's paper and was signed, "Your poor prisoner M.S." [41] The correspondence with the Swiss cities continued.

On September 22, Servetus sent another petition to the Council. Calvin had falsely accused him, among other things, of denying the immortality of the soul. Servetus agreed that this would be indeed a horrible blasphemy.

> He who thinks this does not believe that there is a God, nor justice, nor resurrection, nor Jesus Christ, nor Holy Scripture nor anything. If I had said that, I should condemn myself to death. Wherefore, I ask, honored sirs, that my false accuser be made a prisoner like me until the matter be settled by my death or his or another penalty ... And I shall be glad to die if he be not convicted of this and other things which I mentioned below. I demand justice, my Lords, justice, justice!

Appended was a list of questions on which Calvin should be interrogated:

> 1. Whether in the month of March he had not written by Guillaume Trie to Lyons disclosing the doings of Michel Villanovanus, called Servetus?
>
> 2. Whether with this letter he had not sent half of the first quire of the work of the said Servetus entitled *Christianismi Restitutio?*
>
> 3. Whether he had not sent these to the officials at Lyons in order to accuse Servetus?
>
> 4. Whether fifteen days later he had not sent by the same Guillaume Trie twenty letters in Latin which Servetus had sent to him?
>
> 5. Whether he was aware that in consequence of this accusation Servetus had been burned in effigy?
>
> 6. Whether he did not well know that it is not the office of a minister of the gospel to make a capital accusation and to pursue a man at law to the death?

Then follows an indictment:

> Messieurs, there are four great and infallible reasons why Calvin should be condemned:
>
> 1. This first is that a matter of doctrine should not be subject to criminal prosecution as I can amply show from the ancient doctors of the Church.
>
> 2. The second is that he is a false accuser.

3. The third is that by his frivolous and calumnious reasons he opposes the truth of Jesus Christ.

4. The fourth is that in large measure he follows the doctrine of Simon Magus. Therefore as a sorcerer he should be not only condemned but exterminated and driven from this city and his goods should be adjudged to me in recompense for mine.

Michel Servetus in his own cause. [42]

There is nothing in the records until October 10. On that date we find the following note, which explains much as to the prisoner's lapses from clarity and his fluctuations of feeling. The Libertines were not in such intimate contact with Servetus as were the lice. He wrote:

> Honored sirs, It is now three weeks that I have sought an audience and have been unable to secure one. I beg you for the love of Jesus Christ not to refuse me what you would not refuse to a Turk, who sought justice at your hands. I have some important and necessary matters to communicate to you.
>
> As for what you commanded that something be done to keep me clean, nothing has been done and I am in a worse state than before. The cold greatly distresses me, because of my colic and rupture, causing other complaints which I should be ashamed to describe. It is great cruelty that I have not permission to speak if only to remedy my necessities. For the love of God, honored sirs, give your order whether for pity or duty. Done in your prisons of Geneva, October 10, 1553.
>
> Michael Servetus. [43]

The Council voted again to give him a change of clothing. This ends the third phase of the trial.

Magnifiques seigneurs

Il y a bien troys semmaines, que je desire et demande auoyr audiance, et nay jamays peus lauoyr. Je vous supplie pour lamour de Iesu Christ, ne me refuser ce que vous ne refuseries a vn turc, en vous demandant iustice. Jay a vous dire choses dimportance, et bien necessaires.

Quant a ce que auies commande, quon me fit quelque chose pour me tenir net, nen a rien este faict, et suys plus pietre que jamais. Et dauantaige le froyt me tormante grandamant a cause de ma colique et rompure, la quelle mengendre daultres pauretes, que ay honte vous escrire. Cest grand cruaulte, que je soye constrainct de garder seulement pour remedier a mes necessites. pour lamour de dieu messeigneurs donnes y ordre, ou pour pitie, ou pour le deuoyr. Faict en vous prisons de Geneue le dixiema octobre. 1553.

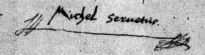
Michel seruetus.

The Last Request of Servetus

Chapter 11

The Stake at Champel

In its fourth phase the trial assumed a national character. The magistrates and ministers of the Swiss cities were alike invited to give their opinions. A uniform letter from the Council at Geneva was addressed to the councils of Zurich, Berne, Basel, and Schaffhausen:

> Magnifficques Seigneurs, We do not know whether you are aware that we have a prisoner by name Michael Servetus who has published a book containing many things against our religion. We have submitted this to our ministers and, though we have no lack of confidence in their judgment, we should like to know also the opinion of your ministers. We have written to them directly and we beg you affectionately to use your good offices that they may examine everything and give their replies in order that the affair may be brought to a proper termination. We pray God that he may increase the prosperity of your commonwealth.
>
> Your good neighbors and great friends the Syndics and Council of Geneva, September 21, 1553.[1]

The replies of the magistrates were comparatively brief. A little glimpse is given into their attitude in a letter from Haller, the minister at Berne, to Bullinger, the minister at Zurich. "We explained," he wrote, "the primary errors of Servetus point by point to our council[a] at their request. On hearing this they were all so indignant that I doubt not they would have burned him had he been detained in their prisons. But since the matter went over their heads they wanted us to write privately to the Genevan council."[2] The magistrates of Berne, therefore, replied very briefly. The ministers of the same city sent a long disquisition in their dialect in which they pointed out that the doctrine of the impossi-

---

[a] i.e. the magistrates

bility of a mortal sin before the twentieth year would be subversive of public morality "especially in these days when the young are so corrupt."[3] There was also a letter in Latin in which these same ministers said, in part:

> We see that Satan operates most persistently in a thousand ways to hinder the progress of the light of truth so that if he cannot extinguish it he may at least obscure it with clouds of pernicious and intricate dogma ... Servetus is a man of little modesty, who calls in question the fundamentals of the Christian religion, revives the errors of the ancient heretics and does not hesitate to adhere to the sects of our own time, reviling infant baptism. We pray God to give you a spirit of prudence, wisdom and fortitude that this pest may be averted from your church and others.[4]

The ministers at Schaffhausen said, "We do not doubt that you, in your wisdom, will repress his attempts lest his blasphemies like a cancer despoil the members of Christ."[5]

Zurich did not mention the rejection of infant baptism for which so many had suffered there. The ministers were shocked rather that Servetus repudiated the doctrine of the Trinity, which was unanimously accepted by the universal church. "We judge that one should work against him with great faith and diligence especially as our churches have an ill repute abroad as heretics and patrons of heretics. God's holy providence has now indeed provided this occasion whereby you may at once purge yourselves and us from this fearful suspicion of evil." The means of coercion were left to the judgment of Geneva.[6]

The ministers of Basel said that they agreed with Zurich and need not repeat what had already been said. Like Berne, Basel was distressed because the Prince of Darkness strained every nerve to overthrow the fundamentals. Paul called such a pest a gnawing cancer, and both the apostle and the fathers regarded heresy as worse than crime. Servetus "exceeds all the old heretics since he vomits their combined errors from one impudent and blasphemous mouth ... Like an excited snake he hisses curses and contumely against Calvin, that most sincere servant of God." Geneva should try to cure him, but if he is incurable "he should be coerced by your office and the power conceded by the Lord lest he be able to give further trouble to the Church of Christ."[7]

These replies appear as unanimous as they were rigorous. But throughout the Swiss cities there was an undercurrent of dissent which comes to light in the private correspondence of the period. Calvin wrote to Sulzer, minister at Basel, commending a certain magistrate for his zeal against Servetus and then adding very significantly, "I wish that your former disciples were as enthusiastic." [8]

Evidence of very considerable disaffection was declared by a distinguished refugee from Italy, a one-time papal nuncio, Vergerio by name, now a simple minister for the Gospel in the Grisons. From Chur he wrote to Bullinger on the 3rd of October, to say that he detested such monsters as Servetus. "Nevertheless I should not think that fire and sword should be used against them." [9] Again, on the 8th, he wrote that "he was terrified by the tragedy of Servetus. The Papists would now scoff that under the guise of reformation the churches were being deformed and the fundamentals shaken."

One needs to read a letter like this to understand the attitude of the men of that period. They had given up country, home, property, and honor for the sake of the gospel. Vergerio himself had renounced a position of eminence. He was deeply concerned that the Reform should not issue in the complete doctrinal disintegration of Christianity. Nevertheless he would not countenance such means to arrest it. His letter continues:

> I have seen your responses to the Genevan council. They will do. You do not say expressly that the heretic should be put to death, but the reader may readily infer that this is your opinion. I have written to you what I think and I will leave the matter to the Lord. I hate such disturbers more than a dog and a snake, but I should have preferred that they be incarcerated in the foulest dungeons rather than that they be destroyed by fire and sword. It is to be regretted that the scamp has supporters among the doctors and among those who are not just nominally for the Gospel, but wish to be considered as pillars. I say what I know, not what I suspect. I have heard it from themselves, not from others, recently and not a long time ago. But I do not wish to write. You will hear when we are together.[10]

In a communication on the 14th he said, "Copies of your responses to the Genevan council I have sent to many in Italy. They will do good." Vergerio evidently did not mean to press his objections. He went on: "A friend has written me from Basel that Servetus has supporters there. This confirms what I wrote you the other day."[11]

On the 19th, a friend at Basel informed Bullinger that a distinguished scholar lately come from Italy had espoused the cause of Servetus. Among the learned in the city there were others of the same mind.[12]

While the trial of Servetus was in progress, one protest indeed came from Basel, an anonymous letter in Dutch. This was the work of David Joris, a one-time leader of the Anabaptists now living under the assumed name of Johan van Brugge. The communication was addressed to the "Noble, honorable, worthy, pious, prudent, wise Lords of the evangelical cities of Switzerland." The letter continues:

I have heard how the good pious Servetus was delivered into your hands through no kindness and love, but rather through envy and hate, as will be made manifest at the last judgment to those whose eyes are now darkened by base cunning, and to whom the truth is unknown. God give them to understand, for the report has gone far and wide and even to my ears that the ministers have written to several places and have determined among themselves to pass sentence of death, which has so troubled me that I could have no peace until I had lifted up my voice as a member of the body of Christ, and poured forth my heart briefly before your Highnesses and freed my conscience. I hope that the bloodthirsty counsel of the learned will not weigh with you. Consider rather the precepts of our only Lord and Master Christ, who taught not only in human and literal fashion in Scripture, but also in a divine manner by word and example that we should crucify and kill no one for his faith, but should rather be crucified and killed ourselves.[13]

The Council at Geneva probably never saw this appeal. The responses of the magistrates and ministers indicated unanimity in favor of extreme measures.

The evidence was now fully assembled. The court could proceed to the verdict. Calvin wrote to Farel on the 26th of October that Perrin had made one more futile attempt to save the prisoner by an appeal to the Two Hundred. "Nevertheless he was condemned without dissent. Tomorrow he will be led to execution. We tried to change the mode of his death but in vain."[14] Of this attempt on the part of the ministers, the public records are silent. But there can be no doubt that Calvin preferred the sword to the stake on humanitarian grounds.[15]

The sentence is dated the 27th. On only two counts, significantly, was Servetus condemned – namely, anti-Trinitiarianism and anti-paedobaptism. There is nothing about pantheism and the denial of immortality, nothing about the Ptolemy or the Pagnini Bible, nothing about the moral offenses. The judges apparently felt that these charges had not been substantiated. There is absolutely nothing about any political offense. Servetus died as a heretic.

This is the verdict:

The sentence pronounced against Michel Servet de Villeneufve of the Kingdom of Aragon in Spain who some twenty-three or twenty-four years ago printed a book at Hagenau in Germany against the Holy Trinity containing many great blasphemies to the scandal of the said churches of Germany, the which book he freely confesses to have printed in the teeth of the remonstrances made to him by the learned and evangelical doctors of Germany. In consequence he became a fugitive from Germany. Nevertheless he continued in his errors and, in order the more to spread the venom of his heresy, he printed secretly a book in Vienne of Dauphiny full of the said heresies and horrible, execrable blasphemies against the Holy Trinity, against the Son of God, against the baptism of infants and the foundations of the Christian religion. He confesses that in this book he called believers in the Trinity Trinitarians and atheists. He calls this Trinity a diabolical monster with three heads. He blasphemes detestably against the Son of God, saying that Jesus Christ is not the Son of God from eternity. He calls infant baptism an invention of the devil and sorcery. His execrable blasphemies are scandalous against the majesty of God, the Son of God and the Holy Spirit. This entails the murder and ruin of many souls. Moreover he wrote a letter to one of our ministers in which, along with other numerous blasphemies, he declared our holy evangelical religion to be without faith and without God and that in place of God we have a three-headed Cerberus. He confesses that because of this abominable book he was made a prisoner at Vienne and perfidiously escaped. He has been burned there in effigy together with five bales of his books. Nevertheless, having been in prison in our city, he persists maliciously in his detestable errors and calumniates true Christians and faithful followers of the immaculate Christian tradition.

Wherefore we Syndics, judges of criminal cases in this city, having witnessed the trial conducted before us at the instance of our Lieutenant against you "Michel Servet de Villeneufve" of the Kingdom of Aragon in Spain, and having seen your voluntary and repeated confessions and your books, judge that you, Servetus, have for a long time promulgated false and thoroughly heretical doctrine, despising all remonstrances and corrections and that you have with malicious and perverse obstinacy sown and divulged even in printed books opinions against God the Father, the Son and the Holy Spirit, in a word against the fundamentals of the Christian religion, and that you have tried to make a schism and trouble the Church of God by which many souls may have been ruined and lost, a thing horrible, shocking, scandalous and infectious. And you have had neither shame nor horror of setting yourself against the divine Majesty and the Holy Trinity, and so you have obstinately tried to infect the world with your stinking heretical poison ... For these and other reasons, desiring to purge the Church of God of such infection and cut off the rotten member, having taken counsel with our citizens and having invoked the name of God to give just judgment ... having God and the Holy Scriptures before our eyes, speaking in the name of the Father, Son and Holy Spirit, we now in writing give final sentence and condemn you, Michael Servetus, to be bound and taken to Champel and there attached to a stake and burned with your book to ashes. And so you shall finish your days and give an example to others who would commit the like. [And we command our lieutenant to execute this present sentence upon you.][16]

Calvin tells how Servetus received the news. "At first he was stunned and then sighed so as to be heard throughout all the room; then he moaned like a madman and had no more composure than a demoniac. At length his cries so increased that he continually beat his breast and bellowed in Spanish, 'Misericordia! misericordia!'"[17]

When he came to himself his first request was that he might see Calvin, who obtained permission from the Council for the visit.[18] Calvin himself gives us the account of the interview.

When he was asked what he had to say to me he replied that he desired to beg my pardon. Then I protested simply, and it is the truth, that I had never entertained any personal rancor against him. I reminded him gently how I had risked my life more than sixteen years ago to gain him for our Savior. If he would return to reason I would faithfully do my best to reconcile him to all good servants of God. And although he had avoided the contest I had never ceased to remonstrate with him kindly in letters. In a word I had used all humanity to the very end, until he being embittered by my good advice hurled all manner of rage and anger against me. But I told him that I would pass over everything which concerned me personally. He should rather ask the pardon of God whom he had so basely blasphemed in his attempt to efface the three persons in the one essence, saying that those who recognize God the Father, Son and Holy Spirit, with a real distinction, created a three-headed hound of hell. I told him to beg the pardon of the Son of God, whom he had disfigured with his dreams, denying that he came in our flesh and was like us in his human nature, and so denying that he is a sole Redeemer. But when I saw that all this did no good I did not wish to be wiser than my Master allows. So following the rule of St. Paul, I withdrew from the heretic who was self-condemned.[19]

Nowhere does Calvin more clearly disclose himself as one of the last great figures of the Middle Ages. To him it was all so perfectly clear that the majesty of God, the salvation of souls, and the stability of Christendom were at stake. Never for a moment did he suppose that he was acting simply on behalf of the laws of a single city. The law under which Servetus had first been imprisoned was that of the Holy Roman Empire; the law by which he was in the end condemned was that of the Codex of Justinian, which prescribes the penalty of death for two ecclesiastical offenses — the denial of the Trinity and the repetition of baptism.

Here again in variant form was a revival of the ecclesiastical state in the sense of an entire society operating under the law of God.

Servetus was resolved at last to stand to his watch, but was not unduly confident of his resolution and requested that he might die by the sword lest in the extremity of his anguish he should recant and lose his soul.[20] The request was denied. But he was not deprived of the consolations of religion and of the opportunity to repent up to the very last. Farel, who happened to be in Geneva, served as the minister of the gospel who should accompany the criminal to the stake. Perhaps he would find the task less distasteful than Calvin, whose desire to mitigate the penalty seemed to Farel too soft.[21]

From Farel's pen we have this account of the *via dolorosa*:

On the way to the stake, when some brethren urged him to confess freely his fault and repudiate his errors, he said that he suffered unjustly and prayed that God would forgive his accusers. I said to him at once, "Do you justify yourself when you have sinned so fearfully? If you continue I will not go with you another step, but will leave you to the judgment of God. I intended to go along and ask everybody to pray for you, hoping that you would edify the people. I did not wish to leave you until you should draw the last breath." Then he stopped and said nothing more of the sort. He asked forgiveness for his errors, ignorance and sins, but never made a full confession. He often prayed with us while we were exhorting, and asked the spectators several times to pray the Lord for him. But we could not get him openly to admit his errors and confess that Christ is the eternal Son of God.[22]

The account of the end is from an anonymous source hostile to Calvin.[23] We are told that Servetus was led to a pile of wood still green. A crown of straw and leaves sprinkled with sulphur was placed upon his head. His body was attached to the stake with an iron chain. His book was tied to his arm. A stout rope was wound four or five times about his neck. He asked that it should not be further twisted. When the executioner brought the fire before his face he gave such a shriek that all the people were horror-stricken. As he lingered, some threw on wood. In a fearful wail he cried, "O Jesus, Son of the Eternal God, have pity on me!" At the end of half an hour he died.

Farel noted that Servetus might have been saved by shifting the position of the adjective and confessing Christ as the Eternal Son rather than as the Son of the Eternal God. That expiring cry was therefore one last gesture of defiance to man and confession to God.

Yet the purpose of this recital has not been to recount one more example of integrity unbroken, of which in our own day we have seen so many noble examples. The point is rather that the execution of Michael Servetus posed the question of religious liberty for the evangelical churches in an unprecedented manner. Murmurs of criticism so speedily reached Calvin that in the following year he issued his *Defense of the Orthodox Trinity Against the Errors of Michael Servetus.* In that same year the dissent became vocal in a work issued anonymously at Basel with the title *Concerning Heretics and Whether They Should be Punished by the Sword of the Magistrate.* We now know this work to have been in part compiled, in part composed, by Sébastien Castellion. Again in that same year Théodore de Bèze on Calvin's behalf replied to Castellion and he in turn penned a response to Calvin's *Defense* in a tract entitled *Against Calvin's Book.* Publication of this refutation was denied during Castellion's lifetime, and not until half a century after his death did it appear in the

---

Farel's Account on the Title Page of His Copy of De Trinitatis Erroribus
(see illustration opposite):

Praeter antiquos auctores Oecolampadius in suis epistolis ac alii in hanc scripserunt non sanam opinionem, sancta pure sunt colenda, non ita impure tractanda. Nullis piorum scriptis haereticus abduci potuit, sed semper magis ac magis erravit, demum cum maximo in Deum contumeliosa scripsisset, ac typis mandaret scripta tam sacrilega, capitur Viennae et morti et igni adiudicatus ope et consilio eorum qui athei sunt, carcares evasit, et Genevam sese contulit, ubi agnitus captus iterum fuit, sua impia dogmata fassus, vera voluit asserere; Scripturis victus, sese ad contumelias pro rationibus conuersus, tanto superior fuit conuitijs, quanto pii rationibus et Scripturis superiores haeretico Serueto fuerunt. Collecta fuere in unum omnia tum a piis, tum a Serueto dicta, et per senatum Genevensem ad Helueticas Ecclesias missa, quarum calculis damnatus Servetus cum suis haeresibus per senatum igni iussus est viuus exuri 27 octobris 1553. Satanas tam selecto se videns priuatum ministro, suos armauit tam amantes reipublicae christianae et tam bene consulentes, quam fuit Satanas ipse primae mulieris, ac quam bene illi consuluit. Cum non possent Serueti causam tueri, licet ipsum in eo haberent ordine quo seipsos ducunt, cum satis norint si patefacerent quae sentiunt, fern nulla possent ratione, ideo celant, nec nisi inter se mussitant, non tamen omnia, et quamvis sibi placeant in absurdissimis, tamen et Deo non credunt, nec iudicant Deum opem ipsis laturum si proponant quae norunt, et damnant iudicium de Serveto pronunciatum. Scripserunt haereticos non plectendos esse. Sed Calvinus prius ita scripserat de tota causa ut constet nihil aequius vmquam in sontem pronunciatum fuisse. Vnde coacti fuere Servetiani pro Serveto agere non aperte, nec nomine eius doctrinam tam impiam attingere, sed tantum in genere pro haereticis. Et non sunt veriti scribere, nihil innocentius haereticis. Sed tam improbos pro dignitate excepit Beza, causam veritatis tutatus potenter. Et futilia tela hostium utcumque fucis aculeis vana prorsus reddidit.

DE TRINI-
TATIS ERRORIBVS
LIBRI SEPTEM.

Per Michaelem Serueto, alias
Reues ab Aragonia
Hispanum.

Anno M. D. XXXI.

Farel's Account on the Title Page of His Copy of De Trinitatis Erroribus

Netherlands. Here his influence was persistent, and here thoroughgoing religious liberty was first achieved.

The story of Calvin and Servetus should demonstrate for us that our slogans of liberty need continually to be thought through afresh. The severity of Calvin was born of zeal for truth and even concern for the victim. Death itself seemed to him not too harsh a penalty for perversion of the truth of God. Today any of us would be the first to cast a stone against Calvin's intolerance; and seldom do we reflect that we who are aghast at the burning of one man to ashes for religion do not hesitate for the preservation of our culture to reduce whole cities to cinders.

The Place of Execution at Champel

Appendix A

An Account of the Death of Servetus

Historia Mortis Serveti (1554)

Translated from the Latin by Alexander Gordon

At the time when Michael Servetus caused his books on the Trinity[a] to be printed at Vienne, there was a certain Lyonese[b] living at Geneva, who wrote letters to a Lyonese friend of his[c] living at Lyons; in which letters, among other things, he made the following statement: "We cherish no heretics; whereas you tolerate among you Michael Servetus, a man most heretical, who is getting books printed, full of errors; and this man is now at Vienne, in such a house," &c. From the similarity of the style, those who have seen these letters think they were written by Calvin, and that the Lyonese had not sufficient power of language to be able to write with so much point. The Lyonese himself said, indeed, that they were his own productions. In any case, they were skillfully sent, in such a way (according to our information from those who have themselves seen these letters) as to arrive at the hands of the magistracy, and thereby of Cardinal Turonius[d] himself. Some say that Calvin personally wrote direct to the Cardinal[e] to this effect: "Were you as zealous for religion as you pretend to be, you would not tolerate Servetus, who is among you," &c. Be this as it may, when these letters were read, Servetus was made prisoner at Vienne, and likewise the printer[f] of said book.

Originally published in *Christian Life*, November 2, 1878. Footnotes are those of Alexander Gordon.

[a] *Christianismi Restitutio*, which opens with five Books and two Dialogues on the Trinity.

[b] Guillaume Trie.

[c] Antoine Arneys.

[d] François de Tournon.

[e] Bolsec even alleges that the Cardinal's secretary, de Gaure, had shown him the letter.

[f] Balthasar Arnoullet.

Subsequently, having furtively escaped from prison, he came to Geneva, and on the very same day, namely, Sunday,[a] he heard sermon after dinner. As he sat there, along with others, before sermon began, he was recognised by certain persons,[b] who at once went to convey the news to Calvin. Calvin immediately laid information, or caused information to be laid, before the magistracy, for them to fetch Servetus to prison for heresy. The magistracy made answer that a man could not be arrested in their free city, unless there were some one as prosecutor, who should present himself to be imprisoned, &c., along with the accused. Calvin put in the name of a domestic of his who would give himself up as prosecutor. This domestic[c] was formerly cook to a certain noble, named Falesius,[d] and Calvin formerly held this Falesius in such esteem for his religious zeal, as to laud him to the skies in a certain epistle. But subsequently, when Falesius appeared to favour a certain physician, named Hieronymus[e] (who was detained in prison about the affair of Predestination, since he had dissented on that point), by Calvin he was condemned[f] in the public congregation as a heretic. The domestic, who gave himself up as prosecutor, is sent there by this same Calvin. Servetus, called out from sermon, and having confessed his name, was thrown into prison, and likewise Calvin's domestic too, who soon after,[g] having given sureties, was set at liberty. Servetus was held so closely in prison that no one, unless a person of great authority, could get access to him; except, indeed, he were a friend of Calvin.

On the arrest of Servetus, a messenger was despatched[h] by the magistracy to Vienne, to bring back the sentence passed on Servetus by the Viennese. The Viennese supplied the messenger with this, and added the following intelligence: that Servetus had fallen into the hands of the Viennese owing to a cue furnished by the chief preacher of the Genevese. Having brought back the sentence,[i] the messenger was des-

---

[a] 13th August, 1553.

[b] The Geneva Pastors' Register says *par quelsque frères*, i.e., ministers.

[c] Nicolas de la Fontaine.

[d] Jacques de Bourgogne, Seigneur de Falais et de Bredam.

[e] Jérome Bolsec.

[f] *judicatus*, perhaps we ought to read *indicatus*, pointed out.

[g] 15th August.

[h] 22nd August.

[i] 31st August.

patched[a] to the Swiss Churches, Berne, Zürich, Schaffhausen, and Basle, taking Servetus' book, the articles of accusation drawn up the preachers, and letters from the Genevan magistracy to the ministers of those Churches, or to the magistrates, asking their opinions respecting Servetus. Meantime, one Thomas, a domestic of Robert Stephanus,[b] was despatched[c] to Frankfort, who, to prevent their distribution, burnt the stock of Servetus' books, which had been forwarded there for the Fair. The other messenger brought back[d] letters from the preachers of the said Churches, in which Servetus was condemned as a heretic. Accordingly, the Genevan magistracy was immediately[e] called together on this business of Servetus.

Amadaeus Gorrius,[f] the head of the military force, and at the same time first Syndic of the city, as he saw the minds of the senators inclined to the slaughter of the man, refused to be present at the judgment, and said he would not be partaker in his blood. Some others did the same; the rest gave sentence, but not all alike; some were for banishment, some for perpetual imprisonment; the majority were for burning, unless he were willing to recant. They say that Cellarius, too, chief professor of theology in that city,[g] never gave his consent to the death of Servetus, or of any other heretic. The same is also thought respecting some inferior ministers of the city, who on that account were not called upon to deliver their opinion concerning Servetus.

So he was led to the tribunal, and there condemned to be burned, and reduced to ashes. When he heard this sentence, in suppliant attitude he pleads with the magistracy that he might be allowed to perish by the sword, lest they should drive him to desperation by the greatness of the agony, and so he should lose his soul; that if he had committed any sin, he had sinned in ignorance; that, indeed, he was so constituted in mind and will as to long to promote the glory of God. These entreaties of his, Farel laid more explicitly before the magistracy. But the magistracy

---

[a] 21st September.

[b] The famous printer, then living at Geneva.

[c] 27th August.

[d] 20th October.

[e] 23rd October.

[f] Amy Perrin.

[g] Martin Borrhaus; but he was never professor at Geneva; he died rector of the High School at Basle.

turned a deaf ear to the prayer of Servetus. So Servetus was led away, exclaiming ever and anon: "O God, keep my soul! O Jesus, Son of God Eternal, have mercy on me!" When they arrived at the place of execution,[a] he fell on his face in prayer, and lay some time thus stretched out, Farel addressing the populace in these words: "Ye see what force hath Satan, when he taketh possession of anyone. This man is a scholar of the first rank, and deemed perchance that he was acting rightly; but now is he possessed of the devil; the very same fate might have overtaken one of you." Meanwhile, when Servetus rose, Farel continued exhorting him to make some declaration. He, with groans and sighs, kept on crying: "O God! O God!" When Farel asked, had he nothing else to say, he replied: "What else can I speak, save of God?" On Farel advising him that, if he had wife or children, and wished to make a will, there was a notary present, he gave no response.

So he was led to the pile of logs. There were, moreover, green oaken faggots, still in leaf, and sticks heaped together with the logs. Servetus was placed upon a stump set on the ground, his feet hanging down to touch the earth. On his head was placed a wreath of straw or leaves, and this was sprinkled with sulphur. His body was bound to a stake with an iron chain; his neck to the same with a thick rope, loosely folded four or five times round; his book bound to his thigh. He prayed the executioner not to let him be in torment long. Meanwhile, the executioner flourished the fire in his face, and then whirled round the flame. At the sight of the fire, the man raised a cry so dreadful as to terrify the whole populace. As he languished long, there were some of the bystanders who threw faggots, to thicken the pile. He, exclaiming with a dreadful sound: "Jesu, Son of God Eternal, have mercy on me!" breathed his last, after an agony of about half an hour. There are persons who affirm that Calvin, when he beheld Servetus led to execution, smiled, dropping his face quietly down to the breast of his robe.

This affair troubled many pious people, and produced a terrible scandal, which it scarcely seems possible ever to wipe off; for in this deed the pious blame many things as criminal.

First, that at Geneva a man was put to death for religion. For they say that no one ought to be put to death for religion; and when the Old Testament passage about killing the false prophets is cited, they quote

---

[a] Champel.

the New Testament on not rooting out the tares till the harvest. If anyone pleads that the Swiss Churches gave their consent to the death of Servetus, they reply that these were not in a position to act as judges, inasmuch as they were defendants in the cause. For Servetus brought his charge of false doctrine against these, as well as against the Genevan Church. Moreover, they are surprised that Calvin conspired against another's life with those very Churches whose doctrines in other respects he condemned. For in his French tract on the Supper he openly condemns Zwingli and Oecolampadius, along with Luther, and says they were in error. But if they were in error in regard to the Supper, they may also be in error in regard to persecution.

The next point is that he was put to death by Calvin's exertions. For he, that he might crush his private enemy, suborned a prosecutor from his own kitchen, a man grossly ignorant of Servetus and of Servetan questions. Now, this, they say, is a procedure as wide apart from the spirit of Christ as earth is from heaven; for Christ came not to destroy, but to save.

The third point is that he was put to death in so cruel a manner, when yet he piteously entreated to be cut off by the sword. This unheard-of cruelty might beget a suspicion of Genevese willingness to return into favour with the Pope, and to demonstrate in act they have no such great abhorrence of him, let their opposition to him in words be as furious as it may.

Fourthly, that Evangelicals entered into a conspiracy with Papists to put him to death. Hence there are those who think that the friendship struck up between these parties resembles that struck up between Pilate and Herod in the matter of the execution of Christ.

The fifth point is that Servetus' books were burned; a trick which (like some others) they seemed to have learned from the Pope. And, indeed, if Calvin's doctrine concerning Predestination and Election is true, there was no ground for fearing that Servetus might lead anyone astray, seeing that the Elect cannot be seduced. Moreover, if sins are committed through necessity, and by a Divine compulsion, Servetus could not act otherwise than he did; nor could Calvinists avoid being deceived by him, if it was to be that they were to be deceived; or, on the other hand, become deceived by him, if it was to be that they were not to be deceived.

The sixth criminal point is that Servetus, after he was dead, was in addition publicly damned in sermons to eternal torment; and damned in such terms that those who heard Farel thundering out the sentence say that a shudder ran through their whole body and soul.

The seventh criminal point is that Calvin appears to be engaged in writing against him, now that he is extinguished, which seems like that act of the Jews, who, when Christ was dead, besought Pilate (calling Christ an impostor) that his corpse might be watched. So, says Calvin, he is afraid, not that Servetus' body may furtively be removed (Calvin's diligence has seen well to it that this cannot be), but that his ashes may speak. Otherwise, if he wished to write against him, it was his duty to write in the man's lifetime, so that he might have power of reply, a right which is accorded even to a cutpurse.

Roland Bainton, Honored Heretic

Roland Bainton knew what it meant to hold an unpopular belief. In 1917 he was a pacifist while almost all around him, including his fellow students and the faculty at the Yale Divinity School, were caught up in the war frenzy. The Dean declared that those students who did not enlist were "morally deficient." While some of his peers devised an accommodation between their anti-German feeling and the Chistian imperative to "love your enemies," Bainton knew that he could not work such a compromise. "I cannot say, 'Christianity does not approve of war. I do approve of war. I am still a Christian.' I must give up one or the other. I can't choose the army and the ministry too."[1]

Because he stood firm in his Christian pacifism, Bainton faced social ostracism and other penalties. A friend convinced him to refrain from submitting an anti-war article to the *Atlantic*, telling him that he might be arrested for sedition. Rather than be interned as a conscientious objector, Bainton volunteered to serve as a relief worker with the American Friends Service Committee in France. Following the war, he remained in France, helping to resettle the interned French, distributing food and clothing, and rebuilding destroyed villages. While thus occupied, he came up with a goal for his life. "I wanted to do something toward the reconciliation of peoples," he later wrote. "Might not a form of scholarship embracing all the lands of the West help, in a measure, to break down the walls of partition? And not only the walls of partition between nations, but also between churches?"[2]

Bainton's self-preparation for this international mission was already well underway. He had been born in England, lived for four years in Canada, and had moved to the United States with his family when eight years old. His father, James Herbert Bainton, an anti-war Independent

Dissenter in Britain who came to America as a Congregationalist missionary, arranged for his young son to be tutored in German and classical languages.[3] Roland pursued classics further at Whitman College in Walla Walla, Washington (1910-14) and specialized in Semitics and Hellenistic Greek as a graduate student at Yale (1917-21). In New Haven he did ministry field work for his Bachelor of Divinity degree in the Italian community, learning to speak and preach in Italian. While serving in France he learned to appreciate French culture, acquiring the language as well. Immediately after the war, while doing research for his thesis in Switzerland, he learned to read Syriac and to read and speak German.[4] He would eventually be able to lecture in French, German, Italian, and Spanish as well as English.

His religion had become polyglot as well. The Italian community amongst whom Bainton served as a student minister were Waldensians, descendants of a movement that had split with the Roman Catholic church prior to the Reformation. During the war he attended Mass with the French and with German prisoners.[5] With the Service Committee work he had begun a lifelong association with the Quakers. He would soon develop a close relationship with Mennonite historians and other scholars in the many churches descended from the Radical Reformation. One of these, Harold Bender, called Bainton the first historian outside their tradition to describe the Reformation Anabaptists sympathetically.[6] For his popular biography of Luther, *Here I Stand*, Lutherans later adopted him. His books were published by Catholic, Methodist, and Unitarian publishing houses. Finding less to divide Christians at the liberal end of the spectrum than at the more conservative end, he enjoyed fellowship with open-minded religious folk across denominational lines.[7]

At Yale Bainton absorbed modern Biblical criticism, which, as he wrote, combined "the breastplate of erudition and the helmet of piety."[8] In his letters home to his father Bainton early showed a propensity to doubt received doctrine. He explained his reasons for wishing to disbelieve in the virgin birth. First, "if Jesus was only a Jewish peasant, the lowliest and most ignorant perhaps of the earth, and was yet able to see the heart of God and live as the perfect son of God, how great are the possibilities of our humanity!" Secondly, "I do not wish to posit a miracle or even a metaphysical character as an explanation of a spiritual miracle . . . I wish to believe that a spiritual miracle may take place in the heart of any man."[9]

On a later occasion, when he was representing "Modernism" in a debate with a Fundamentalist, the rules were laid down that each speaker was to begin with a presentation of a sympathetic account of the other's position. "I spoke first," Bainton recalled, "and said that the infallible Bible was during the Reformation a bulwark against papal infallibility, and against skepticism today. My opponent then affirmed that the first Modernist was the serpent, who insinuated a doubt into the mind of Eve. I replied that the second was the Virgin Mary who, when the angel told her she would bear a son, asked how this could be, thus showing a spirit of critical inquiry."[10]

After the war, Bainton was offered a position teaching Greek and New Testament at the Yale Divinity School. After he had taught New Testament for a term, he began to have doubts about the value of the subject. "We have not enough material to be positive of what Jesus really thought about the most important matters," he wrote to his father. "Consequently the New Testament can never again be for us an absolute authority." And he wondered what ministers in parish practice could do with New Testament criticism and source analysis. Given his own questioning of the resurrection, he doubted that he was the right person to direct his students how to "return to their constituencies" and "wrestle with the problem of how to shed light without extinguishing the candles." He also found himself in trouble with his colleagues at Yale for his dissent from their views. "Don't be too iconoclastic," James Bainton advised his son, "but if you must, let the idols be smashed with as much tenderness and reverence as possible. Truth is so hard to come by that it ill becomes us to become too dogmatic and censorious of opinions opposed to our own."[11]

When an opening became available in 1923, Bainton readily transferred his efforts to teaching Church History. He was able to present this more congenial material in a lively and humorous way that captured his students' imaginations. So successful was he in the new field that he was appointed associate professor in 1932 and in 1936 Titus Street Professor of Church History.[12]

What interested Bainton most in religious history was the issue of liberty of conscience. He wished to understand the problem of coercion and resistance from both sides. "To find an answer," he wrote, "one must understand both the persecuted and the persecutor: the one is not a saint, nor is the other a scoundrel. Both are intensely sincere. The anomaly is that so often the saints persecute the saints: the one who will die for an idea will also kill for it."[13]

Bainton elected to inaugurate his scholarly career in Church History with a study of four men – Michael Servetus, Bernard Ochino, David Joris, and Sébastien Castellion – who had fled Catholic persecution and sought refuge in Switzerland, where they all, in various ways, came into conflict with the Protestant authorities. Until 1926 he pursued this research at Yale, but by that time he had exhausted the sources available locally. With a Guggenheim fellowship he then took a sabbatical trip to England, France, the Netherlands, Italy, and Switzerland. He found additional materials for his study of Servetus at the British Museum in London, the Bibliothèque Nationale in Paris, and at Geneva.[14]

At the British Museum Bainton copied whole volumes of Latin text using a portable typewriter. There he met the elderly Unitarian scholar Alexander Gordon (1841-1931), a prolific writer for the *Dictionary of National Biography,* who considered the study of Servetus one of his special provinces. Gordon had written a major essay on Servetus in 1878, translated into English the important document *Historia mortis Serveti* (c. 1554), and had recently contributed numerous articles on specific aspects of Servetus's life and thought to the Unitarian newspaper, *Christian Life.*[15] He was fluent in more languages than Bainton then knew, was a stern critic of what he deemed poor scholarship, and had a reputation for being gruff and distant. Bainton recorded in his memoir, "While at work, Gordon would put his hat beside him on the desk with the rim uppermost; I looked into the crown and read 'NOT YOURS.' But he was not really crusty."[16]

At the Bibliothèque Nationale in Paris, Bainton studied one of the three surviving original copies of Servetus's *Christianismi Restitutio.* He consulted numerous journal articles on Servetus unavailable in the United States, running into bureaucratic trouble when he asked for too many articles at once. Minister of Education Ferdinand Buisson, a Castellion scholar, pulled some strings for him so that he could look at the journals by the armload. He recalled that "from the larger part I could extract the pertinent portion in fifteen minutes."[17] One French scholar told him that "Calvinism could only be tolerant after it was well established. But if someone like Servetus had been tolerated at the outset, Calvin's whole endeavor to erect the kingdom of God would have collapsed." Bainton answered, "Tant pis" – "Tough!"[18]

The result of this research was not the single book he had planned, but four, one on each of his subjects. The books on Castellion, Joris, and Ochino came out during the six years immediately before the United

States entered the Second World War. The first, *Concerning Heretics: Whether They Are to Be Persecuted and How They Are to Be Treated* (1935) was a translation of Castellion's *De haereticis* (1554) and excerpts of other works by Castellion and Joris. Castellion had gathered opinions on the subject by many earlier authors; Bainton contributed introductory material on all these writers that surpassed the translations in length.[19]

His next book, *David Joris: Wiedertäufer und Kämpfer für Toleranz in 16. Jahrhundert* (1937), although written in English, was translated into German by Hajo and Annemarie Holborn, two recent immigrants from Germany. They did this in exchange for having Bainton translate into English Hajo Holborn's *Ulrich von Hutten and the German Reformation* (1937). All but a few copies of *David Joris* were destroyed in the bombing of Leipzig. The third book was issued in Italian as *Bernadino Ochino, Esule e Riformatore Senese del Cinquecento* (1941). These three works, on the eve of war, brought Bainton friendship with scholars in countries soon to be hostile to his own.[20]

In preparation for his work on Servetus, Bainton wrote three articles: "The Smaller Circulation: Servetus and Colombo" (1931); "Servetus and the Genevan Libertines" (1936), which eventually became a draft for chapter 9 of *Hunted Heretic*; and the most important of the three, "The Present State of Servetus Studies" (1932). "Present State" served both as a general survey of the Servetus literature at that time and as a blueprint for the proposed book, for in it Bainton discussed the various sources, primary and secondary, on a topic by topic – virtually chapter by chapter – basis.[21]

"Present State" made clear the need for a modern book-length biography of Servetus in English – or in any language. The most prolific Servetus scholar, Henri Tollin (1833-1902), had produced only articles and specialized studies. Tollin's work amounted to seventy-five items, which Bainton carefully catalogued and numbered in the bibliography at the end of his article. But Tollin had not lived long enough to produce the great biography for which he had long been preparing himself. The only substantial works of Tollin's disciples Charles Dardier and Alexander Gordon on the subject of Servetus were, in fact, long book reviews. The book that drew their fire was Robert Willis's *Servetus and Calvin* (1877). Dardier and Gordon castigated Willis, a retired physician, for his misreading of and disdain for theology, Servetus's main preoccupation.[22] Bainton agreed, and regretted that Willis's book was unfortunately "the only comprehensive account of the trial in English."[23]

The most recent major work that Bainton respected, Antonius van der Linde's *Michel Servet, Een Brandoffer der Gereformeerde Inquisite* (1891), was then over forty years old. There were in the 1930s only a handful working in the field. Gordon had died the year before "Present State" was published. The aging American Unitarian scholar Earl Morse Wilbur (1866-1956) was preparing to include a study of Servetus in a projected history, but some worried that he would not live to complete the task.[24]

In the 1930s, on the invitation of John Farquhar Fulton, Sterling Professor of Physiology, Bainton lectured students at the Yale Medical School on Servetus's discovery of pulmonary circulation. "My contribution was to make the medical historians aware that Servetus was prompted to engage in dissection by his theology: believing that the soul is in the blood, he set out to discover how blood circulated."[25]

By 1938, work on the Servetus biography had progressed to the point that Bainton thought it nearly finished and tried unsuccessfully to raise the money from Yale for its publication. He already considered it a complete work in January 1940 when he wrote to his friend, the Italian scholar Delio Cantimori, that "Servetus still lies in manuscript."[26] The coming of the Second World War delayed Bainton's publication plans further.

Before the United States entered the war, Bainton co-wrote (with Robert Calhoun) a pamphlet, *Christian Conscience and the State* (1940), recommending changes to the recently-adopted procedures governing conscientious objection. Bainton and Calhoun thought that conscientious objector status should not be tied to membership in certain churches, that these cases ought to be regulated by civil and not military courts, and that exemptions should grant freedom from military service of any kind, not just combat. Bainton later inspected alternative-service camps for conscientious objectors.[27]

During the period of fascist repression of minorities and intellectuals and during the ensuing war, Bainton was preoccupied with tracking the fates of, and aiding when possible, Reformation scholars in Germany, Italy, and occupied Europe. He sent food to Cantimori and helped bring to America endangered Jewish scholars such as Elisabeth Feist (Hirsch) and Paul Oscar Kristeller.[28] He led a Quaker committee to relocate academic refugees. "I recall that for one person I wrote one hundred letters, received ten replies and one job. Enough!"[29]

After the United States declared war on Japan and Germany, Bainton lamented, "The chance of removing more refugees is gone. The possibility of feeding the invaded democracies is probably eliminated." His own plan at that time was not to promote the doctrine of pacifism – that would not be heard kindly – but to "speak constantly a word for the preservation of friendships with individuals in 'enemy' countries." He "pleaded for faith in the common man in all lands." Moreover, he asked that the United States "should not adopt the barbarous methods of our opponents." He drafted a joint article, co-signed by other scholars and printed in the *Christian Century*, asking for a just peace by negotiation rather than imposition, a halt to the internment of Japanese Americans, and the end of American racial discrimination. He felt that only in this way could Americans show themselves sincere in their objection to Nazi intolerance, and ready to deal with their enemies as human beings.[30]

In 1948, on a visit to Europe sponsored by the American Friends Service Committee, Bainton was asked if peace could come about by the renunciation of war. He answered, "Peace will not come through pacifists – there have never been enough of them – but rather through peace minded non-pacifists. The role of pacifists is to bestir others to make every effort to resolve conflict without violence and also to bring reconciliation between all the contending groups within and without their own societies."[31]

Bainton's most celebrated book was intended to be part of the postwar reconciliation between the United States and Germany. During the war he was approached by a New York publisher, who asked him to write a biography of Martin Luther. The publisher's representative told him that "after the war we would like to present to the American public a great German."[32] During the eight years it took to write *Here I Stand*, 1942-50, Bainton's Servetus project remained in the drawer. It was, no doubt, subsequently enriched by his deeper understanding of Luther and his increased command of Lutheran sources.

At the close of the war, Earl Morse Wilbur completed and published the first of the eventual two volumes of his massive work, *A History of Unitarianism*. He and Bainton had long been very friendly: in the preface to volume 1, *Socinianism and Its Antecedents* (1945), Wilbur thanked his colleague for "repeated acts of kindness" and, in a footnote, directed the reader to "The Present State of Servetus Studies" for a literature review.[33] The five chapters on Servetus in Wilbur's volume 1 together form what Bainton, in his review, called "the best biography [of Servetus] now available in any tongue." He criticized Wilbur, however, for his decision not to analyze *Christianismi Restitutio*, while discussing Servetus's work on syrups. "This procedure is seriously open to question in a history of Unitarianism."[34]

In the years after *Here I Stand* (1950), Bainton's *The Travail of Religious Liberty* (1951) and *The Reformation of the Sixteenth Century* (1952) were published. *Travail,* based on a series of lectures given in 1950 at Union Theological Seminary in Richmond, Virginia, was a more popular version of the book Bainton had envisioned at the outset of his Yale career. It had chapter-length treatments of Servetus, Castellion, Joris, and Ochino, framed by biographical essays on Torquemada and Calvin, at one end, and John Milton, Roger Williams, and John Locke, at the other. The Servetus lecture was a précis of the eventual full-length biography, and like *Hunted Heretic,* ended by likening the execution of Servetus to the horrors of the Allied war effort: "We are today horrified that Geneva should have burned a man for the Glory of God, yet we incinerate whole cities for the saving of democracy."[35]

The Reformation of the Sixteenth Century became a standard work on the subject. Bainton identified a fourth strand of the Reformation – along with the Lutheran, Reformed (largely Calvinist), and Anabaptist – which he called "the free spirits." These were mystical and rationalist reformers who tended to eschew organization-building. Coming from lands like Italy and Spain, the most notable of these innovative thinkers found Protestantism "an impossible halfway house" and wished to move beyond such renewed orthodoxy without constraint upon their religious thought.[36] One such free spirit, Michael Servetus, was both a rationalist and a mystic: a rationalist because "he seized upon the acids of decadent scholasticism to corrode the doctrine which he could not find enunciated in Scripture" and a mystic because he believed that human beings could "put off humanity and acquire divinity through union with the divine man, the Son of the eternal God."[37]

The publication of *Hunted Heretic* was precipitated at last in 1953 by the quadricentennial of Servetus's death. The book was, in fact, issued on October 27, the very date that Servetus had been burned at the stake four hundred years before. Bainton's biography was one among several important publications on Servetus issued that year. Others were John F. Fulton's *Michael Servetus: Humanist and Martyr,* Charles Donald O'Malley's *Michael Servetus, a Translation of his Geographical, Medical and Astrological Writings,* Pierre Cavard's *Le procès de Michel Servet à Vienne,* and *Autour de Michel Servet et de Sébastien Castellion,* a collection of essays edited by Bruno Becker. The latter book includes an essay by Bainton,

"Michael Servetus and the Trinitarian Speculation of the Middle Ages." This essay, which was incorporated in altered form in chapter 2 of *Hunted Heretic*, was meant to partly address historian George Foote Moore's assertion, noted two decades earlier in "The Present State of Servetus Studies," that "even an intelligent misunderstanding" of Servetus's theology "requires more than a superficial acquaintance with the transient phase of philosophy to which he was addicted, and a first-hand knowledge of the history of doctrine, heresy, and controversy, from the Fathers to the Reformation."[38]

Reviews of *Hunted Heretic* (sometimes coupled with reviews of *Autour*) were generally enthusiastic. Bainton was complimented on the thoroughness of his scholarship, the clarity of his presentation, his engaging and dramatic writing style, his understated yet incisive criticism of Calvin, and his mastery of the historical background.[39] William Pauck, in two sentences from his review in *Renaissance News*, encapsulated the main themes of this chorus of praise: "No available source has been left unexplored and no phase of earlier interpretations has been overlooked. We now possess a definitive characterization of Servetus and one that is exceedingly well written and colorfully presented."

Not all reviewers were entirely satisfied. Pauck himself expressed concern that "in spite of all his care, [Bainton] has not quite succeeded in making clear the core of Servetus's strangely muddled theology."[40] In the *Journal of Modern History*, Quirinus Breen complained that "the book is too small for the subject, unless it were intended as an *apéritif*." In particular his "expectations on the influence of Florentine Platonism are not satisfied."[41] Readers introduced to Bainton's little masterpiece since the time it was published have felt the same thing: what is there is very good, but it leaves a taste for more.

A number of reviewers noted Bainton's closing sentence, comparing Calvin's burning of Servetus with the bombing of cities during the recently ended Second World War. And during the early 1950s, when many people in the United States were being denounced and blacklisted as Communists and "fellow-travelers," no one could be unaware of the still-powerful instinct for intolerance. "One trembles," wrote Raymond W. Albright in *Church History*, "at the mere thought of a modern revival of such religious and theological zeal."[42]

By the time *Hunted Heretic* came out, the pacifist Bainton was being hunted himself. Although he was not aware of it at the time, he was under investigation by the House Un-American Activities Committee (HUAC) and the Federal Bureau of Investigation (FBI). He found out afterwards that Liston Pope, Dean of the Yale Divinity School between 1949 and 1962, had received (and disregarded), throughout that period, incessant demands that Bainton be dismissed. The FBI briefly investigated a rumor that Bainton was the head of the Communist Party in Connecticut. The Christian Anti-Communist League put out a flyer in 1962, titled "The Facts about Roland Bainton." When Bainton looked into what these "facts" might be, he discovered a HUAC file going back to 1940. Among other things, he stood accused of defending freedom of speech, advocating leniency for those convicted of political crimes, opposing the death penalty, and aiding Spanish refugees. The evidence against him was that his public statements were reported favorably by the *Daily Worker* and that he had signed some petitions that Communists had also signed. Although he personally disapproved of Communism as intolerant and could not understand why his friend Cantimori belonged to the Italian Communist Party, Bainton felt that suppression of Communism was an even greater threat to liberty. "If we by loyalty to liberty should come under the heel of the tyrant," he told the National Council of Churches in 1955, "better to go down uncorrupted than ourselves be the agents in destroying our heritage of freedom."[43]

In a short article on the Servetus anniversary published the day after *Hunted Heretic*, Bainton had noted the progress that had been made towards religious liberty between the sixteenth and twentieth centuries. Although we can feel encouraged by this human achievement, he wrote, "social change is slow," and we yet have another problem, even more dangerous than intolerance – war. "If we take four hundred years to get rid of it, there may not be anybody here to enjoy the ensuing peace. The perfection of modern weapons renders imperative the acceleration of social change. Either we move faster or we perish."[44]

At the end of the 1950s, Bainton assembled a major work, *Christian Attitudes Toward War and Peace* (1960), which, like *Hunted Heretic*, was published after some three decades of preparation. Parts of the book had been presented as lectures in 1939, 1943, and 1958. As he gathered the threads of his historical thinking on the subject, he felt that, under the shadow of the atomic bomb, "the ethical problems of war and peace cry urgently for re-examination."[45] He considered the justifications for war throughout history – crusades, wars of religion, just wars – and rejected them all. He wondered what truly impartial court could ever exist that could rule any country's participation in a war just. "A war to be just must be fought in a spirit of love," he prescribed. "Those who fight in this spirit are to be found, but they are few." Finding and fighting with such virtuous warriors is not, however, a practical strategy, for "although a war may be fought in sorrowful love, it can never be won in this mood." Rejecting the illusion of the just war, Bainton placed his hopes for the maintenance of peace in a combination of Christian renunciation and secularist prudence. He felt that a national renunciation of violence had yet to be tried. "Disarmament and non-violence might revolutionize the world's behavior."[46]

Hopeful, but not optimistic, Bainton ended his book, much as he ended his speech to the National Council of Churches five years earlier, saying that it was better to be annihilated for "honor, shame, mercy and compassion," than to become "unscrupulous in order to survive." Although he devoted much of his life to celebrating the giants who took a stand and the heroes who were persecuted for truth, he did not believe that those who suffered for the truth could count on posthumous success. "As for the impact of martyrdom on public opinion, one never knows," he cautioned. "The scaffold may sway the future, but it may also be buried in oblivion."[47]

Besides his religious connection with the Quakers, and his bond of sympathy with the Mennonites, Hutterites, Brethren, and other pacifist churches descended from the Radical Reformation, Bainton belonged to and served in leadership positions in several non-denominational peace organizations, including the War Resisters League, the Fellowship of Reconciliation, and Promoting Enduring Peace.[48] Because of his contributions to the cause of peace, in 1979 he was awarded the Gandhi Prize.[49] Modest himself, he had earlier noted that when Henry Cadbury, a friend of his, went to Oslo to receive a Nobel Prize for Peace on behalf of the Quakers, Cadbury said, "When the world speaks well of us, that is the time to tremble."[50]

During the 1960s Bainton wrote a number of textbooks on church history and a substantial history of Christianity (which he wrote in bed while recovering from falling off his roof while trying to install a television antenna.)[51] Many of his articles and addresses were gathered together and issued in his three-volume *Collected Papers in Church History*. His major piece of new scholarship was *Erasmus of Christendom* (1969). In his memoir he recalled that his biographies of Luther and Erasmus were influenced by the times in which they emerged: "'Luther' was written in the Joseph McCarthy era, when the great word needed was 'Here I Stand.' But the 'Erasmus' was done while student unrest was rampant and disorganizing the universities, and the proper word then was "Come now, let us reason together."[52]

Bainton had married Ruth Mae Woodruff, whom he had first met at Whitman College, in 1921. Ruth was originally Baptist, then joined the Quakers. The Baintons' five children grew up to be Methodist, Congregational, Presbyterian, Quaker, and Unitarian.[53] Roland was very conscious of his marriage being, among other things, a partnership. In 1957 he wrote a small book, *What Christianity Says about Sex, Love, and Marriage*, telling the history of Christian marriage. He outlined three attitudes — sacramental, romantic, and companionable — each coming into flower in a different era, each contributing an essential ingredient to what he saw as a good marriage, "a union which commences in mutual love and loyalty to God and continues in lifelong fidelity and common labor in the work of the Lord."[54] In 1966 Ruth died after suffering several years with cancer. Three of Bainton's later works, the volumes he wrote on women in the Reformation (1971, 1973, 1977), were dedicated to her memory.[55]

Later in life Bainton broadened his horizons geographically and culturally from the international but still Eurocentric focus with which he had started. With Ruth, who had before marriage wanted to be a missionary, he had toured South America (producing a book of lectures on religious toleration in Spanish) and in her last days they took a brief trip to Africa. On his own, he traveled to Japan, India, the Middle East, and Eastern Europe, all of which served to broaden his sense of the cross-cultural dialogue necessary to hold Christianity, and the world, together.

Bainton died early in 1984. He had had a long career as a scholar and a brilliant communicator, both in the classroom and in print. Gregory I. Jackson wrote, "The labors of Bainton have given America scores of energetic and tolerant historians."[56] Among those who knew him, he left a lasting impression, as a convivial personality, an inveterate bicyclist, and a teacher who brought the thought of the past into effective conversation with the people (not just the scholars) of the present. One Lutheran minister told me that, preaching at a Lutheran church, Bainton gave the best exposition of Luther's doctrine of the Lord's Supper that he had ever heard. "The scholar, the writer, the poet, the preacher are all obliged to reach the people," Bainton said.[57]

Having studied religious leaders and exemplars throughout church history, and having developed a deep appreciation and even affection for many of them, Bainton had his own vision of a Christianity that transcended the knowledge of Calvin and the faith of Luther. Something akin to the justifying love that Servetus expressed in his most profound moments, Bainton's Christianity was a religion of deeds, compassion, universal fraternity, sacrifice, and courage. Using his incisive reason, he thought for himself, doubted much, and came to few firm theological conclusions. But this he knew: how a Christian should act and what a Christian should stand for. He told the history of the past crises that led to the growth of religious toleration and liberty, hoping that we might learn the lessons that would lead away from suspicion and warfare to mutual discovery, friendship, and peace. He cried out for peace with a prophetic voice. He lived the words of Luther, "Here I stand, I cannot do otherwise," and the words of the apostle Paul, that sent Servetus out of hiding to present the world a vision of Christianity restored: "Woe to me if I do not preach the gospel!"

Chronology

1509-1511

Born at Villanueva de Sijena, Spain[1]

1524-1526

Service with Quintana when 14 or 15[2]

1528-1529

Student at Toulouse[3]

1529

July 29   Leaves Toulouse in the train of Quintana and the Emperor[4]

1530

February 24   Witnesses coronation in Bologna[5]

July   In Basel; stays 10 months

Guest of Oecolampadius "a long time"[6]

1531

May   Goes to Strassburg

Persuades Setzer to print *De Trinitatis Erroribus* at Hagenau[7]

July   *De Trinitatis Erroribus* on sale

Again in Basel[8]

1532

In either Lyons or Paris (testified at Vienne that he went to Paris, studied at the college of Calvi, then read mathematics at the college of the Lombards, afterwards went to Lyons; testified at Geneva that he went to Lyons, then to Paris)[11]

Dialogorum Duo printed at Hagenau

April   Aleandro's report on *De Trinitatis Erroribus*

May 24   Inquisition at Zaragoza takes action[9]

June 17   Decree for his apprehension at Toulouse[10]

1533

In Paris, studying at College of Calvi

1534

Fails in rendezvous with Calvin in Paris[12]
In Lyons as editor and corrector of proof for publishing house of Melchior and Gaspard Trechsel

1535

Edition of Ptolemy printed at Lyons

1536

In Leonardum Fuchsium Apologia printed at Lyons

1537

Studying medicine at the University of Paris[13]
Syruporum Universa Ratio printed at Paris

1538

February 12	Observes an eclipse of Mars at Paris[14]
Feb.-March	*Apologetica Disceptatio pro Astrologia* printed at Paris
March 18	Hearing before the Parlement *re* judicial astrology[15]
March 24	Matriculation at the University of Paris[16]
Summer	Residence at Charlieu

1538-1541

At Charlieu for 2 or 3 years[17]

1541

Living at Lyons[18]
February 14   Signs contract to edit Bible in 6 volumes[19]
Second edition of Ptolemy printed at Lyons

1542

Practicing medicine at Vienne
Pagnini Bible and an octavo Bible printed at Lyons[20]

1545

August 20   Completion of the Bible in seven volumes[21]
Reprint of *Syruporum* at Venice

1546-1547

Reprints of *Syruporum* at Lyons
Correspondence with Calvin
Manuscript of *Christianismi Restitutio* sent to Calvin[22]

1548

Reprint of *Syruporum* at Lyons

1551

Arnoullet and Gueroult establish a press at Vienne

1552

September 29   Printing of *Christianismi Restitutio* begun on St. Michael's day

1553

January 3   Printing of *Christianismi Restitutio* completed[23]

February 26   First letter of Guillaume Trie exposing Servetus[24]

Mar. 16-Apr. 6   Trial in Vienne

April 4   Imprisoned in Vienne

April 7   Escapes from prison

June 17   Found guilty (in absentia) by civil tribunal in Vienne

August 13   Recognized and arrested in Geneva[25]

Aug. 14-Sept. 1   Trial in Geneva

September 2-5   Written discussion with Calvin

September 21   Genevan Council writes to Swiss cities

October 27   Sentence and execution

December 23   Posthumous sentence of ecclesiastical court at Vienne[26]

Notes

Chapter 1
Dog of a Marrano

[1] See Chronology, note 1.

[2] [Bainton did not mention the controversy that existed, and continues to exist, between proponents of two towns in Spain which both claim to be Servetus's birthplace. The other candidate is Tudela in Navarre. Since the eighteenth-century discovery of the records of the trial at Vienne, some scholars have believed the answer Servetus gave the Inquisition there: that he was born at Tudela. Among these are Henri Tollin, Charles Dardier, Alexander Gordon, Earl Morse Wilbur, John Fulton, Charles O'Malley, George Huntston Williams, and Francisco González Echeverría. Ranged on the other side, among many others, are Albert Rilliet, Émile Saisset, Robert Willis, Mariano de Paño, Benet Barrios, William Osler, Émile Doumerge, Roland Bainton, Claudio Manzoni, Ángel Alcalá, and Marian Hillar.

Servetus gave Tudela as his birthplace on three recorded occasions while living in France: in 1538 to the University of Paris, in 1548 in the course of becoming a naturalized French citizen, and finally while answering the Inquisition in 1553. On the other side, his early works, written before his long French sojourn, were signed "Michaelem Servetum alias Revés, ab Aragonia hispanum." When on trial in Geneva, he claimed to be from Villaneuva in Aragon. There has also been much research showing that the family of Servetus was long established in Villaneuva.

If he was born in Aragon, why did Servetus so often claim to be from Navarre? The answer that has been proposed by Ángel Alcalá is this: just as Servetus assumed a new name while living in France, so he invented a whole new background to go with this name. He could no longer be Aragonese, but he could not hope to be considered truly French either. So in order to assist his assimilation into French culture, he chose to be from the part of Spain most closely associated with France. He may have chosen Tudela because he had visited there, was familiar with the place, and could plausibly talk about it as his place of origin even amongst those who might have visited there. At the

171

same time, through his choice of alias, he was covertly asserting his true birth-place. "Villeneuve" is a reference to Villanueva de Sijena, but also a legitimate French name which would not necessarily suggest a small town in Aragon to anyone in France.

It must nevertheless be allowed that, absent some conclusive evidence, there remains the remote possibility that Tudela was Servetus's actual birthplace. That throughout a whole period of his life, Michel de Villeneuve a.k.a Servetus asserted that he was born there, gives Tudela a spiritual or cultural claim to him, even if he was not physically born there. He at least adopted Tudela, and may have had good symbolic or emotional reasons for choosing it as the site of his "second birth." And, since then, Tudela has adopted him back. Thus both Tudela and Villenueva have claims to be part of Servetus's background which cannot be negated, even if in future some decisive proof emerges denying one, or indeed both, their claims to be the place of his biological birth.]

[3] These facts were first disclosed by Mariano de Pano in "La familia de Miguel Servet," *Revista de Aragón,* May 1901, 119-121, 151-153. The same ground is covered by Benet R. Barrios, with reproductions of the documents, in *Joventut* no. 198 (19 November 1903), 776f; no. 222 (12 May 1904), 297f. This is sum-marized in *La Chronique Médicale,* 15 August 1905, 556-558. Pano infers that the father died shortly after the last document, in 1538, since on May 3, 1544, the notary was Pedro de Lax.

The date on the altar is not easily legible. It may be 1548 or 1558, MDXXXXVIII or MDXXXXXVIII. [The second date seems more prob-able, given the date of the death of Servetus and the hypothesis that this altar was erected in atonement. The doubt arises from a gap after the D that may or may not once have been filled by a letter – perhaps X, C, or L. A priest of Villanueva told Ángel Alcalá that the altar may have been destroyed during the Spanish Civil War. "If the altar was there, it was burned; it no longer exists."]

[4] [See David Gonzalo Maeso, "Sobre la etimología de la voz 'marrano' (crito-judío)" *Seferad* 15 (1955), 373-385; Norman Roth, *Conversos, Inquisition, and the Expulsion of the Jews from Spain* (Madison: University of Wisconsin Press, 2002).]

[5] Marcel Bataillon, *Érasme et l'Espagne* (Paris, 1937), 180-181.

[6] Bataillon, *Érasme et l'Espagne,* 59-60. [The best work on the movement is Antonio Márquez, *Los alumbrados: orígenes y filosofía, 1525-1559* (Madrid: Taurus, 1972). See also Alastair Hamilton, *Heresy and Mysticism in Sixteenth-Century Spain: the Alumbrados* (Toronto: University of Toronto Press, 1992).]

[7] Benedetto Croce, *La Spagna nella vita italiana durante la Rinascenza* (Bari, 1917), 210-213.

[8] *Tischreden* no. 6145, in *D. Martin Luthers Werke: kritische Gesamtausgabe* (Weimar edition), Abt. 2, 5:511; Arturo Farinelli, *Marrano (storia di un vituperio)* (Geneva, 1925), 57.

[9] *Desiderii Erasmi Roterodami Opera omnia* (Louvain, 1706), 9:352-353; cf. 9:316 and the discussion in Bataillon, *Érasme et l'Espagne,* 98-102.

[10] *De Trinitatis Erroribus*, 22b.

[11] Otto Lehnhof, *Die Beichväter Karls V* (Diss. Göttingen, 1932).

[12] See Chronology, note 3.

[13] Théodore de Bèze, *Histoire ecclésiastique des églises réformées au royaume de France* (Paris, 1883-1889), 1:20.

[14] Henri Tollin, "Toulouser Studentenleben im Anfang des 16. Jahrhunderts. Eine Episode aus dem Leben Michael Servets," *Historisches Taschenbuch* 44 (1874), 77-98; Henri Tollin, "Michael Servets Toulouser Leben," *Zeitschrift für wissenschaftliche Theologie* 20 (1877), 342-386.

[15] John Charles Dawson, "University and Student Life at Toulouse in the Sixteenth Century," in *Toulouse in the Renaissance* (New York, 1923).

[16] *De Trinitatis Erroribus*, 107b; cf. 75a.

[17] *De Trinitatis Erroribus,* 79a.

[18] *Ioannis Calvini Opera quae supersunt omnia* (Corpus reformatorum), 8:780.9.

[19] See Alfred Hackel, *Die Trinität in der Kunst* (Berlin, 1931); Adolphe Napoléon Didron, *Iconographie Chrétienne* (Paris, 1843); Karl von Spiess, *Trinitätsdarstellungen mit dem Dreigesichte* (Vienna, 1914). [See also Germán de Pamplona, *Iconografía de la Santísima Trinidad en el arte medieval español* (Madrid: Consejo Superior de Investigaciones Científicas, Instituto "Diego Velázquez," 1970).]

[20] *De Trinitatis Erroribus*, 42b-43a. Servetus at this time could have found a Latin translation of the Qur'an only in manuscript. It was not until 1543 that Bibliander published at Basel the Latin translation made by Robert of Ketton (Robert of Retina) in 1143. Servetus employed the edition of Bibliander in the *Restitutio,* 35, 46, 399, and 419; cf. *Calvini Opera* 8:770.21.

Statements like the above might well be taken at second hand. Pablo de Burgos, for example, says in his *Scrutinium Scripturarum* (Mantua, 1475), 2:2.6: "In illo n. libro qui dicitur Alcharanus in quo prophana lex Machometi continetur memini me legisse quod in omnibus hominibus habuit aliquam potestatem sathan praeterquam in Jhesu et in matre eius. Ex quo constat quod etiam apud Sarracenos beata virgo reputari debet sancta."[a] [This seems to be based on a strained reading of Qur'an 3:36-37: "'I name her Mary and I commend her and her offspring to Your protection from the rejected Satan.' Her Lord graciously accepted her . . ."

More probable sources for Servetus's knowledge about the Qur'an are Ricoldo of Monte Croce, *Confutatio Alcorani*, and Nicholas of Cusa, *Cribratio Alcorani* (1461). Servetus almost certainly consulted both of these works, in the edition printed in 1543 with the Bibliander Qur'an, while working on the *Restitutio*. Both were available at the time he was writing *De Trinitatis Erroribus*:

---

[a] "In that book called the Qur'an, in which is contained the impious law of Muhammad, I remember reading that he believed that the powers of Satan extended to all human beings except Jesus and his mother. From this it is clear that, even among the Saracens, the blessed virgin must be considered holy."

the Ricoldo of Monte Croce was printed as early as 1500, and the Nicholas of Cusa in 1490, 1505, and 1514. Servetus was much more likely to have seen these books than to have had access to the Latin Qur'an in manuscript.]

For what the Qur'an has about Jesus, see M. Maass, "Bibel und Koran," *Zeitschrift für wissenschaftliche Theologie* 36 (1893), 161-220. [See also Geoffrey Parrinder, *Jesus in the Qur'an* (London: Faber and Faber, 1965); Neal Robinson, *Christ in Islam and Christianity: the representation of Jesus in the Qur'an and the classical Muslim commnetaries* (London: Macmillan, 1991). On the Qur'an in the Reformation era see Hartmut Bobzin, *Der Koran in Zeitalter der Reformation* (Stuttgart: Steiner, 1995).]

[21] *De Trinitatis Erroribus*, 56b (condensed). The reference is to David Kimhi's commentary on Psalm 2. See *The Longer Commentary of R. David Kimhi on the first book of Psalms* (London, 1919), 18-19.

[22] Bataillon, *Érasme et l'Espagne*, 249, 439.

[23] Hans Hogenberg, *The Procession of Pope Clement VII and the Emperor Charles V* (Edinburgh, 1875).

[24] Heinrich Cornelius Agrippa von Nettesheim, "Historiola de duplici coronatione Caroli V," *Opera* (Lyons, 1531; reprint Hildesheim: G. Olms, 1970), 2:1122-1138.

[25] *Christianismi Restitutio*, 462.

Chapter 2
The Errors of the Trinity

[1] The citations by Servetus of these authors in *De Trinitatis Erroribus* (abbreviated *TE*) and *Christianismi Restitutio* (abbreviated *CR*) are as follows:

Augustine, *De Trinitate* – TE 26b, 40b, 41b; CR *passim.*

Peter Lombard, *Sententiae* 1:2.5, 1:13.3, 1:32.6, 1:33.2 – TE 26b, 27b, 28b, 37a, 39a, 42a-b.

Joachim of Fiore – TE 33a, 39a; CR 39, 40.

Richard of St. Victor, *De Trinitate* 3:2 (in Jacques-Paul Migne, *Patrologia Latina*, 196:916) – TE 31b.

Henry of Ghent, *Quodlibeta* 6.2 – TE 31b-32a.

William of Ockham, *Quaestiones et decisiones in Librum I Sententiarum* 26 – TE 42a-b; CR 42, 45.

John Duns Scotus, *Commentaria Oxoniensia ad IV Libros Magistri Sententiarus* 1:25-35 – TE 40b; CR 45.

Robert Holkot, *Super Quatuor Libros Sententiarum* 1:5 – TE 32a-b; CR 29.

Gregory of Rimini, *Lectura super I et II Sententiarum* 1:13 – TE 39b; CR 41.

Pierre d'Ailly, *Quaestiones super Libros Sententiarum* 1:5 – TE 32b; CR 29.

John Major, *In Primum Sententiarum* 1:4.6, 1:5.6 – TE 21a-22a; CR 29.

[2] The statements made in this chapter are more fully elucidated and documented in Roland H. Bainton, "Michael Servetus and the Trinitarian Speculation of

the Middle Ages," in Bruno Becker, ed., *Autour de Michel Servet et de Sébastien Castellion* (Haarlem, 1953).

The first two types of Trinitarian speculation delineated below were first clearly discerned by Théodore de Régnon, *Études de Théologie Positive sur la Sainte Trinité* (Paris, 1892). The third type is well discerned and described by Paul Vignaux, *Luther, Commentateur des Sentences* (Paris, 1935), App. I: "Note sur l'intelligence de la Trinité chez les Théologiens Nominalistes." Many valuable suggestions are to be found in Albert Stohr, "Die Hauptrichtungen der spekulativen Trinitätslehre in der Theologie des 13. Jahrhunderts," *Theologische Quartalschrift* 106 (1925), 113-135.

[3] On Augustine see Michael Schmaus, *Die psychologische Trinitätslehre des Hl. Augustinus,* (Münster, 1927). [A good brief discussion of Augustine's ideas on the Trinity is in Roy W. Battenhouse, ed., *A Companion to the Study of St. Augustine* (New York: Oxford University Press, 1955).]

[4] [See Marcia L. Colish, *Peter Lombard* (New York: E. J. Brill, 1994).]

[5] *De Trinitatis Erroribus*, 27b.

[6] *De Trinitatis Erroribus*, 32a.

[7] *De Trinitatis Erroribus*, 39a, 33a.

[8] On Joachim of Fiore and his school, see Carmelo Ottaviano, *Joachimi Abbatis Liber contra Lombardum (Scuola di Gioacchino da Fiore)* (Rome, 1934), 58, 60. [See also Bernard McGinn, *The Calabrian Abbott: Joachim of Fiore in the History of Western Thought* (New York: Macmillan, 1985); Axel Mehlmann, *De Unitate Trinitatis: Forschungen und Documente zur Trinitätstheologie Joachims von Fiore in Zusammenhang mit seinem verschollenen Traktat gegen Petrus Lombardus* (Diss., Freiburg im Breisgau, 1991).]

[9] The picture of God as self-diffusive being is described in J. Péghaire, "L'axiome 'Bonum est diffusivum sui,' dans le Néo-platonisme et le Thomisme," *Revue de l'Université d'Ottawa*, Section spéciale I (1932), 5-30. [On Richard of St. Victor, see also Heinz Wipfler, *Die Trinitätsspekulation des Petrus von Poitiers und die Trinitätsspekulation des Richard von St. Viktor, ein Vergleich,* Beiträge zur Geschichte der Philosophie und Theologie des Mittelalters 41.1 (Münster, 1965).]

[10] The views of several scholastics including Henry of Ghent are covered in Michael Schmaus, *Der Liber Propugnatorius des Thomas Anglicus und die Lehrunterschiede zwischen Thomas Aquin und Duns Scotus*, part 2, "Die Trinitarischen Lehrdifferenzen," (Münster, 1930). See also Jean Paulus, *Henri de Gand: essai sur les tendances de sa métaphysique* (Paris, 1938), 295f. [See also Josep M. Rovira Belloso, *La visión de Dios según Enrique de Gante* (Barcelona: Editorial Casulleras, 1960).]

[11] *De Trinitatis Erroribus*, 32a.

[12] [See Marilyn McCord Adams, *William Ockham* (Notre Dame: University of Notre Dame Press, 1987), esp. 996-1007; Paul Vincent Spade, ed., *The Cambridge Companion to Ockham* (Cambridge: Cambridge University Press, 1999), esp. 326-349.]

[13] [See Francis Oakley, "Pierre d'Ailly" in Brian Albert Gerrish, ed., *Reformers in Profile* (Philadelphia: Fortress Press, 1967); Leonard A. Kennedy, *Peter of Ailly and the Harvest of Fourteenth-Century Philosophy* (Lewiston, NY: E. Mellen Press, 1986); Eliseo García Lescún, *La Teología trinitaria de Gregorio de Rimini* (Burgos: Aldecoa, 1970); Leonard A. Kennedy, *The Philosophy of Robert Holkot, Fourteenth-Century Skeptic* (Lewiston, NY: E. Mellen Press, 1993).]

[14] *Ioannis Calvini Opera quae supersunt omnia* (Corpus reformatorum), 8:846, 8:767.4.

[15] *Erasmi epistolae* no. 1334, in *Opus epistolarum Des. Erasmi Roterdami* (Oxford, 1906-1947), 5:173-192.

[16] On the introduction of the Reformation in Basel see Rudolf Wackernagel, *Geschichte der Stadt Basel* (Basel, 1924), vol. 3. The documents are published in Paul Roth, ed., *Aktensammlung zur Geschichte der Basler Reformation*, vol. 4: July 1529-September 1530 (Basel, 1941). See also Theophilus Burckhardt-Biedermann, *Bonifacius Amerbach und die Reformation* (Basel, 1894), esp. 63f., 207, 236. [See also Hans Rudolf Guggisberg, *Basel in the Sixteenth Century: Aspects of the city republic before, during, and after the Reformation* (St. Louis: Center for Reformation Research, 1982**)**.]

[17] On Oecolampadius, see Ernst Staehelin, *Das Theologische Lebenswerk Johannes Oekolampads* (Leipzig, 1939), and *Briefe und Akten zum Leben Oekolampads* (Leipzig, 1927-1934). [See also Ernest Gordon Rupp, "Johannes Oecolampadius: The Reformer as Scholar," in *Patterns of Reformation* (Philadelphia: Fortress Press, 1969); Thomas A. Fudge, "Icarus of Basel? Oecolampadius and the Early Swiss Reformation," *Journal of Religious History* 21 (1997), 268-284.]

[18] *Erasmi epistolae* no. 1977, 7:367-368.

[19] On the treatment of the Anabaptists at Basel, see Paul Burckhardt, *Die Basler Täufer* (Basel, 1898).

Chapter 3
The Eternal Word

[1] See Chronology, note 6.

[2] *De Trinitatis Erroribus*, 52b.

[3] *De Trinitatis Erroribus*, 35a.

[4] See Gustave Bardy, *Paul de Samosate* (Louvain, 1923); Friedrich Loofs, *Paulus von Samosata* (Leipzig, 1924); Hugh Jackson Lawlor, "The Sayings of Paul of Samosata," *Journal of Theological Studies* 19 (1917-18), 115-20. On Marcellus of Ancyra, see Friedrich Loofs, "Die Trinitätslehre Marcells von Ancyra," *Sitzungsberichte der Königlich Preussischen Akademie der Wissenschaften zu Berlin* 33 (1902), 764-781. [See also Joseph T. Lienhard, *Contra Marcellum: Marcellus of Ancyra and Fourth Century Theology* (Washington: Catholic University of America Press, 1999).]

[5] Irenaeus, *Adversus Haereses*, 2:22.2.

[6] Tertullian, *Adversus Praxean*. See also James Morgan, *The Importance of Tertullian in the Development of Christian Dogma* (London, 1928).

[7] On the doctrine of the deification of man in early Christian literature, see Ludwig Bauer, "Untersuchungen über die Vergöttlichungslehre in der Theologie der griechischen Väter," *Theologische Quartalschrift* 98 (1916), 467-491; 101 (1920), 28-64, 155-186. Also Karl Bornhäuser, *Die Vergottungslehre des Athanasius und Johannes Damascenus* (Güttersloh, 1903), 7-198; Mirra Ivanovna Lot-Boradine, "La doctrine de la 'déification' dans l'Église grecque jusqu'au XIe siècle," *Revue de l'Histoire des Religions* 150 (1932), 5-43, 525-574; George William Butterworth, "The Deification of Man in Clement of Alexandria," *Journal of Theological Studies* 17 (1915-16), 157-169.

[8] *De Trinitatis Erroribus,* 11b.

[9] *De Trinitatis Erroribus,* 12a.

[10] *De Trinitatis Erroribus,* 102a.

[11] *De Trinitatis Erroribus,* 67a; cf. John 3:8.

[12] *De Trinitatis Erroribus,* 23b; cf. John 17:21, Eph. 4:3.

[13] *De Trinitatis Erroribus,* 9a.

[14] *De Trinitatis Erroribus,* 94b; cf. Isa. 45:15, Ps. 91:1.

[15] *De Trinitatis Erroribus,* 111a.

[16] *De Trinitatis Erroribus,* 64b.

[17] *De Trinitatis Erroribus,* 31b.

[18] *De Trinitatis Erroribus,* 102a.

[19] *De Trinitatis Erroribus,* 65b.

[20] *De Trinitatis Erroribus,* 59b.

[21] *De Trinitatis Erroribus,* 59a; cf. John 6:63.

[22] *De Trinitatis Erroribus,* 53b.

[23] *De Trinitatis Erroribus,* 116b; cf. Dan. 17:13, Ezek. 1, Zech. 1:8-11, Isa. 6:1.

[24] *De Trinitatis Erroribus,* 78a; cf. 1 Cor. 2:8, Rev. 22:16, John 8:12, 9:5, 12:46, Isa. 42:6, Rev. 22:5, Col. 1:16, 1 Cor. 1:23-24.

[25] *De Trinitatis Erroribus,* 59b-60a; cf. Isa. 42:5, Jer. 10:13, Job 26:8, Jer. 5:24.

[26] *De Trinitatis Erroribus,* 81b-82a; cf. 1 Cor. 24-28.

[27] Ernst Staehelin, *Briefe und Akten zum Leben Oekolampads* 2, (Leipzig, 1934), no. 765, no. 766. [The correspondence of Oecolampadius with and concerning Servetus is given in *Ioannis Calvini Opera quae supersunt omnia* (Corpus reformatorum), 8:857-867. On the Anabaptists and their relations with Servetus, see George Huntston Williams, *The Radical Reformation* (Philadelphia: The Westminster Press, 1962), esp. chapters 10, 11, 18.]

[28] *Calvini Opera,* 8:744.1.

[29] Ernst Staehelin, *Das Theologische Lebenswerk Johannes Oekolampads* (Leipzig, 1939), 535.

[30] Staehelin, *Theologische Lebenswerk Oekolampads,* 536; Staehelin, *Briefe und Akten* 2, no. 793. [See also Williams, *Radical Reformation,* chapter 10. On Bucer, see

Martin Greschat, *Martin Bucer: Ein Reformator und seine Zeit* (Munich: Beck, 1990).]

[31] [See Williams, *Radical Reformation,* chapter 10; Miriam Usher Chrisman, *Strasbourg and the Reform: A Study in the Process of Change* (New Haven: Yale University Press, 1967); John D. Derksen, *From Radicals to Survivors: Strasbourg's Religious Nonconformists over Two Generations 1525-1570* ('t Goy-Houton: Hes & de Graaf, 2002).]

[32] Timotheus Wilhelm Röhrich, "Zur Geschichte der strassburgischen Wiedertäufer 1527-1543," *Zeitschrift für historische Theologie* 30 (1860), 30; cf. Henri Tollin, "Strassburger kirchliche Zustände zu Anfang der Reformationszeit. Eine Episode aus dem Leben Servets," *Magazin für die Literatur des Auslandes* 87 (5 June 1875); Henri Tollin, "Michael Servet und Martin Butzer," *Magazin für die Literatur des Auslandes* 89 (10 June 1876).

[33] Camill Gerbert, *Geschichte der Strassburger Sectenbewegung zur Zeit der Reformation 1524-1534* (Strassburg, 1889), 171.

[34] Johann Adam, *Evangelische Kirchengeschichte der Stadt Strassburg bis zur französischen Revolution* (Strassburg, 1922), 109-110. See also Gerbert, *Geschichte der Strassburger Sectenbewegung,* chapter 5. Nikolaus Paulus in his *Protestantismus und Toleranz im 16. Jahrhundert* (Freiburg im Breisgau, 1911), 142-175, collects the harsh utterances of Bucer's later period while conceding an earlier liberalism.

[35] Adam, *Evangelische Kirchengeschichte der Stadt Strassburg,* 116.

[36] Otto Erich Strasser, *Capitos Beziehungen zu Bern* (Leipzig, 1928), 43.

[37] Gerbert, *Geschichte der Strassburger Sectenbewegung,* 137-138.

[38] Timotheus Wilhelm Röhrich, *Mittheilungen aus der Geschichte der evangelischen Kirchen des Elsasses* (Paris and Strassburg, 1855), 3:165-166.

[39] *Bibliotheca Reformatoria Neerlandica,* 7:127.

Chapter 4
Nineveh Unrepentant

[1] K. Steif, "Johannes Setzer (Secerius) der gelehrte Buchdrucker in Hagenau," *Centralblatt für Bibliothekswesen* 9 (1892), 297-317; 10 (1893), 20-22. Also A. Tanauer, "Jean Setzer, l'imprimeur polemiste de Hagenau 1523-32," *Revue d'Alsace,* 4th ser., 3 (1902), 5-34. [See also François Ritter, *Histoire de l'imprimerie alsacienne aux XVe et XVIe siècles* (Strasbourg, 1955), 388-396. On the publisher Conrad Roesch, see *Opere del Dr. Giulio Ceradini* (Milan, 1906), 1:451.]

[2] Ernst Staehelin, *Das Theologische Lebenswerk Johannes Oekolampads* (Leipzig, 1939), 284.

[3] *D. Martin Luthers Werke: kritische Gesamtausgabe* (Weimar edition) Abt. 1, 8:117-118.

[4] Timotheus Wilhelm Röhrich, *Geschichte der Reformation im Elsass und besonders in Strassburg* (Strassburg, 1830), 1:138f.

[5] *Ioannis Calvini Opera quae supersunt omnia* (Corpus reformatorum), 8:869, 8:768, 9:779.5, 9:780.6.

[6] Timotheus Wilhelm Röhrich, *Mittheilungen aus der Geschichte der evangelischen Kirchen des Elsasses* (Paris and Strassburg, 1855), 2:81.

[7] *Calvini Opera*, 8:866.

[8] *Huldreich Zwinglis Sämtliche Werke* (Corpus reformatorum), 11:540.

[9] Karl Rembert, *Die "Wiedertäufer" im Herzogtum Jülich* (Berlin, 1899), 225.

[10] Traugott Schiess, ed., *Briefwechsel der Brüder Ambrosius und Thomas Blaurer 1509-1548* (Freiburg im Breisgau, 1908), 1:306.

[11] Camill Gerbert, *Geschichte der Strassburger Sectenbewegung zur Zeit der Reformation 1524-1534* (Strassburg, 1889), 123.

[12] Ernst Staehelin, *Briefe und Akten zum Leben Oekolampads* 2 (Leipzig, 1934), no. 893; also *Calvini Opera*, 8:866-867.

[13] *Calvini Opera*, 8:868.

[14] Schiess, *Briefwechsel*, 1:306-307. Excerpts in *Calvini Opera*, 8:779 n. 2.

[15] Timotheus Wilhelm Röhrich, "Zur Geschichte der strassburgischen Wiedertäufer 1527-1543," *Zeitschrift für historische Theologie* 30 (1860), 52.

[16] Prior to July 18, 1531: see *Calvini Opera*, 8:866.

[17] *Calvini Opera*, 8:865.

[18] *Zwinglis Sämtliche Werke*, 11:540.

[19] *Calvini Opera*, 8:862.

[20] *Calvini Opera*, 8:767.4.

[21] *Dialogorum de Trinitate libri duo, De justicia regni Christi capitula quatuor*, A1b.

[22] *Dialogorum de Trinitate*, C3b.

[23] *Dialogorum de Trinitate*, C5a-6a.

[24] *Dialogorum de Trinitate*, A5b.

[25] *Dialogorum de Trinitate*, C2a.

[26] *Dialogorum de Trinitate*, C5b.

[27] *Dialogorum de Trinitate*, C6a.

[28] *Calvini Opera*, 8:869.

[29] *Luthers Werke*, Abt. 1, 23:131f., 23:243.

[30] *Dialogorum de Trinitate*, C2a.

[31] *Dialogorum de Trinitate*, C1a; cf. Ps. 104:3, Isa. 40:22, 40:12.

[32] *Luthers Werke*, Abt. 1, 18:622-623.

[33] *Dialogorum de Trinitate*, C1b.

[34] *Dialogorum de Trinitate*, A7b.

[35] On Schwenckfeld, see Karl Ecke, *Schwenckfeld, Luther und der Gedanke einer apostolischen Reformation* (Berlin, 1911); Emanuel Hirsch, "Zum Verständnis Schwenckfelds," in *Festgabe von Fachgenossen und Freunden Karl Müller* (Tübingen, 1922); Frederick Loetscher, *Schwenckfeld's Participation in the Eucharistic Controversy of the Sixteenth Century* (Philadelphia, 1906). [See also André Séguenny, *Homme charnel, homme spirituel: étude sur la christologie de Caspar Schwenckfeld (1489-1561)* (Wiesbaden: Steiner, 1975); R. Emmet McLaughlin, *The Freedom of Spirit, Social Privilege, and Religious Dissent: Caspar Schwenckfeld and the Schwenckfelders* (Baden-Baden: V. Koerner, 1996), esp. "The Politics of Dissent: Martin Bucer, Caspar Schwenckfeld and the Schwenckfelders of Strasbourg," 233-254.]

On Hoffman, see F. O. zur Linden, "Melchior Hoffman," *Teylers Godgeleerd Genootschap*, n.s. 11 (Haarlem, 1885). [See also Klaus Deppermann, *Melchior Hoffman: Social Unrest and Apocalyptic Visions in the Age of Reformation* (Edinburgh: T. & T. Clark, 1987).]

[36] *Dialogorum de Trinitate*, B1a.

[37] *Dialogorum de Trinitate*, B5b.

[38] Ecke, *Schwenckfeld, Luther und der Gedanke einer apostolischen Reformation*, 210; cf. *Corpus Schwenckfeldianorum* (Leipzig, 1936), 14:347f.

[39] *Corpus Schwenckfeldianorum*, 6:384, 6:386.

[40] *Dialogorum de Trinitate*, F7b-8a.

[41] *Tischreden* no. 237, in *Luthers Werke*, Abt. 2, 1:99.

[42] *Tischreden* no. 1327, in *Luthers Werke*, Abt. 2, 2:48; cf. *Tischreden* no. 6143, in *Luthers Werke*, Abt. 2, 5:510; *Luthers Werke*, 50:475. For a refutation of Tollin's conjecture that Servetus visited Luther at the Coburg (Henri Tollin, "Michael Servet über den Geist del Wiedergeburt," *Zeitschrift für wissenschaftliche Theologie* 25 (1882), 310-326), see Gustav Kawerau, "Luther und seine Beziehungen zu Servet," *Theologische Studien und Kritiken* 51 (1878), 479; and Joachim Karl Friedrich Knaake, "Luther und Servet," *Theologische Studien und Kritiken* 54 (1881), 317f. See also Martin Luther, *Briefwechsel*, ed. Ernst Ludwig Enders, et. al. (Frankfurt am Main, etc., 1884-1932), 9:207, 9:253.

[43] *Philippi Melanthonis Opera quae supersunt omnia* (Corpus reformatorum), 2:630, 2:640, 2:660-661.

[44] *Melanthonis Opera*, 21:262; cf. 21:263, 21:359.

[45] *Melanthonis Opera*, 21:619, 21:622-623; cf. 3:746, 3:748-9. Melanchthon repudiated the letter to the Venetian senate warning against Servetus, 3:745f. See also Karl Benrath, "Notiz über Melanchthons angeblichen Brief an den Venetianischen Senat (1539)," *Zeitschrift für Kirchengeschichte* 1 (1877), 469-471. Tollin deals with Melanchthon and Servetus in *Ph. Melanchthon und M. Servet* (Berlin, Mecklenburg, 1876).

[46] Johannes Cochlaeus, *Commentaria Ioannis Cochlaei de actis et scriptis Martini Lutheri Saxonis* (1549), 233-236.

[47] Hugo Laemmer, ed., *Monumenta Vaticana Historiam Ecclesiasticam saeculi XVI* (Freiburg im Breisgau, 1861), 109-110.

[48] Marcel Bataillon, "Honneur et Inquisition: Michel Servet poursuivi par l'Inquisition espagnole," *Bulletin Hispanique* 27 (January-March, 1925).

[49] Jean Crespin, *Histoire des martyrs* (Geneva, 1582), 163f.

[50] Victor-Louis Bourrilly and Nathanaël Weiss, "Jean du Bellay, les Protestants et la Sorbonne 1529-1535," *Bulletin de la Société pour l'Histoire du Protestantisme Français* 53 (1904), 103.

[51] From the ms. pages in the Edinburgh copy of *Christianismi Restitutio;* text in Roland H. Bainton, "The Present State of Servetus Studies," *Journal of Modern History* 4 (1932), 89, translation by Alexander Gordon in *Christian Life*, 18 May 1912. This passage throws light on the curious statement of Servetus to Calvin that he would raise up against him witnesses from Nineveh and the New Isles, *Calvini Opera*, 8:xxxi.

[52] [In 1528 the German banking house of Welser, in consideration of funds advanced to Emperor Charles V, obtained the governorship of Venezuela and the right to exploit its natural and mineral wealth. Their expeditions in 1529 and 1534 were marked by great brutality toward, and violent reprisals by, the native population, as well as by disease, starvation, and cannibalism. It was fortunate for Servetus that he never pursued his fantasy of escape to America. See Jules Humbert, *L'occupation allemande du Venezuela au XVIe siècle: période dite des Welser, 1528-1556* (Paris, Bordeaux, 1905); John Hemming, *The Search for El Dorado* (London: Michael Joseph, 1978).]

Chapter 5
Michel de Villeneuve, Editor

[1] See Chronology, note 11.

[2] Nathanaël Weiss, *La Chambre ardente: étude sur la liberté de conscience en France sous François I et Henri II* (Paris, 1889). [See also Nancy Lyman Roelker, *One King, One Faith: The Parlement of Paris and the Religious Reformations of the Sixteenth Century* (Berkeley: University of California Press, 1996).]

[3] Théodore de Bèze, *Epistola magistri Benedicti Passavantij: Responsiua ad commissionem sibi datam a venerabili d. Petro Lyseto* (Geneva, c. 1600). [A French translation has been published as *Le Passavant: édition critique, introduction, traduction, commentaire*, ed. J. L. R. Ledegang-Keegstra (Leiden: Universiteit Leiden, 2001).]

[4] F. de Larfeul, *Études sur Pierre Lizet* (Clermont-Ferrand, 1856).

[5] *Petri Lizeti Alverni Montigenae, utroque iure consulti, primi dum hos libros componeret, officium Praesidis in supremo regio Francorum consistorio exercentis* (Paris, 1551).

[6] Charles Fleury-Ternal, *Histoire du cardinal de Tournon, ministre de France, sous quatre de nos rois* (Paris, 1728). Also J. Isaac, "Le cardinal de Tournon lieutenant général du roi," *Revue d'Histoire de Lyon* 12 (1913), 321-362; Jacques Moulard, "Le Cardinal François de Tournon," *Le Correspondant* 296 (10 July 1924), 51-63; Michel François, *Le Cardinal François de Tournon, homme d'état, diplomate, mécène et humaniste, 1469-1562* (Paris, 1951).

[7] Fleury-Ternal, *Histoire du cardinal de Tournon*, 208-209.

[8] Fleury-Ternal, *Histoire du cardinal de Tournon,* 372.

[9] For a brief biographical sketch, see Jacobus Echard, *Scriptores ordinis praedicatorum* (Paris, 1721), 2:162.

[10] The argument appears in two tracts: *F. Matthaei Ory Dominicae familiae theologi haereticae pravitatis per Gallies inquisitoris* (Paris, 1544); and *De quinque verbis Pauli* (Venice, 1558).

[11] Jean Crespin, *Histoire des martyrs* (Geneva, 1582), 4:234b.

[12] See Chronology, note 12.

[13] On Palmier, see Claude Charvet, *Histoire de la sainte église de Vienne* (Lyons, 1761), 536-549.

[14] On previous Ptolemys, see Lucien Gallois, *Les géographes allemands de la Renaissance* (Paris, 1890). See also Siegmund Gunther, "Der Humanismus in seinem Einfluss auf die Entwicklung der Erdkunde," *Geographische Zeitschrift* 6 (1900), 65-89.

[15] Leonardo Olschki, *Storia letteraria delle scoperte geografiche* (Florence, 1937).

[16] Geoffroy Atkinson, *Les nouveaux horizons de la renaissance française* (Paris, 1935).

[17] *Christianismi Restitutio,* 373.

[18] Henri Gaidoz and Paul Sébillot, *Blason populaire de la France* (Paris, 1884), 7; cf. Archer Taylor, *The Proverb* (Cambridge: Harvard University Press, 1931), 99-102.

[19] Eloy Bullón y Fernández, *Miguel Servet y la geografía del renacimiento* (Madrid, 1929) reprints the comparison of France and Spain as well as the prefaces to the two editions. [For an English translation of Servetus's prefaces and other contributions to the 1535 and 1542 editions of Ptolemy, see Charles Donald O'Malley, *Michael Servetus, a Translation of his Geographical, Medical and Astrological Writings* (Philadelphia: American Philosophical Society, 1953), 15-37, 190-194.]

[20] Albin Eduard Beau, *As Relações Germanicas do Humanismo de Damião de Góis* (Coimbra, 1941), 151-164, discusses the episode and also reprints the passage. [See also Elisabeth Feist Hirsch, *Damião de Góis: the Life and Thought of a Portuguese Humanist* (The Hague: Nijhoff, 1967).]

[21] [The Latin under consideration is "quare promissam terram pollicitam et non vernacula lingua laudantem pronuncies." Robert Willis, in *Servetus and Calvin* (London, 1877), translated the passage as "wherefore you may say that the land was promised, indeed, but it is of little promise when spoken of in everyday terms." Alexander Gordon, in "Miguel Serveto-y-Revés," *Theological Review* 15 (1878), took Willis to task for this translation, since Willis ignored information available in earlier Servetus literature, including "Tollin's exhaustive article [which] Dr. Willis refers to, but seemingly has not read." Henri Tollin's article "Michael Servet als Geograph," *Zeitschrift der Gesellschaft für Erdkunde zu Berlin* 10 (1875), 182-222, would have explained to Willis that "vernacula lingua" meant not "in everyday terms" but "in the vernacular language," i.e. in

German; and that "laudantem" (praising) was a misprint for "laudatam" (having been praised). The passage thus alludes to a pun in German between "das Gelobte Land" (the Promised Land) and "gelobt," the past participle of "loben" (to praise). Bainton's translation has replaced this German pun with a somewhat different one in English, in which three different Latin words, including "laudatam," are rendered as forms of "promise." Bainton might have omitted mention of these details, had he not worried that his own translation might otherwise have been questioned by some latter-day Alexander Gordon.]

[22] Carl Erdmann, *Die Entstehung des Kreuzzugsgedankens* (Stuttgart, 1935), 279 n. 121.

[23] Julien Baudrier, "Michel Servet, ses relations avec les libraires et les imprimeurs lyonnais," *Mélanges offerts à Émile Picot* (Paris, 1913), 1:41-56.

[24] See the bibliography of Servetus's works by Madeline E. Stanton in John F. Fulton, *Michael Servetus, Humanist and Martyr* (New York: H. Reichner, 1953), 79-82.

[25] Gordon, "Miguel Serveto-y-Revés," 298.

[26] Cf. *Christianismi Restitutio*, 69.

Chapter 6
Doctor of Medicine

[1] On the relations of Servetus and Champier, see J. Andry, "Michel Servet et Symphorien Champier," *Lyon Médical* (1935), 293-303, 328-336.

[2] [See Georgette de Groër, *Réforme et contre-réforme en France: le collège de la Trinité au XVIe siècle à Lyon* (Paris: Publisud, 1995).]

[3] Paul Auguste Allut, *Étude biographique et bibliographique sur Symphorien Champier* (Lyons, 1859). [See also Brian P. Copenhaver, *Symphorien Champier and the Reception of the Occultist Tradition in Renaissance France* (New York: Mouton, 1978).]

[4] Eberhard Stübler, *Leonhart Fuchs Leben und Werk* (Munich, 1928). [A facsimile edition of the herbal has been published as *The new herbal of 1543 / New Kreüterbuch* (New York: Taschen, 2001).]

[5] Henri Tollin, "Michael Servets Brevissima pro Symphoriano Campeggio *Apologia in Leonardum Fuchsium*," *Deutches Archiv für Geschichte der Medizin* 7 (1884), 409-442.

[6] Symphorien Champier, *Le Myrouel des apothiquaires et pharmacopoles* (Paris, 1894), 45-47.

[7] Ernest Wickersheimer, "Sur la syphilis aux XVe et XVIe siècles," *Humanisme et Renaissance* 4 (1937), 157-207. [Fifty years after Bainton wrote, the question of the origin of syphilis has not been resolved. See Carl Zimmer, "Can genes solve the syphilis mystery?" *Science* 292 (11 May 2001), 1091. Evidence for and against the American origin of syphilis is presented in Olivier Dutour, ed.,

The Origin of Syphilis in Europe: before or after 1493? (Toulon: Centre archéologique du Var; Paris: Editions Errance, 1994).]

8 [See Charles Donald O'Malley, *Andreas Vesalius of Brussels, 1514-1564* (Berkeley: University of California Press, 1964).]

9 Johann Guenther von Andernach, *Institutionum Anatomicarum* (Basel, 1538), preface a5 and verso.

10 Richard Copley Christie, *Étienne Dolet: the Martyr of the Renaissance 1508-1546* (London, 1899), 378-379.

11 Thomas Platter, *Thomas und Felix Platter: zur Sittengeschichte des XVI. Jahrhunderts* (Leipzig, 1878), 233-234, 237.

12 The tract is fully analyzed and the formulae for many of the syrups given in Jose M. Castro y Calvo, "Contribución al estudio de Miguel Servet y de su obra 'Syruporum,'" *Universidad* 8 (1931), 797-830, 977-1030; 9 (1932), 3-71.

13 Dedication of the 1541 Ptolemy. [See Charles Donald O'Malley, *Michael Servetus, a Translation of his Geographical, Medical and Astrological Writings* (Philadelphia: American Philosophical Society, 1953), 192.]

14 [For the background of astrological medicine, see Karl Sudhoff, *Iatromathematiker, vornehmlich im 15. und 16. Jahrhundert* (Breslau, 1902).]

15 *Tischreden* no. 6250, in *D. Martin Luthers Werke: kritische Gesamtausgabe* (Weimar edition), Abt. 2, 5:557-558.

16 See Franz Boll, *Sternglaube und Sterndeutung* (Leipzig, 1931); also Theodore O. Wedel, "The Medieval Attitude toward Astrology," *Yale Studies in English* 60 (1920); Don Cameron Allen, *The Star-Crossed Renaissance* (Durham, NC, 1941); Eugène Defrance, *Catherine de Médicis, ses Astrologues . . .* (Paris, 1911). [See also Eugenio Garin, *Astrology in the Renaissance: The Zodiac of Life* (London: Routlege & Kegan Paul, 1983).]

17 *Opere del Dr. Giulio Ceradini* (Milan, 1906), 1:260, note.

18 Henri Tollin, "M. Servets Pariser Prozess urkundlich dargestellt," *Deutches Archiv für Geschichte der Medizin* 3 (1880), 183-221; cf. also "Der königliche Leibarzt und Hofastrologe Johann Thibault, Michael Servets Pariser Freund," *Archiv für pathologische Anatomie und Physiologie* 78 (November 1879), 302-318; "Zu Thibaults Prozess urkundlich dargestellt," *Deutches Archiv für Geschichte der Medizin* 3 (1880), 332-347.

19 *Ioannis Calvini Opera quae supersunt omnia* (Corpus reformatorum), 8:767.5, 8:776.12, 8:780.12.

20 George Sarton, *Introduction to the History of Science* (Baltimore, 1927), 1:268 n. 32.

21 The passages in Galen on which the above statements rest are, in order: *Claudii Galeni Opera Omnia* (Leipzig, 1822), 4:703ff; 3:497; 2:208; 3:455-456, 3:509; 4:489-492; 5:150f; 3:510; 3:539-541; 3:412; 3:545. See also James S. Prendergast, *Galen's View of the Vascular System in Relation to that of Harvey* (London, 1928).

[An English translation of Galen's *De usu respirationis, An in arteriis natura sanguis contineatur, De usu pulsuum,* and *De causis respirationis* is in *Galen on Respiration and the Arteries,* ed. David J. Furley and J.S. Wilkie (Princeton: Princeton University Press, 1984). See also Donald F. Proctor, "Galen: His Genius and His Shadow" in *A History of Breathing Physiology* (New York: Marcel Dekker, 1995).]

[22] The contribution of Servetus is discussed by Tollin in *Die Entdeckung des Blutkreislaufs durch Michael Servet* (Jena, 1876) and in the following articles:

"Matteo Realdo Colombos Sektionen und Vivisektionen," *Archiv für gesammte Physiologie* 11 (1880), 349-360.

"Matteo Realdo Colombo, ein Beitrag zu seinem Leben aus seinen L. XV, de re anatomica (1559)," *Archiv für gesammte Physiologie* 12 (1880), 262-290.

"William Harvey, eine Quellenstudie," *Archiv für pathologische Anatomie und Physiologie* 81 (July 1880), 114-157.

"Kritische Bemerkungen über Harvey," *Archiv für gesammte Physiologie* 28 (1882), 581-630.

"Über Colombos Antheil an der Entdeckung des Blutkreislaufs," *Archiv für pathologische Anatomie und Physiologie* 91 (January 1883), 39-66.

"Die Spanier und die Entdeckung des Blutkreislaufs," *Archiv für pathologische Anatomie und Physiologie* 91 (March 1883), 423-433; "Die Italiener und die Entdeckung des Blutkreislaufs," *Ibid.* 93 (July 1883), 64-99; "Die Franzosen und die Entdeckung des Blutkreislaufs," *Ibid.* 94 (October 1883), 86-135; "Die Engländer und die Entdeckung des Blutkreislaufs," *Ibid.* 97 (March 1883), 431-482; *Ibid.* 98 (November 1884), 193-240.

"Harvey und seine Vorgänger," *Biologisches Zentralblatt* 3 (1 October, 15 October, and 1 November 1883), 461-496, 513-537.

"Ein italienisches urteil über die ersten Entdecker des Blutkreislaufs," *Archiv für gesammte Physiologie* 33 (1884), 482-493.

"Robert Willis' neuer William Harvey," *Archiv für gesammte Physiologie* 34 (1884), 1-21.

"Andreas Caesalpin," *Archiv für gesammte Physiologie* 35 (1884), 295-390.

"Andreas Vesals Verhältnis zu Servet," *Biologisches Zentralblatt* 5 (1 July, 1 August, 15 August, 1 September, 15 September, and 1 October 1885), 242-255, 271-278, 366-349, 373-383, 404-414, 440-448, 471-480.

See also the works listed in bibliography under Bayon, Fulton, Hemmeter, Izquierdo, Neuberger, Osler, Temkin, and Wickersheimer.

[23] Max Neuberger, "Zur Entdeckungsgeschichte des Lungenkreislaufes," *Sudhoffs Archiv für Geschichte der Medizin* 23 (1930), 7-9; José Joaquín Izquierdo, "A New and More Correct Version of the Views of Servetus on the Circulation of the Blood," *Bulletin of the Institute of the History of Medicine* 5 (1937), 914-932.

[24] *Christianismi Restitutio,* 169-171.

[25] The references to Clement of Alexandria in *Christianismi Restitutio* are as follows. These references are not found in the corresponding pages in the Paris manuscript.

CR 140, citing *Stromata* 5:3 (ms. p. 49).
CR 223, citing *Stromata* 5:13 (ms. p. 92).
CR 224 (ms. p. 93).

[26] The references to Philo of Alexandria in *Christianismi Restitutio*, and the corresponding pages in the Paris manuscript, are as follows.

CR 102 (ms. p. 125).
CR 131 (ms. p. 42).
CR 139 (ms. p. 49).
CR 204 (ms. p. 75).
CR 240 (ms. p. 110).

See Roland H. Bainton, "The Smaller Circulation, Servetus and Colombo," *Sudhoffs Archiv für Geschichte der Medizin* 24 (1931), 371-374.

[27] Professor Charles O'Malley writes from Stanford University: "As for *Ebenefis philosophi ac medici expositio super quintum canonem Avicennae ad Andrea Alpago Bellunensi* . . . Venice, 1547, we have it in the Lane Library. Regrettably it deals only with drugs and their therapeutic values. I may say that we also have three sections of a ms. of Ibn Nafis (about 300 leaves) which Hitti declared to be the autograph copy. Unfortunately the case is the same – it is the wrong part. But what I should like to know more about is Andrea Alpago, a physician, who certainly must in his translating have run across the pertinent bits in Ibn Nafis – reputedly the pulmonary circulation is mentioned five times throughout the work."

[28] Oswei Temkin, "Was Servetus influenced by Ibn An-Nafis?" *Bulletin of the Institute of the History of Medicine* 8 (May 1940), 731-734, concludes in the negative because the Arab explicitly denied pores in the septum and because he assumed that the blood filters through the wall of the pulmonary artery, mixes with air in the lungs and then filters into the pulmonary vein; whereas Servetus believed that the blood passes from the pulmonary artery into the pulmonary vein by way of intermediate vessels.

[29] The attitude is well described by Walter Pagel in "Religious Motives in the Medical Biology of the Seventeenth Century," *Bulletin of the Institute of the History of Medicine* 3 (1935), 98-128. He is mistaken, I think, in finding the beginning only in Paracelsus.

[30] *Christianismi Restitutio,* 168-169.

[31] Gen. 9:4, Lev. 17:11.

[32] *Christianismi Restitutio,* 170.

[33] Lynn Thorndike, *History of Magic and Experimental Science* (New York: Macmillan, 1941), 5:116.

[34] *Christianismi Restitutio,* 178, 182.

Chapter 7
The Restoration of Christianity

[1] *Ioannis Calvini Opera quae supersunt omnia* (Corpus reformatorum), 8:769.17.

[2] *Calvini Opera*, 8:765, 8:769.18, 8:777, 8:781.28.

[3] *Christianismi Restitutio*, 430.

[4] *Calvini Opera*, 8:846, 8:767.5.

[5] Antoine Gachet d'Artigny, "Mémoires pour servir à l'histoire de Michel Servet," *Nouveaux mémoires d'histoire, de critique et de littérature* (Paris, 1749-1756), 2:68; Émile Doumergue, *Jean Calvin, les hommes et les choses de son temps* (Lausanne, 1899-1927), 6:254 n. 4. Cf. *Calvini Opera*, 8:834-835.

[6] [These two paragraphs, taken from Bainton's Foreword to the 1960 paperback edition of *Hunted Heretic*, are based on Pierre Cavard, *Le Procès de Michel Servet à Vienne* (Vienne, 1953). Cavard's book was among those published in 1953 in connection with the four hundredth anniversary of the execution of Servetus, too late to be included in the first edition of *Hunted Heretic*.]

[7] Humbert de Terrebasse, *Histoire et généalogie de la famille de Maugiron en Viennois, 1257-1767* (Lyons, 1905), 32-33.

[8] The Hermetic literature is so important for Servetus's thought that I venture to list the citations and allusions. References in *Christianismi Restitutio* to the *Corpus Hermeticum* (abbreviated *CH*) and *Asclepius* (abbreviated *As*) are as follows:

    CR 132 – *CH* 3:1, 5:10, [8:5], 9:9, [9:5]; *As* 34; *CH* 2:12, 1:31, [5:2, 12:23].
    CR 133 – *As* 17, 18; [*CH* 3:1, 9:9].
    [*CR* 137 – *CH* 1:5-6, 1:9.]
    CR 138 – *CH* [11:16], 11:20.
    CR 144 – *CH* 2:12.
    [*CR* 145 – *CH* 1:8.]
    [*CR* 152 – CH 5:9, 5:11; see also 12:21-23, 13:19.]
    CR 180 – *CH* 1:21.
    CR 212 – *CH* 8:1; see also 10:14, 9:8, [12:15].
    CR 213 – *CH* [5:10, 13:12], 12:15, [3:3]; see also 1:11.
    [*CR* 229 – 1:24.]
    CR 261 – *CH* [11:15], 8:1, [12:15-16].
    CR 262 – 13:5, 13:7, 13:10; 12:8, [12:9, 12:12], 12:19 .
    CR 271 – *CH* 8:5.
    CR 465 – *As* 41; see also *CH* 13:16.
    CR 567 – *CH* 13:7-9.
    CR 624 – *CH* 13.

Additional references to Hermes Trismegistus are found in *CR* 130, 155, 161, 162, 174, 260, 728, 733.

[9] *Christianismi Restitutio*, 110-111.

[10] *Christianismi Restitutio*, 138, 595, 728-729.

[11] *Christianismi Restitutio,* 138-139, 588.

[12] *Christianismi Restitutio,* 130, citing Moses Maimonides, *Guide of the Perplexed* 1:69 (Servetus incorrectly cited chapter 68).

[13] *Christianismi Restitutio,* 278.

[14] *Christianismi Restitutio,* 128.

[15] *Christianismi Restitutio,* 130.

[16] *Christianismi Restitutio,* 589.

[17] *Christianismi Restitutio,* 240.

[18] *Christianismi Restitutio,* 128.

[19] The biblical passages cited by Servetus in *De Trinitatis Erroribus* (abbreviated *TE*) and *Dialogorum de Trinitate* (abbreviated *DT*) are as follows:
> Gen. 1:3 – *TE* 47a, 90b, 41b; *DT* A3a, A4a.
> Ex. 34:29f, 2 Cor. 3 – *TE* 103b; *DT* A4a.
> Ps. 104:2 – *TE* 90a.
> John 1:1-17 – *TE* 93a, 105a-b, 115b; *DT* A3b-4b.
> John 8:12 – *TE* 47a, 78a; *DT* B4b-5a.
> 2 Cor. 4:6 – *DT* A4a-b.
> Col. 1:12 – *DT* C8b.
> 1Tim. 6:16 – *TE* 45b.
> Jas. 1:17– *TE* 102a.

[20] Plato, *Republic* 6:508b-c.

[21] Plotinus, *Enneads* 1:6.3.

[22] *Corpus Hermeticum* 1:21.

[23] On light metaphysics (*Lichtmetaphysik*), see Clemens Baeumker, *Witelo, ein Philosophe und Naturforscher des XIII. Jahrhunderts* (Münster, 1908), esp. "Gott als Licht," 357-433; Gillis Petersson Wetter, *Phôs: eine Untersuchung über hellenistische Frömmigkeit* (Uppsala, 1915). [See also A. Vogt, "La doctrina de la luz en Paracelso y en Miguel Servet," *Folio Humanística* 64 (1968), 355-366.]

[24] *Christianismi Restitutio,* 147-154, 162. On page 145 he cites Plato, Plotinus, Proclus, and Hermes, but shows no acquaintance with later speculation.

[25] *Christianismi Restitutio,* 151; cf. Gen. 1:2, Eph. 5:13.

[26] *Christianismi Restitutio,* 267, 590-591, 693-694.

[27] *Christianismi Restitutio,* 153, combining 1 Cor. 15:41 and Col. 1:18 with *Lichtmetaphysik.*

[28] *Christianismi Restitutio* 280-281, condensed; cf. Ps. 104:3, Ps. 68, Isa. 40:12, Deut. 23:14, Rev. 1:12-20, Ezek. 43.

[29] *Christianismi Restitutio,* 340-341.

[30] *Christianismi Restitutio,* 259.

[31] *Christianismi Restitutio,* 285, 312-313, 674.

[32] *Christianismi Restitutio,* 279.

[33] *Christianismi Restitutio,* 557-559, condensed; cf. John 17:21-22, 2 Cor. 4:16, Ps. 82:6.

[34] *Christianismi Restitutio,* 434.

[35] *Christianismi Restitutio,* 488-489.

[36] *Christianismi Restitutio,* 545-546.

[37] *Christianismi Restitutio,* 434.

[38] *Christianismi Restitutio,* 495.

[39] *Christianismi Restitutio,* 364.

[40] *Christianismi Restitutio,* 366.

[41] *Christianismi Restitutio,* 412, 372.

[42] *Christianismi Restitutio,* 412.

[43] *Christianismi Restitutio,* 375.

[44] *Christianismi Restitutio,* 555.

[45] *Christianismi Restitutio,* 574; cf. John 3:6.

[46] *Christianismi Restitutio,* 619.

[47] *Christianismi Restitutio,* 575.

[48] *Calvini Opera,* 8:834-835.

[49] *Calvini Opera,* 8:482.

[50] *Calvini Opera,* 8:484-486.

[51] *Calvini Opera,* 8:748.37.

[52] Printed in the *Restitutio* and in *Calvini Opera,* 8:645-714 with the variants of the Paris manuscript.

[53] *Calvini Opera,* 8:833-834.

[54] *Calvini Opera,* 12:283, February 13, 1546. Doumergue, *Jean Calvin,* 6:260-261, regards this as old style, hence 1547. [For an English translation see *Letters of John Calvin,* ed. Jules Bonnet (Edinburgh, 1857), 2:19.]

[55] *Calvini Opera,* 8:xxx-xxxi.

[56] Isa. 61:3.

[57] *Christianismi Restitutio,* 409; cf. Rev. 6:2-8.

[58] *Christianismi Restitutio,* 460.

[59] *Christianismi Restitutio,* 403, 409, 667.

[60] *Christianismi Restitutio,* 628.

[61] Karl Rembert, *Die "Wiedertäufer" im Herzogtum Jülich* (Berlin, 1899), 363 n. 1.

[62] Rev. 12:6.

[63] *Christianismi Restitutio,* 388-410.

[64] *Christianismi Restitutio,* 535; cf. Rev. 7:17, Rev. 19.

[65] *Calvini Opera,* 8:750-751. Servetus said in 1553 that this letter was written more than six years before (*Calvini Opera* 8:769.15). The whole correspondence with the Genevans would then have ended not later than 1547.

Chapter 8
Brush with the Inquisition

[1] *Ioannis Calvini Opera quae supersunt omnia* (Corpus reformatorum), 8:835. Cf. Stanislas Kot, "L'influence de Michel Servet sur le mouvement antitrinitarien en Pologne et en Transylvanie," in Bruno Becker, ed., *Autour de Michel Servet et de Sébastien Castellion* (Haarlem, 1953), 90 n. 39.

[2] DeVaux de Lancey, ed., *Premier livre des Emblèmes composé par Guillaume Guéroult à Lyon* (Rouen: Société Rouennaise de Bibliophiles, 1937), introduction. Cf. *Calvini Opera,* 11:146; Émile Doumergue, *Jean Calvin, les hommes et les choses de son temps* (Lausanne, 1899-1927), 6:255-256.

[3] *Calvini Opera,* 8:852-853, 8:781.21.

[4] Jean Crespin, *Histoire des martyrs* (Geneva, 1582), 4:230a. Cf. Nathanaël Weiss, "Les Cinq Étudiants de Lyon devant le Parlement de Paris 17-18 février 1553," *Bulletin de la Société pour l'Histoire du Protestantisme Français* 41 (1892), 306-308; Nathanaël Weiss, "Calvin, Servet, G. de Trie et le Tribunal de Vienne," *Ibid.* 57 (1908), 396.

[5] This and the following documents were discovered by Abbé d'Artigny and published in Antoine Gachet d'Artigny, "Mémoires pour servir à l'histoire de Michel Servet," *Nouveaux mémoires d'histoire, de critique et de littérature* (Paris, 1749-1756), vol. 2. They were subsequently published in Johann Lorenz Mosheim, *Neue Nachrichten von dem berühmten spanischen Arzte Michael Serveto* (Helmstadt, 1750), and Friedrich Trechsel, *Die protestantischen Antitrinitarier vor Faustus Socin* (Heidelberg, 1844), after independent consultation of the originals which have subsequently been destroyed. The documents and much of the narrative of d'Artigny are given in *Calvini Opera,* 8:833ff.

[6] *Christianismi Restitutio,* 199.

[7] *Calvini Opera,* 8:839.

[8] *Calvini Opera,* 8:839-840.

[9] *Calvini Opera,* 8:840-844.

[10] Nikolaus Paulus, in *Protestantismus und Toleranz im 16. Jahrhundert* (Freiburg im Breisgau, 1911), 228ff., lists many Protestants who consider Calvin to have been the instigator. For the contrary view, see Weiss, "Calvin, Servet, G. de Trie, et le Tribunal de Vienne," 387-404, and Doumergue, *Jean Calvin,* 6:276-301.

[11] *Calvini Opera,* 8:732.5, 8:738.4, 8:789, 8:805. Calvin said that Servetus had circulated this charge in Padua and Venice (*Ibid.,* 8:479).

[12] *Calvini Opera,* 8:479.

[13] The reference is to a letter not extant.

[14] The passage is obscure. The reference cannot be to the printed work, which had not been in Lausanne for two years.

[15] *Calvini Opera,* 8:843-844.

[16] *Calvini Opera,* 8:851.

[17] *Calvini Opera,* 8:844-845.

[18] Weiss, "Calvin, Servet, G. de Trie, et le Tribunal de Vienne," 400 n. 1.

[19] *Calvini Opera,* 8:845-847.

[20] *Calvini Opera,* 8:847-850.

[21] *Calvini Opera,* 8:850 n. 1.

[22] In some interrogatories Servetus added details apparently discrepant: that he climbed a wall and got through a window (*Calvini Opera,* 8:746.5; cf. 8:749); that he got away at 9 o'clock in the morning (*Ibid.,* 8:788). Perhaps he meant that he was entirely clear of Lyons by 9 o'clock.

[23] *Calvini Opera,* 8:853.

[24] *Calvini Opera,* 8:784-787.

[25] *Calvini Opera,* 8:855-856.

[26] *Calvini Opera,* 8:791.

[27] On Bertet, see Doumergue, *Jean Calvin,* 6:265 n. 6.

[28] *Calvini Opera,* 8:752-757.

[29] Doumergue, *Jean Calvin,* 6:272-275.

Chapter 9
Why Geneva?

[1] *Ioannis Calvini Opera quae supersunt omnia* (Corpus reformatorum), 8:725.

[2] *Calvini Opera,* 8:770.28. The statement that he went to church comes only from an anti-Calvinist source, *Historia Mortis Serveti,* reprinted in Johann Lorenz Mosheim, *Anderweitiger Versuch einer vollständigen und unpartheyischen Ketzergeschichte* (Helmstadt, 1748), 446-451. [An English translation by Alexander Gordon was printed in *Christian Life,* 2 November 1878, 533-534; see appendix A.]

[3] *Calvini Opera,* 14:602, 8:726.

[4] Calvin accepted responsibility for the arrest. *Calvini Opera,* 8:461, 8:479, 8:726, 14:615.

[5] *Calvini Opera,* 8:727. For the provisions of the Caroline Code observed by Geneva, see Ernst Pfisterer, "Wer trägt die Schuld an Servets Feuertod?" *Die Sammlung* 3 (1948), 114-116. On Fontaine, see Émile Doumergue, *Jean Calvin, les hommes et les choses de son temps* (Lausanne, 1899-1927), 6:312.

[6] *Calvini Opera,* 8:770.28, 8:782.38.

[7] *Calvini Opera,* 8:476.

[8] *Calvini Opera,* 14:589.

[9] For this thesis, see *Calvini Opera,* 14:590 n. 1. Albert Rilliet, in "Relation du procès criminel intenté a Genève, en 1553, contre Michel Servet," *Mémoires et documents publiés par la Société de l'Histoire et d'Archéologie de Genève* 3 (1844), contended that Servetus suffered for sedition rather than heresy. Doumergue *(Jean Calvin,* 6:309 n. 5) linked intimately the cases of Servetus and Berthelier the Libertine, and held that a residence of Servetus in Geneva prior to his arrest could not be disproved. In this he was sustained by Karl Holl, *Johannes Calvin* (Tübingen, 1909), 53.

[10] *Calvini Opera,* 20:438.

[11] *Calvini Opera,* 20:437 and note.

[12] *Calvini Opera,* 21:146, 14:602.

[13] *Calvini Opera,* 14:614.

[14] *Calvini Opera,* 8:782.37, 14:576.

[15] *Calvini Opera,* 8:731.38, 8:734.38.

[16] *Calvini Opera,* 8:740.38.

[17] *Calvini Opera,* 8:768.11, 8:780.15, 8:781.22-25.

[18] Doumergue, *Jean Calvin,* 6:310.

[19] *Calvini Opera,* 8:792.

[20] Jean Calvin, *Déclaration pour maintenir la vraie foi* (Geneva, 1554), 55; cf. *Calvini Opera,* 8:480.

[21] Doumergue, *Jean Calvin,* 6:332-334.

[22] *Calvini Opera,* 14:628.

[23] *Calvini Opera,* 14:624.

[24] *Calvini Opera,* 8:743.

[25] *Calvini Opera,* 14:623-624.

[26] Michel Roset, *Les chroniques de Genève,* ed. Henri Fazy (Geneva, 1894), 355.

[27] *Calvini Opera,* 14:657.

[28] Mosheim, *Anderweitiger Versuch,* 1:449.

[29] *Calvini Opera,* 8:825.

[30] *Calvini Opera,* 20:438.

[31] Amédée Roget, *Histoire du peuple de Genève depuis la réforme jusqu'a l'escalade,* 7 vols. in 3 (Geneva, 1870-1873), vol. 4 appendix.

[32] Roget, *Histoire du peuple de Genève,* 4:167-168.

[33] Roget, *Histoire du peuple de Genève,* 4:291 n. 1.

[34] François Bonivard, *Advis et devis de l'ancienne et nouvelle police de Genève* (Geneva, 1865), 108.

[35] Roget, *Histoire du peuple de Genève,* 4:326-327.

[36] *Calvini Opera,* 14:693.

[37] *Calvini Opera,* 21:146.

[38] Bonivard, *Advis et devis,* 107. Rilliet ("Relation du procès criminel," 104) suggests that Claude was suspect, because on October 23, Servetus was committed to other hands.

[39] *Calvini Opera,* 8:789.

[40] *Calvini Opera,* 8:789, "et mesmes on luy avait cloue les fenestres."

[41] Rilliet, "Relation du procès criminel," 69-70.

[42] *Calvini Opera,* 8:746.5.

[43] Doumergue, *Jean Calvin,* 6:277. *Calvini Opera,* 8:738.4, 8:789, 8:805-806.

[44] *Calvini Opera,* 8:746.5, 8:749, 8:788.

[45] *Calvini Opera,* 8:767.4.

Chapter 10
The Geneva Trial

[1] *Ioannis Calvini Opera quae supersunt omnia* (Corpus reformatorum), 8:731-735.

[2] *Calvini Opera,* 8:735-741.

[3] *Calvini Opera,* 8:741-749.

[4] *Calvini Opera,* 8:759-760.

[5] *Calvini Opera,* 8:496-497.

[6] *Calvini Opera,* 8:496; cf. 8:611.

[7] *Calvini Opera,* 8:550.34; cf. 8:611.

[8] *Calvini Opera,* 8:732.6, 8:746.6.

[9] *Calvini Opera,* 8:739.27, 8:740.28.

[10] *Calvini Opera,* 8:740.30-32.

[11] *Calvini Opera,* 8:738.8, 8:740.37, 8:738.2.

[12] *Calvini Opera,* 8:779:3.

[13] *Calvini Opera,* 8:498.

[14] Irenaeus, *Adversus Haereses* 4.6.2; *Christianismi Restitutio,* 34. *Adversus Haereses,* 4.32.1; *Christianismi Restitutio,* 52, 687. Other references to Justin in *Christianismi Restitutio:* 6, 402, 671, 677, 692. Cf. Alexander Gordon, "Miguel Serveto-y-Revés," *Theological Review* 15 (1878), 429.

[15] *Calvini Opera,* 8:759. Cf. Henri Tollin, "Michael Servets Sprachkentniss," *Zeitschrift für die gesammte lutherische Theologie und Kirche* 38 (1877), 625. The passage is in Justin (Lyons, 1551), 176.

[16] *Calvini Opera,* 8:751-752, 8:761-762.

[17] *Calvini Opera,* 8:762-763.

[18] *Calvini Opera,* 8:771-775. Émile Doumergue, *Jean Calvin, les hommes et les choses de son temps* (Lausanne, 1899-1927), 6:326 n. 4, points out that the granting of counsel was at the discretion of the court.

[19] *Calvini Opera,* 8:774.

[20] *Calvini Opera,* 8:765.20, 8:777.32.

[21] *Calvini Opera,* 8:767.2-3.

[22] *Calvini Opera,* 8:770.21, 8:782.34-35.

[23] Johann Lorenz Mosheim, *Anderweitiger Versuch einer vollständigen und unpartheyischen Ketzergeschichte* (Helmstadt, 1748), 20.

[24] *Calvini Opera,* 8:765.17-19, 8:766.26-29, 8:769.17-19, 8:770.26-29.

[25] *Calvini Opera,* 8:764.13, 8:765.20, 8:768.13, 8:769-70.20.

[26] *Calvini Opera,* 8:783-784.

[27] *Calvini Opera,* 8:789-790.

[28] *Calvini Opera,* 8:791-793.

[29] *Calvini Opera,* 14:611.

[30] *Calvini Opera,* 8:524-525.

[31] *Calvini Opera,* 8:514.

[32] *Calvini Opera,* 8:535-536.

[33] *Calvini Opera,* 8:551.

[34] *Calvini Opera,* 8:517-518.

[35] *Calvini Opera,* 8:606-607.

[36] Jean Calvin, *Déclaration pour maintenir la vraie foi* (Geneva, 1554), 313; *Calvini Opera,* 8:623.

[37] *Calvini Opera,* 8:606-607.

[38] *Calvini Opera,* 8:796.

[39] *Calvini Opera,* 14:600.

[40] *Calvini Opera,* 8:797.

[41] *Calvini Opera,* 8:799-801.

[42] *Calvini Opera,* 8:804-806.

[43] *Calvini Opera,* 8:806-807.

Chapter 11
The Stake at Champel

[1] *Ioannis Calvini Opera quae supersunt omnia* (Corpus reformatorum), 8:803.

[2] *Calvini Opera,* 14:647.

[3] *Calvini Opera,* 8:816.

[4] *Calvini Opera,* 8:818-819.

[5] *Calvini Opera,* 8:810.

[6] *Calvini Opera,* 8:555-558.

[7] *Calvini Opera,* 8:820-823.

[8] *Calvini Opera,* 14:615.

[9] *Calvini Opera,* 14:633.

[10] *Calvini Opera,* 14:635-636.

[11] *Calvini Opera,* 14:642.

[12] *Calvini Opera,* 14:649.

[13] Johann Lorenz Mosheim, *Anderweitiger Versuch einer vollständigen und unpartheyischen Ketzergeschichte* (Helmstadt, 1748), 421-425.

[14] *Calvini Opera,* 14:657.

[15] *Calvini Opera,* 14:590.

[16] *Calvini Opera,* 8:827-829, rephrased, edited and condensed.

[17] *Calvini Opera,* 8:826 n. 3 (French), 8:498 (Latin).

[18] *Calvini Opera,* 8:826; cf. 14:693. Émile Doumergue, *Jean Calvin, les hommes et les choses de son temps* (Lausanne, 1899-1927), 6:356 n. 4.

[19] *Calvini Opera,* 8:826 (French), 8:460 (Latin).

[20] Mosheim, *Anderweitiger Versuch,* 449; *Calvini Opera,* 14:694.

[21] *Calvini Opera,* 14:613.

[22] *Calvini Opera,* 14:694.

[23] *Historia Mortis Serveti*; see chapter 9, note 2.

Appendix B
Roland Bainton, Honored Heretic

[1] Roland H. Bainton, *Roly: Chronicle of a Stubborn Non-Conformist* (New Haven: Yale University Divinity School, 1988), 31-32.

[2] Bainton, *Roly,* 32-46.

[3] Bainton, *Roly,* 1-4.

[4] Bainton, *Roly,* 29-30, 46, 53-54.

[5] Bainton, *Roly,* 29-30, 45.

[6] Bainton, *Roly,* 157.

[7] Bainton, *Roly,* 157-159.

[8] Roland H. Bainton, *Pilgrim Parson: The Life of James Herbert Bainton* (New York: Nelson, 1958), 106.

[9] Bainton, *Roly,* 28.

[10] Bainton, *Roly,* 158.

[11] Bainton, *Roly*, 62-64.

[12] Stephen Simpler, *Roland H. Bainton: An Examination of His Reformation Historiography* (Lewiston, NY: Edwin Mellen Press, 1985), 8-10.

[13] Bainton, *Roly*, 77-78.

[14] Bainton, *Roly*, 78-83.

[15] Alexander Gordon, "Miguel Serveto-y-Reves," *Theological Review* 15 (1878), 281-307, 408-443; "Historia Mortis Serveti," *Christian Life* 3 (2 November 1878). For details on the *Christian Life* articles, see the bibliography.

[16] Bainton, *Roly*, 82.

[17] Bainton, *Roly*, 83-84.

[18] Bainton, *Roly*, 85.

[19] Bainton, *Roly*, 93.

[20] Bainton, *Roly*, 93-95.

[21] Roland H. Bainton, "Servetus and the Genevan Libertines," *Church History* 5 (June 1936), 141-149; "The Smaller Circulation: Servetus and Colombo," *Sudhoffs Archiv für Geschichte der Medizin* 24 (1931), 371-374; "The present state of Servetus studies," *Journal of Modern History* 4 (1932), 72-92.

[22] Charles Dardier, "Michel Servet d'après ses plus récents biographes," *Revue Historique* 10 (May-June 1879), 5. Gordon, "Miguel Serveto-y-Reves," 413.

[23] Bainton, "Present State," 73.

[24] *Correspondence of Roland H. Bainton and Delio Cantimori, 1932-1966: An Enduring Transatlantic Friendship between Two Historians of Religious Toleration*, edited by John Tedeschi (Florence: Leo S. Olschki Editore, 2002), 218.

[25] Bainton, *Roly*, 96.

[26] *Correspondence of Bainton and Cantimori*, 169, 223.

[27] Bainton, *Roly*, 99, 105-108.

[28] *Correspondence of Bainton and Cantimori*, 30, 35-42; Bainton, *Roly*, 95.

[29] Bainton, *Roly*, 101.

[30] Bainton, *Roly*, 104-105.

[31] Bainton, *Roly* 117-118.

[32] Bainton, *Roly*, 98.

[33] Earl Morse Wilbur, *A History of Unitarianism*, Volume 1, *Socinianism and its Antecedents* (Cambridge: Harvard University Press, 1945), ix, 50.

[34] Roland H. Bainton, *Review of Religion* 11 (1946).

[35] Roland H. Bainton, *The Travail of Religious Liberty: Nine Biographical Studies* (Philadelphia: Westminster, 1951), 94.

[36] Roland H. Bainton, *The Reformation of the Sixteenth Century* (Boston: Beacon, 1952), 123-124.

[37] Bainton, *Reformation*, 134-135.

[38] Bainton, "Present State," 78.

[39] Myron P. Gilmore, *American Historical Review* 59:914-916; W. E. Garrison, *Christian Century* (18 November 1953); Raymond W. Albright, *Church History* 23:282-283; E. Harris Harbison, *Theology Today* 11:422-423.

[40] William Pauck, *Renaissance News* 7:45.

[41] Quirinus Breen, *Journal of Modern History* 26:373.

[42] Albright, *Church History* 23:283.

[43] Bainton, *Roly*, 129-131.

[44] Roland H. Bainton, "Burned Heretic: Michael Servetus," *Christian Century* (28 October 1953), 1231.

[45] Roland H. Bainton, *Christian Attitudes toward War and Peace: An Historical Survey and Critical Re-evaluation*, (New York: Abingdon, 1960), 13.

[46] Bainton, *Christian Attitudes*, 246, 266.

[47] Bainton, *Christian Attitudes*, 268, 248.

[48] Bainton, *Roly*, 161.

[49] *Correspondence of Bainton and Cantimori*, 11.

[50] Bainton, *Roly*, 161.

[51] Bainton, *Roly*, 173-174.

[52] Bainton, *Roly*, 193.

[53] Bainton, *Roly*, 158.

[54] Roland H. Bainton, *What Christianity Says about Sex, Love, and Marriage* (New York: Association Press, 1957), 110.

[55] Bainton, *Roly*, 194.

[56] Gregory I. Jackson, *Gospel Herald* (19 October 1976), 802.

[57] Brian Randal Reeves, *Roland H. Bainton: The Historian as Social Activist*, M.A. thesis, Truman State University, 1995.

Chronology

[1] Born in 1509: *Ioannis Calvini Opera quae supersunt omnia* (Corpus reformatorum), 8:780.8. Born in 1511 (20 yrs. old in 1531): *Calvini Opera*, 8:845-846; *Christianismi Restitutio*, Edinburgh ms. Born in 1511-13: *Calvini Opera*, 8:848; cf. Henri Tollin, "Zur Servet-Kritik," *Zeitschrift für wissenschaftliche Theologie* 21 (1878), 425-466.

[2] *Calvini Opera*, 8:846.

[3] Left Spain 1528-29: *Calvini Opera*, 8:766-767. In Toulouse 2 or 3 years: *Calvini Opera*, 8:780.8; cf. 8:767.4.

[4] *Calvini Opera*, 8:846.

[5] *Calvini Opera*, 8:846.

[6] Ernst Staehelin, *Briefe und Akten zum Leben Oekolampads* 2 (Leipzig, 1934), no. 765, no. 1010.

[7] Staehelin, *Briefe und Akten* 2, no. 1010; *Calvini Opera,* 8:767.4, 8:893 n. 4.

[8] *Calvini Opera,* 8:893, 8:895.

[9] Marcel Bataillon, "Honneur et Inquisition: Michel Servet poursuivi par l'Inquisition espagnole," *Bulletin Hispanique* 27 (January-March, 1925).

[10] Victor-Louis Bourrilly and Nathanaël Weiss, "Jean du Bellay, les Protestants et la Sorbonne 1529-1535," *Bulletin de la Société pour l'Histoire du Protestantisme Français* 53 (1904), 103.

[11] *Calvini Opera,* 8:767.4, 8:846.

[12] Théodore de Bèze dates this in 1534 in *Calvini Opera,* 21:123f., but in 1533 in *Histoire ecclésiastique des églises réformées au royaume de France* (Paris, 1883-1889) 1:25, cf. n. 2. Calvin dates it in 1537 in *Calvini Opera,* 8:460, cf. 8:481. Émile Doumergue inclines to 1534 in *Jean Calvin, les hommes et les choses de son temps* (Lausanne, 1899-1927), though less confidently in 6:208 n. 5 than in 1:441.

[13] Tollin, "Zur Servet-Kritik," 449.

[14] *Opere del Dr. Giulio Ceradini* (Milan, 1906), 1:260 n.

[15] Henri Tollin, "M. Servets Pariser Prozess urkundlich dargestellt," *Deutsches Archiv für Geschichte der Medizin* 3 (1880), 186.

[16] Tollin, "Zur Servet-Kritik," 449.

[17] *Calvini Opera,* 8:767.5, 8:846.

[18] Julien Baudrier, "Michel Servet, ses relations avec les libraires et les imprimeurs lyonnais," *Mélanges offerts à Émile Picot* (Paris, 1913), 1:41.

[19] Baudrier, "Michel Servet," 1:41.

[20] Baudrier, "Michel Servet," 1:50f.

[21] Baudrier, "Michel Servet," 1:49.

[22] Calvin's letter to Farel, February 13, 1546, *Calvini Opera,* 12:283; cf. Doumergue, *Jean Calvin,* 6:260-261.

[23] *Calvini Opera,* 8:853, 8:781.21.

[24] *Calvini Opera,* 8:835-838.

[25] *Calvini Opera,* 8:725.

[26] *Calvini Opera,* 8:851-855.

Bibliography

Editor's Note:
This bibliography was prepared specifically for this edition of *Hunted Heretic*. It emphasizes works essential to Servetus historiography; works in western European languages; works on Servetus as a religious figure; and works that a researcher can locate with a minimum of trouble and expense. Not every work listed in the original 1953 bibliography has been included here. Mention of some works, which were cited by Bainton for background purposes or to establish a point of detail, has been confined to the endnotes.

For a more detailed bibliography of the earlier literature, see Earl Morse Wilbur, *A Bibliography of the Pioneers of the Socinian-Unitarian Movement* (see under Selected Works about Servetus below). Wilbur's bibliography includes dramas about Servetus, which are not included here, and a much greater selection from the medical literature, here held to a minimum.

Annotations in this bibliography are taken from the following sources. For full citations, see the bibliography. Annotations not otherwise credited are those of the editor.

Alcalá, Ángel. 1973. Epilogue to *Miguel Servet, el hereje perseguido.*
Alcalá, Ángel. 1980. Introduction to *Restitución del cristianismo.*
Alcalá, Ángel. 2004. Annotations supplied by Alcalá for this edition.
Bainton, Roland H. 1932. "The present state of Servetus studies."
Bainton, Roland H. 1953. Bibliography of *Hunted Heretic.*
Bainton, Roland H. 1960. Introduction to paperback edition of *Hunted Heretic.*
Dardier, Charles. 1879. "Michel Servet d'après ses plus récents biographes."
Friedman, Jerome. 1974. "Michael Servetus: Exegete of Divine History."
Friedman, Jerome. 1978. *Michael Servetus: a case study in total heresy.*
Goldstone, Lawrence, and Nancy Goldstone. 2002. *Out of the Flames.*
Gordon, Alexander. 1878. "Miguel Serveto-y-Reves."
Hillar, Marian. 2002. *Michael Servetus: Intellectual Giant, Humanist, and Martyr.*
Howe, Charles. 1997. *For Faith and Freedom.*

Ladame, Paul Louis. 1913. *Michel Servet, sa réhabilitation historique.*

Mackall, Leonard L. 1919. "Servetus Notes."

Mackall, Leonard L. 1924. "A Manuscript of the 'Christianismi Restitutio.'"

Norton, Andrews. 1813. "Life of Michael Servetus."

Osler, William. 1909. "Michael Servetus."

Schaff, Philip. 1890. *History of the Christian Church.*

Simpler, Steven. 1985. *Roland H. Bainton: An Examination of His Reformation Historiography.*

Wilbur, Earl Morse. 1932. Introduction to *The two treatises of Servetus on the Trinity.*

Wilbur, Earl Morse. 1950. *A bibliography of the pioneers of the Socinian-Unitarian movement.*

Works by Servetus

Note: A detailed bibliography of Servetus's works prepared by Madeline E. Stanton, giving a census of copies, and location of rare editions, is found in John Fulton, *Michael Servetus, Humanist and Martyr* (see below).

Apologetica disceptatio pro astrologia. Paris, 1538. Reprinted by Henri Tollin. Berlin, 1880.

> [English trans.] In *Michael Servetus, a Translation of his Geographical, Medical and Astrological Writings.* Translated by Charles Donald O'Malley. Philadelphia: American Philosophical Society, 1953.
>
> [Spanish trans.] In *Obras Completas,* vol. 3 (see below).

Christianismi Restitutio. Vienne, 1553. Reprint, Nuremberg, 1790; Frankfurt am Main: Minerva, 1966.

> [German trans.] *Wiederherstellung des Christentums.* Translated by Bernhard Spiess. Contains the *Apologia to Melanchthon* in Latin. 3 volumes. Wiesbaden, 1892-96.
>
> [Spanish trans.]
>
> 1. *Restitución del cristianismo.* Translated by Ángel Alcalá and Luis Betés; edited by Ángel Alcalá. Madrid: Fundación Universitaria Española, 1980. Reviewed by Bainton in *Renaissance Quarterly* 34 (Winter 1981), 583-584.
>
> 2. *Treinta cartas a Calvino; Sesenta signos del Anticristo; Apología de Melanchton.* Translated by Ángel Alcalá. Madrid: Castalia, 1981.
>
> [English trans.]There is no complete translation into English. A translation of the section describing the lesser circulation may be found in O'Malley, *Michael Servetus, a Translation of his Geographical, Medical and Astrological Writings* (see under *Apologetica disceptatio pro astrologia* above).

De justicia regni Christi, capitula quatuor. Hagenau, 1532. See *Dialogorum de Trinitate.*

De Regno Christi. Alba Julia, 1569.

> A portion of *Christianismi Restitutio,* issued by Giorgio Biandrata.

De Trinitate Divina. London, 1723.

> A portion of *Christianismi Restitutio,* partly printed, then suppressed.

De Trinitatis erroribus libri septem. Hagenau, 1531. Spurious edition, Regensburg, 1721?

> [Dutch trans.] *Van de Dolinghen in de Drievvldigheyd.* Translated by Reiner Telle. Amsterdam, 1620.
>
> [English trans.] *The two treatises of Servetus on the Trinity: On the Errors of the Trinity, 7 books, A.D. 1531. Dialogues on the Trinity, 2 books. On the righteousness of Christ's kingdom, 4 chapters, A.D. 1532.* Translated and edited by Earl Morse Wilbur. Cambridge: Harvard University Press, 1932.
>
> [Spanish trans.] In *Obras Completas,* vol. 2 (see below).

"Declarationis Jesu Christi filii Dei libri V." Manuscript.

> [Spanish trans.] In *Obras Completas,* vol. 2 (see below).
>
> For details on this work see Stanislas Kot, "L'influence de Michel Servet sur le mouvement antitrinitarien en Pologne et en Transylvanie" (see under Selected Works about Servetus below); and Bainton's "Notes on 'Declarationis Jesu Christi filii Dei libri V'" (at the end of this Bibliography).

Dialogorum de Trinitate libri duo. De justicia regni Christi, capitula quatuor. Hagenau, 1532. Spurious edition, Regensburg, 1721?

> [English trans.] In *The two treatises of Servetus on the Trinity* (see under *De Trinitatis Erroribus* above).
>
> [Spanish trans.] In *Obras Completas,* vol. 2 (see below).

In Leonardum Fuchsium apologia. Lyons, 1536. Reprint, Oxford, 1909.

> [English trans.] In *Michael Servetus, a Translation of his Geographical, Medical and Astrological Writings* (see under *Apologetica disceptatio pro astrologia* above).
>
> [Spanish trans.] In *Obras Completas,* vol. 3 (see below).

In quendam medicum apologetica disceptatio pro astrologia. Paris, 1538.

> See under *Apologetica disceptatio pro astrologia* above.

Syruporum universa ratio. Paris, 1537; Venice, 1545; Lyons, 1546; Lyons, 1547; Lyons, 1548.

> [English trans.] In *Michael Servetus, a Translation of his Geographical, Medical and Astrological Writings* (see under *Apologetica disceptatio pro astrologia* above).
>
> [Spanish trans.] In *Obras Completas,* vol. 3 (see below).

Obras Completas (Zaragoza: Prensas Universitarias de Zaragoza, 2003-). Spanish translation of Servetus's works. Edited by Ángel Alcalá.

> Three volumes have appeared so far. Volume 1 is devoted to documentation of Servetus's life. Volume 2 includes *De Trinitatis erroribus,* "Declarationis Jesu Christi filii Dei," *Dialogorum de Trinitate,* and the introduction and notes to *Biblia Sacra ex Santis Pagnini tralatione.* Volume 3 includes *In Leonardum Fuchsium apologia, Apologetica disceptatio pro astrologia, Syruporum universa ratio,* and the commentaries from *Claudii Ptolomaei Geographicae.* Volumes 4-6 will include *Christianismi Restitutio,* the letters to Calvin, *Signs of the Antichrist,* and *Apology to Melancthon* (the same material published in the 1981 Castalia edition of *Restitución del cristianismo* – see under *Christianismi Restitutio* above).

Works Edited by Servetus

Biblia Sacra cum glossis. Lyons, 1545.

Biblia Sacra ex Santis Pagnini tralatione. Lyons, 1542.
[Spanish trans.] A translation of Servetus's introduction and notes is in *Obras Completas*, vol. 2 (see under Works by Servetus above).
[English trans.] Partial translations into English of Servetus's introduction and notes may be found in *Impartial History*, 46-58; Willis, *Servetus and Calvin*, 146-156; Newman, "Michael Servetus the Anti-Trinitarian Judaizer," 543-547 (see under Selected Works about Servetus below).

Claudii Ptolomaei Geographicae enarrationis libri octo. Lyons, 1535. Second edition, Vienne, 1541.
[Spanish trans.] In *Obras Completas*, vol. 3 (see under Works by Servetus above).
[English trans.] A partial translation into English of the first edition and the introduction to the second may be found in O'Malley, *Michael Servetus, a Translation of his Geographical, Medical and Astrological Writings* (see under *Apologetica disceptatio pro astrologia* above).

Other Sixteenth-Century Works and Documents

Alesius, Alexander. *Contra horrendas Serveti blasphemias.* Leipzig, 1554-1555.
Alexander Alesius was a Scottish theologian and physician, long resident in Germany. An associate of Luther and Melanchthon, he signed the Augsburg Confession in 1530.

Artigny, Antoine Gachet d'. "Mémoires pour servir à l'histoire de Michel Servet" (see under Selected Works about Servetus below).
Contains records of the Vienne trial.

Bèze, Théodore de. *De haereticis a civili magistratu puniendis libellus, aduersus Martini Bellii farraginem, & nouorum academicorum sectam.* Geneva, 1554.
[French version] *Traité de l'autorité du magistrat en la punition des hérétiques.* Geneva, 1560.

Bolsec, Jérôme-Hermès. *Histoire de la vie, mœurs, actes, doctrine, constance et mort de Jean Calvin.* Paris, 1577.

Calvin, John. *Defensio orthodoxae fidei de sacra Trinitate contra prodiciosos errores Michaelis Serveti Hispani* (see under *Ioannis Calvini Opera* below).
[French version.] *Déclaration pour maintenir la vraie foi que tiennent tous Chrestiens de la Trinité des personnes en un seul Dieu.* Geneva, 1554.

————. *Institutio Christianae religionis.* Basel, 1536.
[English trans.] *Institutes of the Christian Religion.* Translated by Ford Lewis Battles. Grand Rapids: Eerdmans, 1975.

————. *Institutio Christianae religionis, in libris quatuor.* Geneva, 1559.
[English trans.] *Calvin: Institutes of the Christian Religion.* Translated by Ford Lewis Battles. Edited by John T. McNeill. 2 volumes. Philadelphia: Westminster, 1960.

This later edition of Calvin's *Institutes* contains a number of references to Servetus and refutations of his theology.
Reviewed by Bainton in *Interpretation* 16 (1962), 98-100.

―――. *Ioannis Calvini Opera quae supersunt omnia* (vol. 29-87 of Corpus reformatorum). Brunswick, 1863-1900.
Volume 8 contains Calvin's *Defensio*, the records of the Geneva trial in French, and letters about Servetus. Volumes 10 through 20 contain Calvin's correspondence. Of special interest is Volume 14 (1551-1553). Volume 20 has a supplement containing letters from various periods. Volume 21 contains the *Annales Calviniani*, a chronology based upon documents from several sources.

―――. *Letters of John Calvin*. Translated and edited by Jules Bonnet. 4 volumes. Philadelphia, 1858.
English translation of Calvin's correspondence.

Castellion, Sébastien. *Contra libellum Calvini in quo ostendere conatur hæreticos jure gladij coercendos esse*. Amsterdam, 1612.
[French trans.] *Contre le libelle de Calvin après la mort de Michel Servet*. Translated by Étienne Barilier. Geneva: Carouge, 1998.

―――. *De haereticis, an sint persequendi et omnino quomodo sit cum eis agendum*. 1554.
[French version] *Traité des hérétiques, à savoir, si on les doit persécuter, et comment on se doit conduire avec eux, selon l'avis, opinion, et sentence de plusieurs auteurs, tant anciens, que modernes*. 1554.
[English trans.] *Concerning heretics: whether they are to be persecuted and how they are to be treated*. Translated and edited by Roland H. Bainton. New York: Columbia University Press, 1935.

Commentarii facultatis medicinae parisiensis, 5:97ff. Reprint, edited by Achille Chéreau, in *Bulletin de l'académie de médicine* (1879), 799-801.
Contains records of Servetus's trial for teaching astrology.

Historia de morte Serveti. (c.1554)
A short narrative of unknown authorship, first found bound with Castellion's *Contra Libellum Calvini*. Reprinted in Allwoerden, *Historia Michaelis Serveti* and Mosheim, *Anderweitiger Versuch*.
[English trans.] "Historia Mortis Serveti," *Christian Life* 3 (November 2, 1878). Translated by Alexander Gordon. Included in this volume as Appendix A.
[Spanish trans.] In *Obras Completas*, vol. 1 (see under Works by Servetus above).
"With the letter written by Farel to Ambrosius Blaurer, 10th December, 1553 . . . it forms the only trustworthy relation of the last moments of Serveto."
Gordon, 1878, introduction to the translation.

Registre de la Compagnie des Pasteurs de Genève au temps de Calvin. Edited by Jean-François Bergier, Robert Kingdon, et al. Geneva: Droz, 1962-1964.
The trial of Servetus is in vol. 2.
Reviewed by Bainton in *Archiv für Reformationsgeschichte* 55 (1964), 279-280.
[English trans.] *Register of the Company of Pastors of Geneva in the time of Calvin*. Translated and edited by Philip Edgcumbe Hughes. Grand Rapids: Eerdmans, 1966.

Schlüsselburg, Konrad. *Haereticorum catalogus.* Frankfurt, 1587-1599.
Konrad Schlüsselburg, Lutheran theologian and controversialist, was a fierce opponent of Calvinism.

Servet: Vida, Muerte, y Obra. Volume 1 of *Obras Completas* (see under Works by Servetus above).
Contains documents in Spanish about Servetus's family; Spanish translations of records of the trials in Vienne and Geneva; letters and excerpts from the controversy that followed Servetus's execution, including portions of Calvin's *Defensio* and works by Castellion.

Wigand, Johann. *De persequutione impiorum.* Frankfurt, 1580.

————. *De Servetianismo, seu de antitrinitatis.* Königsburg, 1575.
Lutheran theologian Johann Wigand denied that Servetus was a true martyr.

Selected Works about Servetus

Alcalá, Ángel. "Los dos grandes legados de Servet." *Turia* 63-64 (2003), 221-242.

————. Introduction to *Restitución del cristianismo,* 7-111 (see under Works by Servetus above).

————. Introduction to *Treinta cartas a Calvino,* 9-76 (see under Works by Servetus above).

————. *Miguel Servet.* Zaragoza: Caja de Ahorros de la Inmaculada de Aragón, 2000.

————. "Nuestra deuda con Servet: de Menéndez Pelayo a la obra de Barón." *Revista de Occidente,* 113-114 (1972), 233-260.

————. *El sistema de Servet.* Madrid: Fundación Juan March, 1978.

Allen, Joseph Henry. "Michael Servetus." *New World* 1 (1892), 639-657.
Eminent Unitarian historian's synopsis of Servetus's life and thought shows familiarity with then-current literature and a sophisticated appreciation of *De Trinitatis Erroribus.*

————. "Servetus." In Joseph Henry Allen and Richard Eddy, *A History of the Unitarians and the Universalists in the United States.* New York, 1894.
A slightly updated version of the above article. Allen's part of the Allen/Eddy work was also published separately, in the same year, as *An Historical Sketch of the Unitarian Movement Since the Reformation.*

Allwoerden, Henrik van. *Historia Michaelis Serveti.* Helmstadt, 1727.
[Dutch trans.] *Historie van Michael Servetus den Spanjaart.* Rotterdam, 1729.
"The first attempt at a life of Servetus." Wilbur, 1932.

Arribas Salaberri, Julio P. *Genealogía y heráldica de Miguel Servet.* Lérida: Instituto de Estudios Llerdenses, 1972.

————. *Miguel Servet, concejal: con una síntesis biográfica.* Lérida: Graficas Larrosa, 1974.

Artigny, Antoine Gachet d'. "Mémoires pour servir à l'histoire de Michel Servet." In *Nouveaux mémoires d'histoire, de critique et de littérature*, 2:55-154. Paris, 1749.
"Contains the only extant records of the Vienne trial." Wilbur, 1932.
"D'Artigny's contributions are now largely available in the Calvini Opera, vol. 8, but for a few details the original must still be consulted." Bainton, 1932.

Aubert, Hippolyte. "L'opinion de Farel sur Servet d'après un texte inédit." *Bulletin de la Société de l'histoire du Protestantisme Français* 69 (1920), 17-24.

Bainton, Roland H. "Burned Heretic: Michael Servetus." *Christian Century*, 70 (1953), 1230-1231.

————. *Hunted Heretic: The Life and Death of Michael Servetus, 1511-1553*. Boston: Beacon Press, 1953. Paperback edition with new foreword, 1960.
[French edition] *Michel Servet; hérétique et martyr, 1511-1553*. Geneva: Droz, 1953.
[German trans.] *Michael Servet, 1511-1553*. Translated by Senta Bergfield, Agnes Müller, and Gustav Adolf Benrath. Gütersloh: Gerd Mohn, 1960.
[Spanish trans.] *Miguel Servet, el hereje perseguido* (1511-1553). Translated by Ángel Alcalá. Madrid: Ediciónes Taurus, 1973.
"A towering little book." Alcalá, 1973.
"The best recent work on Servetus and the modern starting point for all Servetus scholarship . . . The ideas of the Restitution are nicely described with many of its new ideas cited. One great strength of this volume is the author's non-polemical and non-ideological approach." Friedman, 1978.
"The best tool that the most demanding Servetian researcher could hope for." Alcalá, 1980.

————. "Michael Servetus and the Pulmonary Transit." *Bulletin of the History of Medicine* 25 (1951), 1-7.

————. "Michael Servetus and the trinitarian speculation of the Middle Ages." In Becker, *Autour de Michel Servet* (see below).
"This article has been largely incorporated into chapter 2 of the present work, but without the Latin citations from the scholastics in the footnotes." Bainton, 1960.

————. "New Documents on Early Protestant Rationalism." *Church History* 7 (1938), 179-187.

————. "The present state of Servetus studies." *Journal of Modern History* 4 (1932), 72-92.

————. *The Reformation of the Sixteenth Century*. Boston: Beacon Press, 1952.
Chapter 7, "The Free Spirits," places Servetus in the context of a mystical and rationalist strand within the Reformation.
[Italian trans.] *La Riforma protestante*. Translated by Francesco Lo Bue. Turin: Einaudi, 1958.

————. "Servetus and the Genevan Libertines." *Church History* 5 (June 1936), 141-149.

————. "The Smaller Circulation: Servetus and Colombo." *Sudhoffs Archiv für Geschichte der Medizin* 24 (1931), 371-374.

————. "The Struggle for Religious Liberty." *Collected Papers in Church History.* Series Two. Boston: Beacon Press, 1963.

————. *The Travail of Religious Liberty: Nine Biographical Studies.* Philadelphia: Westminster, 1951.
> Chapters 2-4 are on Calvin, Servetus, and Castellion.
> [Italian trans.] *La Lotta per la libertà religiosa.* Translated by Franca Medioli Cavara. Bologna: Il Mulino, 1963.

Balázs, Mihály. "Die osteuropäische Rezeption der *Restitutio Christianismi* von Servet." In Róbert Dán and Antal Pirnát, ed., *Antitrinitarianism in the Second Half of the 16th Century.* Leiden: E.J. Brill, 1982.

————. *Early Transylvanian Antitrinitarianism (1566-1571): from Servet to Palaeologus.* Baden-Baden: Éditions Valentin Koerner, 1996.
> Includes a chapter on the relationship between *Christianismi Restitutio* and Francis Dávid's *De regno Christi.*

Balmas, Enea Henri. "Tra umanesimo e riforma: Guillaume Gueroult, 'terzo uomo' del proceso Serveto." In *Montaigne a Padova: e altri studi sulla letteratura francese del cinquecento.* Padua: Liviana, 1962.

Barón Fernández, José. *Miguel Servet: su vida y su obra.* Madrid: Espasa-Calpe, 1970.
> "Very worthy for many reasons, although deficient for many others . . . [Serving truth is] not done by 'removing the theological chaff,' as Barón says. On the contrary, everything in Servetus's work is 'chaff' except his thought, his speculative theories, and his honest life commitment to a radical reformation at any price, even the price of his own life." Alcalá, 1973.
> "Most complete in many points, above all on Servetus as a physician. He does poorly in his exposition of [Servetus's] intellectual system, to the study of which he admitted himself to be incompetent; restricting himself to stating that it was characterized by 'mysticism toward Jesus,' the influence of Neoplatonism, pantheism, and anabaptism, taking these concepts from Bainton without further personal investigation." Alcalá, 1980.

Barrios, Benet Roura. "Sobre M. Servet." *Joventut* 5, no. 222 (12 May 1904), 297-299.
> Summarized in *La Chronique Médicale* (15 August 1905), 556-558.

Bataillon, Marcel. "Honneur et inquisition: Michel Servet poursuivi par l'Inquisition espagnole." *Bulletin Hispanique* 27 (January-March, 1925).
> Based upon Inquisition documents preserved in the National Historical Archive in Madrid.

Baudrier, Julien. "M. Servet, ein Vorläufer K. Ritters und Alex. von Humboldts." *Zeitschrift der Gesellschaft für Erdkunde zu Berlin* 14 (1879), 356-368.

————. "Michael Servet als Geograph." *Zeitschrift der Gesellschaft für Erdkunde zu Berlin* 10 (1875), 182-222.

————. "Michel Servet, ses relations avec les libraires et les imprimeurs lyonnais." *Mélanges offerts à Émile Picot,* 1:41-56. Paris, 1913.

Bayon, H. P. "Calvin, Serveto, and Rabelais." *Isis* (1947).

————. "William Harvey, Physician and Biologist: his precursors, opponents, and successors." *Annals of Science* 3 (October 1938), 434-457; 4 (January 1939), 65-107.

Beach, Seth Curtis. "Michael Servetus," *Unitarian Review* 22 (1884), 429-445; 24 (1885), 149-164.
> An American Unitarian historian. Does not claim Servetus as Unitarian. Accepts Saisset's characterization of Servetus as "pantheist." Derivative, but decent for its time.

Becker, Bruno, ed. *Autour de Michel Servet et de Sébastien Castellion.* Haarlem: H.D. Tjeenk Willink, 1953.
> Reviewed by Bainton in *Theologische Lituraturzeitung* 80 (1955), 356-358.
> Reviewed by George Huntston Williams in *Proceedings of the Unitarian Historical Society* 11/2 (1957), 29-35.

Buisson, Ferdinand Edouard. *Sébastien Castellion, sa vie et son oeuvre (1515-1563).* Nieuwkoop: B. de Graaf, 1964.

Bullón y Fernández, Eloy. *Miguel Servet y la geografía del renacimiento.* Madrid, 1929.
> "Knowledgeable exposition of Ptolemy's Renaissance editions, with superficial, uncritical summary of Servetus's purported additions. He... believed that those scholia are by Servetus, while ... all of them, with three or four minor corrections, except those on four countries, were already in the 1525 Pirckheimer edition." Alcalá, 2004.

Castro y Calvo, José. "Contribución al estudio de Miguel Servet y de su obra 'Syruporum.'" *Universidad* 8 (1931), 797-830, 977-1030; 9 (1932), 3-71.

Cavard, Pierre. *Le procès de Michel Servet à Vienne.* Isère: Syndicat d'Initiative Vienne, 1953.
> "Many illuminating details are given regarding those with whom he consorted and those who were to have a part in his trial: the inquisitor Matthew Ory, the Cardinal Tournon, the Lieutenant Governor Guy de Maugiron, the printer Arnoullet, and others. As for the trial, only two items are new. First: The prison in which Servetus was detained has been carefully mapped and the precise course of his escape has been traced. Second: Cavard reports that Calvin, in the French version of his *De scandalis*, printed in 1550 and reprinted in 1551, declared that Michael Servetus was operating in France under the pseudonym of Michel de Villeneuve. This must mean that the literary circles in Lyons and Vienne knew who he was, yet were content to leave him unmolested, so long as he deported himself inoffensively." Bainton, 1960.

Chauffepié, Jacques Georges de. "Servet." *Nouveau dictionnaire historique et critique,* 4:219-245. Amsterdam, 1753.
> [English trans.] *The Life of Servetus.* Translated by James Yair. London, 1771.
> "Violent prejudice against Servetus." Wilbur, 1950.

Chauvet, Adolphe. *Étude sur le système théologique de Servet.* Strassburg, 1867.

"I have not seen Chauvet's article, but from the citations of others I judge that he rightly emphasized the importance of the Neoplatonists and Philo without adequately showing the precise nature of their influence." Bainton, 1932. See also Alcalá comment on Saisset, below.

Choisy, Eugène. *Le journal de Genève*. 3 November 1903.
Newspaper article by the Genevan minister and president of the church who led the ceremonies dedicating the expiatory monument to Servetus in Geneva.

————. "Le procès et le bûcher de Michel Servet." *Revue Chrétienne* 18 (1903), 269-292.

————. *La théocratie à Genève au temps du Calvin*. Geneva, 1897.

[Crellius, Samuel.] "Annotationes quaedam de Michaele Serveto." *Bibliotheca historico-philologico-thelogica* 1 (1719), 739-760.
"Gives Servetus's theological system, enlarging and correcting de la Roche." Wilbur, 1950.

Cuthbertson, David. *A Tragedy of the Reformation*. Edinburgh and London, 1912.
"Consists of scrappy quotations and a few bibliographical notes." Bainton, 1932.

Dardier, Charles. "Michel Servet d'après ses plus récents biographes." *Revue Historique* 10 (May-June 1879).
Reviews recent work on Servetus, esp. Tollin and Willis. The review functions as Dardier's own biography of Servetus, though he disclaimed that purpose. He also wrote an entry on Servetus in *Encyclopédie des Sciences religieuses*. [Spanish translation] In *Anfiteatro anatomico* (30 June 1879-31 March 1880).

Dide, Auguste. *Michel Servet et Calvin*. Paris, 1907.
"Follows Tollin blindly, and bitter against Calvin." Wilbur, 1950.

Doumergue, Émile. "L'emplacement du bûcher de Michel Servet." *Bulletin de la Société d'histoire et d'archéologie de Genève* 2 (1903), 357-363.

————. *Jean Calvin, les hommes et les choses de son temps*. Lausanne, 1899-1927. On Servetus, see esp. 6:171-369.
"The best account of the details of [the] whole correspondence between Servetus and Calvin . . . Understands Calvin too well to do better than he in understanding his opponents." Bainton, 1932.

Drummond, William Hamilton. *The life of Michael Servetus, the Spanish physician*. London, 1848.

Eliot, Thomas Lamb. "The Martyrdom of Servetus." *Unitarian Review* 19 (1883), 58-87.
Slight and melodramatic article by an American Unitarian minister, father-in-law of E. M. Wilbur. No discussion of theology. Identifies Servetus as Unitarian.

Emde, W. "Michael Servet als Renaissance Philosoph und Restitutions-Theologie." *Zeitschrift für Kirchengeschichte* 60 (1941), 96-131.
"Valuable for its study of Servetus's theological ideas." Bainton, 1960.

Emerton, Ephraim. "Calvin and Servetus." *Harvard Theological Review* 2 (1909), 139-160.

>Harvard professor of church history, teacher of E. M. Wilbur. Fair short telling of the story, with brief exposition of Servetus's theology, pigeon-holing Servetus as Sabellian and pantheist. Critical of Servetus's "erratic" personality and somewhat lenient towards Calvin. Accounts for religious persecution as being caused by "the fatal union of civil and religious power."

Fox, Arthur Wilson. *Michael Servetus*. London: British & Foreign Unitarian Association, 1914.

>Unitarian tract based upon information supplied by Alexander Gordon. Stresses Servetus's independence of thought, sees Unitarian leanings, avoids coming to grips with his theology.

Friedman, Jerome. "The Archangel Michael vs. the Antichrist: The Servetian Drama of the Apocalypse." *Renaissance and Reformation* 11 (1975), 45-51.

―――. "Michael Servetus: the Case for a Jewish Christianity." *Sixteenth Century Journal* 4 (April 1973), 87-110.

―――. *Michael Servetus: a case study in total heresy*. Geneva: Droz, 1978.

>"A very suggestive work, relatively superior to what has been done until now regarding Servetus's theological thinking, although he did not use Kot's material." Alcalá, 1973, commenting on the book in its pre-publication form.

>"Not always successful in solving the apparent contradictions in Servetus's argumentation . . . Friedman has covered the major issues raised by Servetus." Elisabeth Feist Hirsch, review in *Archive for Reformation History* 8 (1979).

>"Mixes what is Hebrew and what is Jewish, i.e. the linguistic and the religious values." Alcalá, 1980.

―――. "Michael Servetus: Exegete of Divine History." *Church History* 43 (1974), 460-469.

―――. "Michael Servetus: Unitarian, Antitrinitarian, or Cosmic Dualist." *Proceedings of the Unitarian Universalist Historical Society* 20/2 (1985-86), 11-20.

―――. "The Reformation Merry-Go-Round: The Servetian Glossary of Heresy." *Sixteenth Century Journal* 7 (April 1976), 73-80.

―――. "Servetus and Antitrinitarianism: A Propos Antonio Rotondò." *Bibliothèque d'Humanisme et Renaissance* 35 (1973), 543-545.

Fuentes Sagaz, Manuel de. *Michael Servetus (1511-1553)*. Barcelona: Uriach, 1999.

Fulton, John F. *Michael Servetus, humanist and martyr*. New York, 1953. Includes a bibliography of Servetus's works by Madeline E. Stanton.

>"[The Stanton bibliography] is especially valuable because it locates all the known copies of the works of Servetus both in Europe and the United States." Bainton, 1960.

>"A good exposition of the priority of the blood circulation discovery in favor of Servetus." Alcalá, 1973.

————. "Michael Servetus and the lesser circulation of the blood through the lungs." In Becker, *Autour de Michel Servet* (see above).

> "Here a judicious account is given of the contributions of Servetus to pharmacology and physiology." Bainton, 1960.

Gauss, Julia. "Der junge Michael Servet." *Zwingliana* 12 (1966), 410-459.

> "She insists that Servetus owed Erasmus more than what has been shown . . . Erasmus's attacks against the scholastics, which he shared with Servetus, can also be found in Vives, another great Spaniard." Alcalá, 1973.

Gener, Pompeyo. *Servet: Reforma contra Renacimiento, calvinismo contra humanismo.* Barcelona, 1911.

> "A commendable, though unfocused, effort. His opposition of Servetus the Renaissance man with Calvin the reformer does not correspond to reality – as if Servetus were not a reformer, and Calvin were not a magnificent humanist . . . Called [Servetus] 'a philosopher of a great vision, clear, superhuman. For him the love of humanity is paramount,' in a philosophical system which 'is that of his time: naturalistic pantheism' . . . Apart from this childish distortion of doctrine, Gener invents facts and sources . . . Lamentably, this superficial and irresponsible tone was influential in its time, and many of Gener's affirmations are still transcribed without attribution by Servetians who do not submit them to independent criticism." Alcalá, 1980.

Geymonat, Jean. *Michel Servet et ses idées religieuses.* Geneva, 1892.

> "Superficial." Bainton, 1932.

Goldstone, Lawrence, and Nancy Goldstone. *Out of the Flames: the Remarkable Story of a Fearless Scholar, a Fatal Heresy, and One of the Rarest Books in the World.* New York: Broadway Books, 2002.

> Written by book collectors about *Christianismi Restitutio*, the ultimate in rare books. It tells the story of printing and includes biographical material about Servetus and about Sir William Osler, a collector of Servetus publications.
>
> "In this lively account, the authors vividly recreate a Renaissance world of revolution and reform in which the dissemination of ideas flourished thanks to the printing press . . . The Goldstones offer both a portrait of an important but neglected Renaissance humanist and a testimony to the power of books to shape minds and hearts." Publishers Weekly, 2002.
>
> "A well written monument of bibliographical research, but a monumental series of errors and misunderstandings, [showing] complete ignorance of philosophical, biblical, and theological ideas." Alcalá, 2004.

González Echeverría, Francisco Javier. *Hans Holbein el Joven y Miguel Servet: Retratos o tablas de las historias del Testamento Viejo, Lyón 1543.* Pamplona: Gobierno de Navarra, Departamento de Salud y Caja Navarra, 2001.

> *Retratos o tablas de las historias del Testamento Viejo* (Lyons: Jean and François Frellon, 1543) is the Spanish version of *Historiarum Veteris Testamenti icones*, a collection of woodcuts by Hans Holbein accompanied by short texts in Latin, which was published in a number of variant forms. An edition with Spanish verses (anonymous, except for a preface signed by the publisher) was published

in 1543. González Echeverría argues that the Spanish text – which has been edited so as to omit almost all passages in which Old Testament events and figures are interpreted as prophetic or allegorical references to Christ – was the work of Servetus. Alcalá disputes this in *Obras Completas*, vol. 2.

————. *Miguel Servet, editor del Dioscórides*. Villanueva de Sijena: Instituto de Estudios Sijenenses Miguel Servet, 1997.
"It is not impossible that Servetus had a hand in the Dioscorides, but the reasons given by González are insufficient." Alcalá, 2004.

————. "Miguel Servet pertenecía a la famosa familia de judeoconversos de los Zaporta." *Pliegos de bibliofilia* 7 (1999), 33-42.
Argues that Servetus's grandmother was a *conversa*.
"That the Zaporta family were Servetus's ancestors has been known at least since the beginning of the twentieth century, but [the connection] still has not been well researched. This article does not present the original document." Alcalá, 2004.

Gordon, Alexander. "Miguel Serveto-y-Reves." *Theological Review* 15 (1878), 281-307, 408-443.
Review of Tollin's *Charakterbild* and Willis's *Servetus and Calvin*. The review contains Gordon's own biography of Servetus. It is harshly critical of Willis, admiring of Tollin and sometimes guilty of Tollinesque excess. Compares the literary style of Servetus favorably with that of Emerson. Gordon also wrote the entry on Servetus for the *Encyclopaedia Britannica*, 1911.
"The chief living authority on Servetus." Mackall, 1924.
"For a period of nearly fifty years the late Alexander Gordon contributed articles on this subject, every one worthy of careful reading." Bainton, 1932.

————. "The personality of Michael Servetus." In *Addresses Biographical and Historical*. London, 1922.

————. Articles in *Christian Life*.
1. Review of Cuthbertson, *Tragedy of the Reformation*. 18 May 1912.
2. "Servetus and America." 24 October 1925.
3. "Servetus and the art of healing." 6 February 1926.
4. "Servetus on church and scripture." 30 January 1926.
5. "Servetus on creation." 23 January 1926.
6. "Servetus on moral freedom." 19 June 1926.
7. "Servetus and the Spanish Inquisition." 12 December 1925.
8. "Villanueva." 29 September 1888.
9. "Villanueva Revisited." 2 December 1911.

Goyanes Capdevila, José. *Miguel Serveto, teólogo, geógrafo y médico, descubridor de la circulación de la sangre*. Madrid, 1933.

Guttmann, Jacob. "Michael Servet in seinen Beziehungen zum Judentum." *Monatsschrift für Geschichte und Wissenschaft des Judenthums* n.f. 51 (1907), 77-94.
"An admirable study of the Jewish influences on the *Restitutio*." Bainton, 1932.

Harnack, Adolf von. *Lehrbuch der Dogmengeschichte.* Freiburg and Leipzig: Mohr, 1894-1897.

[English trans.] *History of Dogma.* Volume 7. Translated by William M'Gilchrist. New York: Russell and Russell, 1958.

"Bainton's interpretation of Servetus's thought follows the traditional lines developed by Adolph von Harnack." Simpler, 1985.

Heberle, Wilhelm. "Michael Servets Trinitätslehre und Christologie." *Tübinger Zeitschrift für Theologie* (1840).

Hemmeter, John C. "Michael Servetus, Discoverer of the Pulmonary Circulation: His Life and Work." *Janus* 20 (1915), 331-364. Reprinted in *Johns Hopkins Hospital Bulletin* 26 (1915), 318-326.

Hillar, Marian. *The case of Michael Servetus (1511-1553): the turning point in the struggle for freedom of conscience.* Lewiston, NY: Edwin Mellen Press, 1997.

"Hillar, a Polish expatriate and Socinian scholar, is vitriolic in his denunciations of both Calvin and the Catholic Church, but there is no doubting the depth of his research." Goldstone and Goldstone, 2002.

————— with Claire S. Allen. *Michael Servetus: Intellectual Giant, Humanist, and Martyr.* Lanham, MD: University Press of America, 2002.

The only recent major biography of Servetus in English, not as impartial as Bainton but deals with some issues omitted in *Hunted Heretic.* Includes results of more recent scholarship. Grapples with some of the more difficult aspects of Servetus's thought and looks at Servetus from a humanist and political perspective.

"Since the epoch-making book on Servet by Roland Bainton in 1953, none has been written on his life, death, and doctrines and their consequences with more clarity, authority and usefulness for the general public, while at the same time avoiding abstruse theological discussions presented in other recent books, than this remarkable work." Alcalá, 2002, from the Foreword.

Hirsch, Elisabeth Feist. "Michael Servetus and the neoplatonic tradition: God, Christ, and man." *Bibliothèque d'Humanisme et Renaissance* 42 (1980), 561-575.

—————. "Servetus and the Early Socinians." *Proceedings of the Unitarian Universalist Historical Society* 20/2 (1985-86), 21-32.

Howe, Charles A. *For Faith and Freedom: A Short History of Unitarianism in Europe.* Boston: Skinner House, 1997.

Includes chapters on the life and legacy of Servetus. Intended as a précis of the first volume of Wilbur's history of Unitarianism, supplemented with material from Williams and Bainton.

"I wrote it to bring the essence of Wilbur's and Williams's work to the general reader." Howe, 1997.

Impartial history of Michael Servetus. London, 1724.

"Hardly more than a reprint of de la Roche. Sometimes wrongly ascribed to George Benson." Wilbur, 1950.

"The most complete treatment [of Servetus's exegetical views]." Friedman, 1974.

Instituto de Estudios Sijenenses Miguel Servet, Villanueva de Sijena. Booklets on Servetus and related topics.

Instituto de Estudios Sijenenses Miguel Servet / Michael Servetus Institute was founded by Julio Arribas Salaberri in 1975 for the study of "the life and works of Michael Servetus and spreading his intellectual and scientific legacy." It sponsors lectures, publications, exhibitions, and events related to Servetus and the history of Villanueva de Sijena. Among its publications:

Alcalá, Ángel. *Servet en su tiempo y en el nuestro: el nuevo florecer del servetismo.* 1978.

Arribas Salaberri, Julio P. *En torno a Miguel Servet.* 1975.

————. "El famoso retablo de la Trinidad en Villanueva." *Circular Informativa* 5 (1978), 8-24.

————. *Fisiología y psiquis de Miguel Servet: homenaje nacional al ilustre sabio en Villanueva de Sijena.* 1975.

————. *Miguel Servet: geógrafo, astrónomo, astrólogo.* 1976.

————. "El patronímico Serveto." *Circular Informativa* 4 (1978), 11-19.

Betés Palomo, Luis. *Anotaciones al pensamiento teológico de Miguel Servet.* 1975.

Cavero Lacambra, B. "La fecha del retablo de la Trinidad costeado por la familia Serveto." *Circular Informativa* 6 (1979), 1-14.

Ferrer Benimeli, José A. *Voltaire, Servet y la tolerancia.* 1980.

Gracia Guillén, Diego. *Teología y medicina en la obra de Miguel Servet.* 1981.

Sánchez-Blanco, Francisco. *El pensamiento filosófico de Miguel Servet.* 1978.

Vega Díaz, Francisco. *Propuesta para una interpretación antropobiográfica de Miguel Servet (Mitificación, desmitificación y remitificación).* 1977.

Izquierdo, José Joaquín. "A New and More Correct Version of the Views of Servetus on the Circulation of the Blood." *Bulletin of the Institute of the History of Medicine* 5 (1937), 914-932.

Jacquot, Jean. "L'affaire Servet dans les controverses sur la tolérance au temps de la Révocation de l'Edit de Nantes." In Becker, *Autour de Michel Servet* (see above).

Karmin, Otto. *Michel Servet et Voltaire.* Lausanne, 1908.

Kot, Stanislas. "L'influence de Michel Servet sur le mouvement antitrinitarien en Pologne et en Transylvanie." In Becker, *Autour de Michel Servet* (see above). "Announcing the discovery of a new Servetus manuscript." Bainton, 1953.

————. "Michel Servet et Sébastien Castellion: Martyre et tolérance." *Bibliothèque d'Humanisme et Renaissance* 16 (1954) 222-234.

Ladame, Paul Louis. *Michel Servet, sa réhabilitation historique.* Geneva, 1913. "Respectable survey . . . nothing new save for the vagary of Ladame, who would interpret the character of Servetus from his handwriting." Bainton, 1932.

La Roche, Michel de. *Historical account of the life and trial of Michael Servetus.* London, 1712.

[French trans.] "Histoire de M. Servet," *Bibliothèque Angloise, ou histoire littéraire de la Grande Bretagne,* 3:76-198. Amsterdam, 1717-1727. "First reports from the records of the Geneva trial." Wilbur, 1932.

Larson, Martin A. "Milton and Servetus: a study in the sources of Milton's theology." *Publications of the Modern Language Association* 41 (1926), 891-934.

Latassa y Ortín, Felix de. *Biblioteca nueva de los escritores aragoneses que florecieron desde el año de 1500 hasta el de 1599*, 1:146-155. Pamplona, 1798.
Did not discuss the *Restitutio*, which he thought negligible.
"Interesting points on Quintana and Servetus." Alcalá, 1973.
"Though containing only a very brief biographical and bibliographical account, with some inconsistencies which are now superseded, it was the first step [in Spanish Servetus literature]." Alcalá, 1980.

Leibowitz, Joshua Otto. "Annotations on the Biblical aspects of Fulton's Servetus." *Journal of the History of Medicine and Allied Sciences* 10 (1955).
"Leibowitz and Margalith emphasize the influence of old Hebrew texts, especially some from Genesis referring to blood, in Servetus's investigations." Alcalá, 1973.

————. "Medical aphorisms and quotations from old Hebrew sources." *Israel Journal of Medical Sciences* 4 (1968), nos. 1, 2, 4-6.

Linde, Antonius van der. *Michel Servet, Een Brandoffer der Gereformeerde Inquisite*. Groningen, 1891.
Especially celebrated for its bibliography, which stood as the best survey until Bainton's "Present State of Servetus Studies" in 1932.
"Tollin made some errors of detail which were minutely and pitilessly revealed by Prof. van der Linde, 1891 . . . In spite of his errors, Tollin grasped the spirit of Servetus and penetrated and understood his personality better than van der Linde, who, in turn, had a better hold on the literature of the subject and had studied Servetus more from the outside." Ladame, 1913.
"Even professional bibliographers like van der Linde become careless [when writing on Servetus]." Mackall, 1919.
"His biography of Servetus was a reaction against the hagiography of Tollin, and sought to disparage the achievements and magnify the inconsistencies of Servetus." Bainton, 1932.

Mackall, Leonard L. "Servetus Notes." In *Contributions to Medical and Biological Research, dedicated to Sir William Osler, in honour of his seventieth birthday, July 12, 1919, by his pupils and co-workers*. New York, 1919.
"One of the most accurate Servetists ever." Alcalá, 1973.

————. "A Manuscript of the 'Christianismi Restitutio' of Servetus, placing the discovery of the pulmonary circulation anterior to 1546." *Proceedings of the Royal Society of Medicine* 17 (1924), 35-38.
"The author did not write this title. For 'anterior to' he would substitute 'as early as.'" Bainton, 1953.

Manzoni, Claudio. *Umanesimo ed eresia: Michele Serveto*. Naples: Guida, 1974.
"Brings into bold relief the importance of understanding Servetus's neoplatonic ideas." Friedman, 1978.

"[A] brilliant and beautiful book about the real scope of another set of sources for the Servetian system: the humanist ones, and particularly Italian humanism . . . It perhaps extrapolates conclusions which are not guaranteed nor supported by facts." Alcalá, 1980.

————. "Logica nominalistica e filosofia umanistica nel *De Trinitatis erroribus* di Michaele Serveto." *Annali della Faccoltà Filosofia e Lettere, Triste* 3 (1966), 91-112.

Margalith, David. "The first anticipations of the idea of circulation in ancient Jewish sources." *Hebrew Medical Journal* 2 (1957), 79-98, 130-134.
See Alcalá comment on Leibowitz, "Annotations," above.

Martínez Laínez, Fernando. *Miguel Servet: Historia de un fugitivo.* Barcelona: Rueda, 1991.
"A beautifully written popular biography that uses literary imagination too much . . . contains errors and inaccuracies not to be expected [in such a recent work]." Alcalá, 2004.

Menéndez y Pelayo, Marcelino. *Historia de los Heterodoxos Españoles.* Madrid, 1877.
"Relies mainly on Tollin and Willis." Wilbur, 1950.
"Incomprehensibly, ironically, not known to Bainton or included in his original Servetian bibliography . . . This work . . . [has] become very outdated. His opinions about Servetus are excessively passionate and, being extremely subjective, they are also false. However, he was the only Spanish writer who studied the Servetian texts." Alcalá, 1973.
"The first attempt to place Servetus within the context of heterodox Spanish thought." Friedman, 1978.
"His precise erudition, his clear style, his forceful turns of phrase never cease to amaze . . . His analysis of the doctrine can still be read with pleasure [but] he was not able to maintain his evaluative composure . . . the key to Servetus's system, according to Don Marcelino, was pantheism, an error into which, he said, all Spanish heretics fall 'when they dispense with logic.'" Alcalá, 1980.
"Set the tone and trend for further attempts to diminish and sidetrack the figure of Servetus in history." Hillar, 2002.

Mosheim, Johann Lorenz. *Neue Nachrichten von dem berühmten spanischen Arzte Michael Serveto.* Helmstadt, 1750.

————. *Versuch einer unpartheyischen und gründlichen Ketzergeschichte.* Helmstadt, 1746; *Anderweitiger Versuch einer vollständigen und unpartheyischen Ketzergeschichte.* Helmstadt, 1748.
"Did not sufficiently examine the works of the Spanish doctor." Dardier, 1879.
"For years the common tap from which all Servetus knowledge was derived." Osler, 1909.
"Superior to all his predecessors, though often obscure and prolix." Ladame, 1913.
"Of the works prior to van der Linde, the first of any moment, and one still worth reading, is that of Mosheim, not only for the balance of judgment,

but for the evidence which later accounts give in abbreviated form on his authority . . . Some of the documents published by Mosheim are still not readily available elsewhere, such as the apology of David Joris for Servetus." Bainton, 1932.

"Supersedes Allwoerden." Wilbur, 1932.

"Critical of d'Artigny." Wilbur, 1950.

"Approached Servetianism through his peculiar prism . . . [To Mosheim] Servetus was a fanatic, bordering on madness, who wrote without order or harmony and did not understand the most elementary philosophical and theological terms, thus resulting in an obscure and boring work, an authentic 'model of disorder.'" Alcalá, 1980.

Neuberger, Max. "Zur Entdeckungsgeschichte des Lungenkreislaufes." *Sudhoffs Archiv für Geschichte der Medizin* 23 (1930) 7-9.

Newman, Louis Israel. "Michael Servetus the Anti-Trinitarian Judaizer." In *Jewish Influence on Christian Reform Movements*. New York: Columbia University Press, 1925.

"Nowhere in this hundred-page 'investigation' of Servetus does Dr. Newman give the smallest intimation of the contention of Servetus, consistently maintained and passionately affirmed, that Jesus Christ was God . . . Newman flounders in the most elementary of Latin . . . The quotations in the footnotes swarm with transcriptional and typographical blunders." George Foote Moore, review in *American Historical Review* 32 (1926), 100-102. (For Moore's own take on Servetus, see his *History of Religions*, 2:336-337. New York: Scribner's, 1920.)

"Incorporates [Guttmann's] results and extends the study to cover the earlier theological works of Servetus." Bainton, 1932.

Norton, Andrews. "Life of Michael Servetus." *General Repository and Review* 4 (1813), 31-78.

This article, by a distinguished early American antitrinitarian theologian, scholar, and Unitarian leader, is based upon a manuscript, "Historical Sketches on Calvin and Servetus," by Francis Adrian van der Kemp, a Unitarian immigrant from the Netherlands. Norton also used d'Artigny, Mosheim, the *Impartial History*, de la Roche etc. A scholarly piece, for its time, and well balanced. Norton had no direct access to Servetus's writings. The van der Kemp manuscript was written in 1811 and deposited at Harvard University.

Odhner, Carl Theophilus. *Michael Servetus: His Life and Teachings*. Philadelphia, 1910.

"A Swedenborgian interpretation." Wilbur, 1950.

O'Malley, Charles Donald. *Michael Servetus, a Translation of his Geographical, Medical and Astrological Writings*. Philadelphia: American Philosophical Society, 1953. Contains a set of introductions to the translations.

"His translations were very difficult to do and they will be most useful, but I am slightly taken aback by his obviously acidulous attitude to Servetus." Letter, Stanislas Kot to Roland Bainton, 3 February 1954.

Ongaro, G. "La scoperta della *Christianismi Restitutio* di Michele Serveto nel XVI seclo in Italia e nel Veneto." *Episteme* 5 (1971), 3-44.

Osler, Sir William. *Bibliotheca Osleriana.* Oxford, 1929.
   A catalogue of the Osler collection at McGill University in Montréal, Québec, with annotations by Osler. Nos. 839-896 are items about Servetus. Osler's story is told by the Goldstones in *Out of the Flames.*

―――. "Michael Servetus." In *Selected Writings.* Oxford: Oxford University Press, 1951. Reprinted as *A Way of Life and other selected writings.* New York: Dover, 1958.
   A classic 1909 address by the distinguished Canadian physician. No new scholarship, relies on quotations from Emerton for Servetus's religious thought.

Pagel, Walter. "Vesalius and the pulmonary transit of venous blood." *Journal of the History of Medicine* 19 (1964), 327-334.
   "Pagel's studies have clarified some aspects of [Servetus's] medical contributions in relation to Vesalius and Harvey." Alcalá, 1973.

Palacios Sánchez, Juan Manuel. *El ilustre aragonés Miguel Servet: breve biografía del sabio español, descubridor de la circulación de la sangre.* Huesca: Consejo Superior de Estudios Oscenses, 1956.

Pano, Mariano de. "La familia de Miguel Servet." *Revista de Aragón,* May 1901, 119-121, 151-153.
   "The facts as to [Servetus's] childhood in Villanueva de Sijena . . . were disclosed by Mariano de Pano." Bainton, 1932.

Podach, E. F. "De la diffusion du *Christianismi Restitutio* (1553) au XVIe siècle." *Bulletin de la Société pour l'Histoire du Protestantisme Français* 101 (1952), 251-264.

―――. "Die Geschichte der *Christianismi Restitutio* im Lichte ihrer Abschriften." In Becker, *Autour de Michel Servet* (see above).

Pünjer, Bernhard. *De Michaelis Serveti doctrina commentationum dogmatico-historicam.* Jena, 1876.
   "Content to point out that Servetus was unorthodox and inconsistent." Bainton, 1932.
   "Accused Mosheim and other predecessors of partiality and of ignorance of the core of Servetus's system, [which he found to be] perfectly coherent and clearly expressed." Alcalá, 1980.

Rilliet, Albert. "Relation du procès criminel intenté a Genève, en 1553, contre Michel Servet." *Mémoires et documents publiés par la Société de l'Histoire et d'Archéologie de Genève* 3 (1844).
   [English trans.] *Calvin and Servetus: the reformer's share in the trial of Michael Servetus historically ascertained.* Translated and edited by William King Tweedie. Edinburgh, 1846.
   "An original work of great importance." Ladame, 1913.
   "Extracts from the Geneva records of the trial." Wilbur, 1932.

Roget, Amédée. *Histoire du peuple de Genève.* 7 volumes in 3. Geneva, 1870-1883.
"Unlike many others, Roget thinks that Michael Servetus had no acquaintance with the adversaries of Calvin, the Perrinists, either before his imprisonment or during the trial. He gives proofs which appear quite convincing." Ladame, 1913.
"The importance of the Libertines is minimized." Bainton, 1932.

Rotondò, Antonio. *Calvin and the Italian Antitrinitarians.* St. Louis: Foundation for Reformation Research, 1968.
A critique of those who connect Servetus to Socinianism and Unitarianism, arguing for Italian anti-Trinitiarianism independent of Servetus.
"If Rotondò consistently overemphasizes the importance of Lelio [Socinus]'s contribution, he consistently underestimates or misinterprets the place of Michael Servetus." Friedman, 1973.

Rude, F. "Michel Servet et l'astrologie." *Bibliothèque d'Humanisme et Renaissance* 20 (1958), 377-387.

———. "La naturalisation de Michel Servet." In Becker, *Autour de Michel Servet* (see above).
"Contains the documents on the naturalization of Michel de Villeneuve as a citizen of Vienne." Bainton, 1960.

Saisset, Émile Edmond. "Doctrine philosophique et religieuse de Michel Servet." *Revue des deux mondes* 21 (15 February 1848), 586-618. Reprinted in *Mélanges d'histoire, de morale et de critique*, Paris, 1859.
"Saisset correctly highlighted the great philosophical range of the writings of Servetus . . . But he wrongly ascribed to him pantheistic tendencies." Dardier, 1879.
"Rightly discerned some of the influences which affected Servetus' thought, but went no further than to describe it as 'pantheist.'" Bainton, 1932.
"The first systematic study of Servetus's thought . . . followed soon afterward by that of his countryman Chauvet, both from a Calvinist perspective. Both analyzed in detail all the theoretical works of Servetus, especially *Restitutio*, and their conclusions could not be more devastating. There was not one single dogma of orthodox Christianity that Servetus had understood, nor one single error of the two Christian millennia that he had not reproduced." Alcalá, 1980.

———. "Le procès et la mort de Michel Servet." *Revue des deux mondes* 21 (1 March 1848), 818-848.

Sánchez-Blanco, Francisco. *Michael Servets Kritik an der Trinitätslehre: Philosophische Implikationen und historische Auswirkungen.* Frankfurt am Main, 1977.
"A profound and important little book on Servetus's philosophy and its relationship to Neoplatonism, Aristotelianism, and the ideals of the Enlightenment." Alcalá 2004.

Secret, François. "Postel et Servet." *Bibliothèque d'Humanisme et Renaissance* (1961), 132-134.

Solsona, Fernando. *Miguel Servet.* Zaragoza: Diputación General de Aragón, Servicio de Publicaciones, 1988.
"A popular though superficial biography of Servetus by a distinguished Aragonese medical doctor." Alcalá 2004.

Temkin, Oswei. "Was Servetus Influenced by Ibn An-Nafis?" *Bulletin of the Institute of the History of Medicine* 8 (May 1940), 731-734.

Tollin, Henri. [Tollin's works listed as Bainton organized and numbered them]
"He will have the credit for erecting a lasting monument to the memory of Michael Servetus... One can perhaps reproach our learned critic for having over-praised the noble martyr. One will not be able, however, to join in this reproach until one has thoroughly studied, as he did himself, all of Servetus's writings." Dardier, 1879.

"The greatest Servetus scholar and vindicator... He makes Servetus a real hero, the peer of Calvin in genius... But he has overdone the subject, and put some of his own ideas into the brain of Servetus, who, like Calvin, must be studied and judged in the light of the sixteenth, and not of the nineteenth, century." Philip Schaff, 1890.

"No one has ever had a more enthusiastic biographer, and to the writings of the Magdeburg clergyman we owe the greater part of our modern know-ledge of Servetus." Osler, 1909.

"Nothing which Tollin wrote on Servetus can be neglected, and nothing can be believed without corroboration, except the documents which he reprinted." Bainton, 1932.

"Tollin's work [is] tremendously admirable despite its tremendous defects." Alcalá, 1980.

1. "Des Arztes Michael Servet Lehrer in Lyon, Dr. Symphorien Champier." *Archiv für pathologische Anatomie und Physiologie* 61 (September 1874), 377-382.
2. "Der königliche Leibarzt und Hofastrologe Johann Thibault, Michael Servets Pariser Freund." *Archiv für pathologische Anatomie und Physiologie* 78 (November 1879), 302-318.
3. "Anleitung zum Studium der Medizin aus den Jahren 1553 und 1540." *Archiv für pathologische Anatomie und Physiologie* 80 (April 1880), 47-78.
4. "William Harvey, eine Quellenstudie." *Archiv für pathologische Anatomie und Physiologie* 81 (July 1880), 114-157.
5. "Über Colombo's Antheil an der Entdeckung des Blutkreislaufs." *Archiv für pathologische Anatomie und Physiologie* 91 (January 1883), 39-66.
6. "Die Spanier und die Entdeckung des Blutkreislaufs." *Archiv für pathologische Anatomie und Physiologie* 92 (March 1883), 423-433.
7. "Die Italiener und die Entdeckung des Blutkreislaufs." *Archiv für pathologische Anatomie und Physiologie* 93 (July 1883), 64-99.
8. "Die Franzosen und die Entdeckung des Blutkreislaufs." *Archiv für pathologische Anatomie und Physiologie* 94 (October 1883), 86-135.
9. "Die Engländer und die Entdeckung des Blutkreislaufs." *Archiv für pathologische Anatomie und Physiologie* 97 (September 1884), 431-482.

10. "Die Engländer und die Entdeckung des Blutkreislaufs," continuation. *Archiv für pathologische Anatomie und Physiologie* 98 (November 1884), 193-230.

11. "Saint Vertunien Delavau." *Archiv für pathologische Anatomie und Physiologie* 101 (July 1885), 44-70.

12. "Matteo Realdo Colombos Sektionen und Vivisektionen." *Archiv für die gesammte Physiologie* 11 (1880), 349-360.

13. "Matteo Realdo Colombo, ein Beitrag zu seinem Leben aus seinen L.XV, de re anatomica (1559)." *Archiv für die gesammte Physiologie* 22 (1880), 262-290.

14. "Kritische Bemerkungen über Harvey." *Archiv für die gesammte Physiologie* 28 (1882), 581-630.

15. "Ein italienisches Urteil über die ersten Entdecker des Blutkreislaufs." *Archiv für die gesammte Physiologie* 33 (1884), 482-493.

16. "Robert Willis' neuer William Harvey." *Archiv für die gesammte Physiologie* 34 (1884), 1-21.

17. "Andreas Caesalpin." *Archiv für die gesammte Physiologie* 35 (1884), 295-390.

18. "Des Paulus Burgensis Schriftbeweis gegen die Juden." *Beweis des Glaubens* [later *Geisteskampf der Gegenwart*] 10 (June 1874), 241-246.

19. "Harvey und seine Vorgänger." *Biologisches Zentralblatt* 3 (1 October, 15 October, 1 November 1883), 461-496, 513-537.

20. "Andreas Vesals Verhältnis zu Servet." *Biologisches Zentralblatt* 5 (1 July, 1 August, 15 August, 1 September, 15 September, 1 October 1885), 242-255, 271-278, 336-349, 373-383, 404-414, 440-448, 471-480.

21. "Wie Michael Servet ein Mediciner wurde." *Deutsche Klinik* 27 (20 February, 27 February 1875), 57-59, 65-68.

22. "M. Servets Pariser Prozess urkundlich dargestellt." *Deutsches Archiv für Geschichte der Medizin* 3 (1880), 183-221.

23. "Zu Thibaults Process urkundlich dargestellt." *Deutsches Archiv für Geschichte der Medizin* 3 (1880), 332-347.

24. "Michael Servet, der Mann des Experiments." *Deutsches Archiv für Geschichte der Medizin* 7 (1884),171-176.

25. "Michael Servets Brevissima pro Symphoriano Campegio Apologia in Leonardum Fuchsium." *Deutsches Archiv für Geschichte der Medizin* 7 (1884), 409-442.

26. "Michael Servet in Charlieu." *Deutsches Archiv für Geschichte der Medizin* 8 (1885), 76-96.

27. "Servet auf dem Reichstag zu Augsburg." *Evangelisch-Reformierte Kirchenzeitung* 26 (1876), 138-192.
"Irrelevant for Servetus." Bainton, 1932.

28. "Toulouser Studentenleben im Anfang des 16. Jahrhunderts. Eine Episode aus dem Leben Michael Servets." *Historisches Taschenbuch* 44 (1874), 77-98.
"Describes what might have been." Bainton, 1932.

29. "Die Toleranz im Zeitalter del Reformation." *Historisches Taschenbuch* 45 (1874), 37-77.

30. " Eine italienische Kaiserreise in den Jahren 1529 und 1530." *Historisches Taschenbuch* 47 (1877), 51-103.
31. "Der Reichstag von Augsburg." *Historisches Taschenbuch* 50 (1880), 61-108. "Irrelevant for Servetus." Bainton, 1932.
32. "Servets Lehre von del Gotteskindschaft." *Jahrbücher für protestantische Theologie* 2 (1876), 421-450.
33. "Alex. Alesii Widerlegung von Servets Restitutio Christianismi." *Jahrbücher für protestantische Theologie* 3 (1877), 631-652.
34. "Servets christologische Bestreiter." *Jahrbücher für protestantische Theologie* 7 (1881), 284-325.
"Reviews a number of treatments, none of them valuable." Bainton, 1932.
35. "Der Verfasser de Trinitatis Erroribus L.VII, und die zeitgenössischen Katholiken." *Jahrbücher für protestantische Theologie* 17 (1891), 384-429.
36. "Die Beichtväter Karls V." *Magazin für die Literatur des Auslandes* 85 (4 April, 18 April, 2 May 1874), 201-204, 230-233, 259-263.
37. "Buchdrucker-Strike in Lyon in der Mitte des 16. Jahrhunderts." *Magazin für die Literatur des Auslandes* 87 (13 February 1875), 99-101.
38. "Strassburger kirchliche Zustände zu Anfang der Reformationszeit. Eine Episode aus dem Leben Servets." *Magazin für die Literatur des Auslandes* 87 (5 June 1875), 333-336.
39. "Michael Servet und Martin Butzer." *Magazin für die Literatur des Auslandes* 89 (10 June 1876), 333-336.
"To make Servetus Bucer's secretary . . . is sheer guess work." Bainton, 1932.
40. "Zur Ehrenrettung Servets." *Protestantische Kirchenzeitung* 22 (2 October 1875), 932-935.
41. "Michel Servet." *Revue Scientifique* IIe série, 17 (12 June 1880), 1180-1187.
42. "Trois médecins du XVIe siècle, Champier, Fuchs, Servet." *Revue Scientifique* 35 (16 May, 23 May 1885), 613-620, 651-654.
43. "Butzers Confutatio der Libri VII de Trinitatis erroribus." *Theologische Studien und Kritiken* 48 (1875), 711-736.
44. "Michael Servets Dialoge van der Dreieinigkeit." *Theologische Studien und Kritiken* 50 (1877), 301-318.
45. "Ein Beitrag zur Theologie Servets." *Theologische Studien und Kritiken* 52 (1879), 111-128.
46. "Servet über Predigt, Taufe, und Abendmahl." *Theologische Studien und Kritiken* 54 (1881), 279-310.
47. "Michael Servet als Geograph." *Zeitschrift der Gesellschaft für Erdkunde zu Berlin* 10 (1875), 182-222.
48. "M. Servet, ein Vorläufer K. Ritters und Alex. van Humboldts." *Zeitschrift der Gesellschaft für Erdkunde zu Berlin* 14 (1879), 356-368.
49. "Servets Kindheit und Jugend." *Zeitschrift für die historische Theologie* 45 (1875), 545-616.
"Describes what might have been." Bainton, 1932.

50. "Michael Servets Sprachkenntniss." *Zeitschrift für die gesammte lutherische Theologie und Kirche* 38 (1877), 608-638.

51. Review of Pünjer, *De Michaelis Serveti doctrina. Zeitschrift für die gesammte lutherische Theologie und Kirche* 39 (1878), 342-343.

52. "Servet und die Bibel." *Zeitschrift für wissenschaftliche Theologie* 18 (1875), 75-116.

53. "Servets Pantheismus." *Zeitschrift für wissenschaftliche Theologie* 19 (1876), 241-263.

54. "Servets Teufelslehre." *Zeitschrift für wissenschaftliche Theologie* 19 (1876), 371-387.

55. "Michael Servets Toulouser Leben." *Zeitschrift für wissenschaftliche Theologie* 20 (1877), 342-386.

56. "Zur Servet-Kritik." *Zeitschrift für wissenschaftliche Theologie* 21 (1878), 425-466.

57. "Servets Lehre von der Welt." *Zeitschrift für wissenschaftliche Theologie* 22 (1879), 239-249.

58. "Der Antichrist Michael Servets." *Zeitschrift für wissenschaftliche Theologie* 22 (1879), 351-374.

59. "Servets Anthropologie und Soteriologie." *Zeitschrift für wissenschaftliche Theologie* 23 (1880), 323-343.

60. "Luther und Marheineke." *Zeitschrift für wissenschaftliche Theologie* 23 (1880), 464-471.

61. "Die Zeugung Jesu in Servets *Restitutio Christianismi*." *Zeitschrift für wissenschaftliche Theologie* 24 (1881), 68-88.

62. "Michael Servets Positivismus." *Zeitschrift für wissenschaftliche Theologie* 24 (1881), 420-454.

63. "Michael Servet über den Geist del Wiedergeburt." *Zeitschrift für wissenschaftliche Theologie* 25 (1882), 310-326.

64. "Die bisherigen Darstellungen der Eschatologie Michael Servets." *Zeitschrift für wissenschaftliche Theologie* 25 (1882), 483-488.

65. "Thomas von Aquino der Lehrer Michael Servets." *Zeitschrift für wissenschaftliche Theologie* 35 (1892), 220-243, 347-373, 436-444.

66. "Thomas von Aquino," continuation. *Zeitschrift für wissenschaftliche Theologie* 36 (1893), 1:171-195.

67. "Thomas von Aquino," continuation. *Zeitschrift für wissenschaftliche Theologie* 36 (1893), 2:280-304.

68. "Thomas von Aquino," continuation. *Zeitschrift für wissenschaftliche Theologie* 37 (1894), 261-303.

69. *Dr. M. Luther und Dr. M. Servet*. Berlin, 1875.
"Must be read with caution since he sometimes applies to Servetus references which were meant for Campanus." Bainton, 1932.

70. *Ph. Melanchthon und M. Servet*. Berlin, 1876.
"The comments of Luther and Melanchthon [on Servetus] are collected." Bainton, 1932.

71. *Charakterbild Michael Servets*. Berlin, 1876.

[English trans.] "Character-Portrait of Michael Servetus." Translated by F. A. Short. *Christian Life* (27 October-1 December 1877), 518-519, 524-525, 569-570, 580.

[French trans.] *Michel Servet, portrait-caractère.* Translated and expanded by A. Picheral-Dardier. Paris, 1879.

"In the brief compass of the vivid Character-Portrait . . . there is more matter of value for the right understanding of Serveto than in the whole of Dr. Willis's volume of 541 unprofitable pages." Gordon, 1878.

72. *Das Lehrsystem Michael Servets, genetisch dargestellt,* 3 vols. Gütersloh, 1876-1878.

"Locates a number of the biblical and patristic sources but is distinctly weak on the philosophy of the Middle Ages, and never shows in any discriminating fashion how diverse traditions were fused in the passionate heat of religious enthusiasm." [This applies also to nos. 32-35, 44-46, 52-59, and 61-68.] Bainton, 1932.

73. *Die Entdeckung des Blutkreislaufs durch Michael Servet 1511-1553.* Jena, 1877.

74. *Mich. Servet und Mart. Butzer.* Berlin, 1880.

75. *Michaelis Villanovani (Serveti) apologetica disceptatio pro astrologia,* Reprint with introduction and notes by Tollin. Berlin, 1880.

Trechsel, Friedrich. *Michael Servet und seine Vorgänger.* Heidelberg, 1839.

Vol. 1 of *Die protestantischen Antitrinitarier vor Faustus Socin;* contains reprint of the Berne ms. copy of the Geneva trial.

"Solid, if unimaginative. The first volume on the anti-Trinitiarianism of the period is indispensable for the background." Bainton, 1932.

Valayre, G. de [pseud. of Gustave-Charles-Ferdinand de Bonstetten]. *Légendes et chroniques Suisses.* Paris, 1842.

Contains records of Geneva trial once considered lost.

Valtueña Borque, José Antonio. *Proceso y rehabilitación de Miguel Servet.* Madrid: Historia Hispana, 1994.

Verdú Vicente, Francisco Tomás. *Astrología y hermetismo en Miguel Servet.* Doctoral thesis, Universidad de Valencia, 1998.

"Amply covers many topics related to astrology . . . [though] not always without errors." Alcalá, 2004.

Vogt, A. "La doctrina de la luz en Paracelso y en Miguel Servet." *Folia Humanistica* 6 (1968), 355-367.

Voltaire, François Marie Arouet de. "De Genève et de Calvin" and "De Calvin et de Servet." In *Essai sur les mœurs et l'esprit des nations et sur les principaux faits de l'histoire depuis Charlemagne jusqu'à Louis XIII.* Paris: Garnier, 1963.

Historically important 1756 essays against intolerance. Genevan ministers reacted by making the Servetus trial documents unavailable for nearly a century.

Weiss, Nathanaël. "Calvin, Servet, G. De Trie et le Tribunal de Vienne." *Bulletin de la Société pour l'Histoire du Protestantisme Français* 57 (1908), 387-404.

"Demonstrated that Servetus was examined at Vienne not on the printed *Restitutio* but on the copy of Calvin's *Institutes* which Servetus had marked with scurrilous comments and returned to the author, who now supplied it to the inquisition." Bainton, 1932.

Wickersheimer, Ernest. "À propos d'un livre sur Michel Servet," *La France médicale* (25 November 1907), 423f.

"A discriminating article . . . makes Servetus and Columbo mutually independent." Bainton, 1932.

Wilbur, Earl Morse. *A bibliography of the pioneers of the Socinian-Unitarian movement in modern Christianity, in Italy, Switzerland, Germany, Holland.* Rome, 1950.

————. *A History of Unitarianism.* Vol. 1, *Socinianism and its antecedents.* Cambridge: Harvard University Press, 1945.

"On every count this is the best biography [of Servetus] now available in any tongue. For precision of statement and balance of judgment it is unsurpassed." Bainton, review in *Review of Religion* 11 (1946), 82-84.

"Chapters 5 and 9-12 constitute an admirable treatment of Servetus." Bainton, 1953.

"A traditional treatment of Servetus as part of a larger Unitarian tradition." Friedman, 1974.

————. *The two treatises of Servetus on the Trinity* (see under Works by Servetus above).

Reviewed by Bainton in *Church History* 2 (1933), 60-61.

Contains an introductory biographical article on Servetus by Wilbur.

Williams, George Huntston. *The Radical Reformation.* Philadelphia: Westminster, 1962.

A Unitarian Universalist scholar who saw his own denomination in a larger historical perspective and whose writing on the Radical Reformation reflects an appreciation of the several strands of Reformation thought, piety, and practice to which Servetus belonged.

"Has also contributed to our understanding of this complex radical thinker. Several new tendencies found in the Restitution are described in the Radical Reformation, and the probability of gnostic influence is brought to the reader's attention." Friedman, 1978.

"No Servetist should ignore the approach and perspectives of such a complex, as well as indispensable, work as that of Professor Williams about the Radical Reformation." Alcalá, 1980.

Willis, Robert. *Servetus and Calvin.* London, 1877.

"Tedious and trifling . . . Considering his superior advantages, his book, as a whole, compares unfavourably with the old *Impartial History* of 1724 . . . Take on trust no exposition by Dr. Willis which [you] have not verified, and accept no translation of his which [you] have not tested . . . In many cases he makes [Servetus] speak in terms which express a sense the very opposite of his real meaning." Gordon, 1878.

"The best account in English." Osler, 1909.

"Negligible were it not the only comprehensive account of the trial in English." Bainton, 1932.

"The most useful work on Servetus." Goldstone and Goldstone, 2002.

Wolf, Ernst. "Deus Omniformis. Bemerkungen zur Christologie des Michael Servet." In *Theologische Aufsätze: Karl Barth, zum 50. Geburtstag.* Munich, 1936.

Wotton, William. *Reflections upon ancient and modern learning.* London, 1694, 211-213.

"First to reprint Servetus's account of the circulation of the blood." Wilbur, 1950.

Wright, Richard. *An apology for Dr. Michael Servetus: including an account of his life, persecution, writings and opinions: being designed to eradicate bigotry and uncharitableness: and to promote liberality of sentiment among Christians.* Wisbech [Cambridgeshire], 1806.

"His Apology would have been much more valuable, if he had quoted his authorities particularly; if he had been much more accurate in his translations; if he had not given some things, for which there is no good authority; and if he had been less diffuse in his reflections and remarks." Andrews Norton, 1813.

"Uses de la Roche entire, also [*An Impartial History*] and Chauffpié." Wilbur, 1950.

Zweig, Stefan. *The right to heresy; Castellio against Calvin.* New York: Viking, 1936.

Reviewed by Bainton in *Review of Religion* 1 (1937), 414-416, and in *Christian Century* 68 (1952), 19.

"The book abounds in errors and inconsistencies, and even if they were corrected it would still be amateurish." Bainton, 1937, review.

"Zweig chose to project the conflict [Hitler vs. 1930s dissidence] backwards into a period where any resemblance could be disclaimed as purely coincidental." Bainton, 1952 review.

Selected Books by Roland H. Bainton

Note: For a more detailed bibliography see Cynthia Wales Lund, *A Bainton Bibliography* (Kirksville, MO: Truman State University Press, 2000). For an extended critical evaluation of Bainton's writing, see Steven Simpler, *Roland H. Bainton: An Examination of His Reformation Historiography* (Lewiston, NY: Edwin Mellen Press, 1985).

The Age of the Reformation. Princeton: Van Nostrand, 1956.

"Basilidian Chronology and New Testament Interpretation." *Journal of Biblical Literature* 42 (1923), 81-134. Yale thesis.

Bernard Ochino, Esule e Riformatore Senese del Cinquecento, 1487-1563. Translated into Italian by Elio Gianturco. Florence: Sansoni, 1941. English version in manuscript, "Bernardino Ochino of Siena." Typescript in Roland Bainton Papers, Manuscripts and Archives, Yale Divinity Library.

Bibliography of the Continental Reformation: Materials Available in English. Chicago: American Society of Church History, 1935. Second edition, revised and enlarged, with Eric W. Gritsch. Hamden, CT: Archon Books, 1972.

Castellion, Sébastien. *Concerning Heretics: Whether They Are to Be Persecuted and How They Are to Be Treated; A Collection of the Opinions of Learned Men, Both Ancient and Modern*. Translated by Roland H. Bainton, together with excerpts from other works by Sébastien Castellion and David Joris. New York: Columbia University Press, 1935. Reprinted with a new introduction. New York: Octagon Books, 1965.

Christian Attitudes toward War and Peace: An Historical Survey and Critical Re-evaluation. New York: Abingdon, 1960.
    Several times reprinted and translated into other languages.

The Church of Our Fathers. New York: Scribner's, 1941.
    Several times reprinted and translated into other languages.

Collected Papers in Church History. Series One: Early and Medieval Christianity. Boston: Beacon Press, 1962.

Collected Papers in Church History. Series Two: Studies on the Reformation. Boston: Beacon Press, 1963.

Collected Papers in Church History. Series Three: Christian Unity and Religion in New England. Boston: Beacon Press, 1964.

Correspondence of Roland H. Bainton and Delio Cantimori, 1932-1966: An Enduring Transatlantic Friendship between Two Historians of Religious Toleration. Edited by John Tedeschi. Florence: Leo S. Olschki Editore, 2002.

David Joris: Wiedertäufer und Kämpfer für Toleranz im 16. Jahrhundert. Translated into German by Hajo Holborn and Annemarie Holborn. Leipzig: M. Heinsius Nachfolger, 1937. English version "A Refugee from the Netherlands: David Joris." Zug: Inter Documentator, 19--. Microfiche.

Early Christianity. Princeton: Van Nostrand, 1960.

Erasmus of Christendom. New York: Scribner's, 1969.
    Several times reprinted and translated into other languages.

George Lincoln Barr: His Life. With selections from Barr's writings edited by Lois Oliphant Gibbons. Ithaca: Cornell University Press, 1943.

Here I Stand: A Life of Martin Luther. New York: Abingdon-Cokesbury, 1950.
    Several times reprinted and translated into other languages.

The Horizon History of Christianity. New York: American Heritage and Harper & Row, 1964. Later reworked in 2 volumes as *Christendom: A Short History of Christianity*, New York: Harper & Row, 1966; and as *The Penguin History of Christianity*, Harmondsworth: Penguin, 1967.
    Translated into French, 1969.

Hunted Heretic: The Life and Death of Michael Servetus, 1511-1553. Boston: Beacon Press, 1953. Paperback edition with new foreword, 1960.
> Several times reprinted and translated into other languages. (See under Selected Works about Servetus for details.)

Luther's Meditations on the Gospels. Translated and arranged by Roland H. Bainton. Philadelphia: Westminster, 1962.

The Medieval Church. Princeton: Van Nostrand, 1962.
> Several times reprinted.

Pilgrim Parson: The Life of James Herbert Bainton, 1867-1942. New York: Nelson, 1958.

The Reformation of the Sixteenth Century. Boston: Beacon Press, 1952.
> Several times reprinted and translated into other languages.

Roly: Chronicle of a Stubborn Non-Conformist. Edited by Ruth C. L. Gritsch. New Haven: Yale Divinity School, 1988.

The Travail of Religious Liberty: Nine Biographical Studies. Philadelphia: Westminster, 1951.
> Several times reprinted and translated into Italian, 1963.

What Christianity Says about Sex, Love, and Marriage. New York: Association Press, 1957. Originally published as "Christianity and Sex: An Historical Survey," *Pastoral Psychology* 3:26 (September 1952), 10-26; 4:21 (February 1953), 12-29.

Women of the Reformation in Germany and Italy. Minneapolis: Augsburg, 1971. Reprint, Boston: Beacon Press, 1974.
> Translated into Italian, 1992, and German, 1995.

Women of the Reformation in France and England. Minneapolis: Augsburg, 1973. Reprint, Boston: Beacon Press, 1975.

Women of the Reformation from Spain to Scandinavia. Minneapolis: Augsburg, 1977.

Yale and the Ministry: A History of Education for the Christian Ministry at Yale from the Founding in 1701. New York: Harper, 1957.

Yesterday, Today, and What's Next? Reflections on History and Hope. Minneapolis: Augsburg, 1978.

Notes on "Declarationis Jesu Christi filii Dei libri V"

from the Bibliography, 1953

This work has just been discovered in the Stuttgart State Archives (call number A63, B25), by the Polish scholar Dr. Stanislas Kot, who has been pursuing the trail of Polish students in western Europe in the sixteenth century. A number of them studied at Basel, Strassburg and Tübingen. From the former city to the latter they carried the ideas of Servetus. The murder of one of these students brought to light among his effects a manuscript of Servetus with a preface by Alphonsus Lyncurius Tarraconensis, a friend and compatriot of Servetus, who had committed to his care a body of manuscripts. After disillusioning experiences in Germany and in France Servetus had decided to go to Venice to edit the text of the Bible. "But alas, this man of genius has been cut off" – such is the account.

The pseudonym is otherwise known through an apology for Servetus after his execution but the identity has never been satisfactorily explained. Professor Kot has discovered that, when the scandal broke at Tübingen, Vergerio identified this Alphonsus Lyncurius as Celio Secundo Curione of Basel. This is extremely interesting because it shows that Servetus was in continuous friendly intercourse with the liberal circle at Basel. It may also explain how the Paris manuscript of the *Christianismi Restitutio,* which is earlier than the printed book, happened once to have been in the possession of Caelius Horatius Curione, the son of Celio Secundo. (See Tollin, No. 9, p. 448; and Bainton's article in *Sudhoffs Archiv.*[a]) We have already known from Castellion that Servetus sent a manuscript for approval to Martin Borrhaus of Basel (Ferdinand Buisson, *Sebastien Castellion,* p. 2:478[b]). This makes it extremely probable that the letter from Basel to Servetus telling him that the *Restitutio* could not be printed there was not from "Marrinus," as D'Artigny read the signature, but from Martinus – namely, Martin Borrhaus.

Professor Kot says that this manuscript makes less appeal to Scripture and has fewer citations from the scholastics than the other works, with a larger dependence on Irenaeus. This means no more than a shift in emphasis, and one may expect that the new and eagerly awaited work will not seriously alter the delineation of the thought of Servetus.

---

[a] Henri Tollin, "Die Engländer und die Entdeckung des Blutkreislaufs," *Archiv für pathologische Anatomie und Physiologie* 97 (September 1884), 431-482; Roland H. Bainton, "The Smaller Circulation: Servetus and Colombo," *Sudhoffs Archiv für Geschichte der Medizin* 24 (1931), 371-374.
[b] Ferdinand Edouard Buisson, *Sébastien Castellion, sa vie et son oeuvre (1515-1563)* (Nieuwkoop: B. de Graaf, 1964).

from the Epilogue to the Spanish edition, 1973

The original document appears to have been written by five different hands. The sections of the text do not come from transcriptions of any of Servetus's published works, but the topics are the same and there are no significant theological differences. There are no words written in Greek or Hebrew, nor is there any mention of scholastic philosophers.

The only point in Kot's conclusions with which we may have to disagree concerns the date. Kot places the new material between *De Trinitatis Erroribus* and *Christianismi Restitutio*, and believes that it is a simplification intended for a less learned audience. However, an author is generally more inclined to add than to remove text. Several clues would seem to indicate that, on the contrary, what we have is a draft that is less mature than *De Trinitatis*. Its date must be later than 1525, because of its references to the Anabaptists, who only began to act in that year (and also because of the extreme youth of Servetus, born in 1511). Servetus refutes the idea of the Anabaptist Melchior Hoffman (although he does not mention him by name) that Jesus came through Mary as through a channel with no contamination. And this is a relevant detail: Hoffman had been in Spain.

Index

This book is a joint publication of Blackstone Editions and the Unitarian Universalist Historical Society.

Blackstone Editions

Mail:	60 12th Street
	Providence, RI 02902
Web:	www.BlackstoneEditions.com
E-mail:	editor@BlackstoneEditions.com

Unitarian Universalist Historical Society

Web:	www.uua.org/uuhs

The collection of six volumes comprising the bilingual edition, Spanish and Latin, of *Obras Completas* (of which three have already appeared) can be purchased at its publisher, PUZ (Prensas Universitarias de Zaragoza).

Prensas Universitarias de Zaragoza

Mail:	Edificio de Ciencias Geológicas
	Pedro Cerbuna, 12
	50009 Zaragoza
	Spain
Phone:	+34 976 76 13 30
Fax:	+34 976 76 10 63
Web:	puz.unizar.es
E-mail:	puz@posta.unizar.es

Servetus studies are presently promoted and centralized by two institutions: the venerable Instituto de Estudios Sijenenses and the recently founded Servetus International Society.

Instituto de Estudios Sijenenses

Mail:	Casa Natal
	22231 Villanueva de Sijena
	Huesca
	Spain
Phone:	+34 974 57 81 37
Web:	www.miguelservet.org
E-mail:	mail@miguelservet.org

Servetus International Society

Web:	www.servetus.org
E-mail:	info@servetus.org